Praise for
The Whole Brain Business Book

"Ned Herrmann knows more about the brain than anyone. If you want to function better, this is a must read."

—Ken Blanchard
co-author of *The One Minute Manager*

"A comprehensive, readable and useful work. In *The Whole Brain Business Book*, Ned Herrmann has distilled his many years of research and hands-on experience into a practical approach for translating Whole Brain theory into on-the-job results. A must read for line or staff practitioners."

—Richard C. Whiteley
Vice Chairman, The Forum Corporation and
author of *The Customer-Driven Company*

"Ned's research started at General Electric and continues in the corporations of the world. His four-quadrant perspective has important applications at all levels of organizational life. Individuals and executives, teams and top management, tools and techniques for everyone! Here is your opportunity to share in a lifetime of learning from a man who has successfully dedicated himself to understanding how we all think!"

—Geoff Bellman
Author of *The Consultant's Calling* and
Getting Things Done When You Are Not In Charge

"It is best to buy a book from an author who practices what he preaches. As an individual, Ned Herrmann has excelled in the arts, the sciences, and business. *The Whole Brain Business Book* is the formula that has made him an outstanding success in each of these fields. Read it and follow in his footsteps."

—Tony Buzan
President, The Brain Foundation and
author of *The Mind Map Book, Use Both Sides of Your Brain* and
Buzan's Book of Genius

THE
WHOLE BRAIN
BUSINESS BOOK

NED HERRMANN

McGraw-Hill
New York   San Francisco   Washington, D.C.   Auckland   Bogotá
Caracas   Lisbon   London   Madrid   Mexico City   Milan
Montreal   New Delhi   San Juan   Singapore
Sydney   Tokyo   Toronto

Library of Congress Cataloging-in-Publication Data

Herrmann, Ned.
   The whole brain business book / Ned Herrmann.
      p. cm.
   Includes index.
   ISBN 0-07-028462-8 (alk. paper)
    1. Success in business. 2. Leadership—Psychological aspects.
   3. Personality and occupation. 4. Typology (Psychology) 5. Brain
   —Physiology. I. Title.
   HF5386.H434 1996
   650.1'3—dc20   95-53334
                                           CIP

McGraw-Hill

*A Division of The **McGraw·Hill** Companies*

7 8 9 0 QWF/QWF 0 9 8 7 6 5 4 3 2

ISBN 0-07-028462-8

The sponsoring editor for this book was Richard Narramore, the editing supervisor was Jane Palmieri, the designer was Laura Herrmann, and the production supervisor was Pamela Pelton. It was set in ITC Berkeley Book by Laura Herrmann of the Ned Herrmann Group's publication department.

Printed and bound by Quebecor/Book Press.

McGraw-Hill books are available at special quantity discounts to use as premiums and sales promotions, or for use in corporate training programs. For more information, please write to the Director of Special Sales, McGraw-Hill, 11 West 19th Street, New York, NY 10011. Or contact your local bookstore.

 This book is printed on recycled, acid-free paper containing a minimum of 50% recycled, de-inked fiber.

I dedicate this book to my wife, Margy. She is my life mate, my business partner, and my creative colleague. Her support over a decade of continuous writing has been crucial to the success of my earlier books and articles. Her active involvement in the concentrated writing of this third book deserves special recognition and my heartfelt thanks.

Contents

PART I
Introduction to the Whole Brain Concept

Introduction 3

1. The Organizing Principle: A Four-Quadrant Model of the Brain 6

2. The Link Between Brain Dominance and Thinking Preferences 20

3. Measuring Thinking Styles the Whole Brain Way 34

4. How Your Brain Gets Along with Other People's Brains 44

5. Identifying Brain Dominance Characteristics with the
   Whole Brain Model 58

PART II
The Whole Brain Organization

6. Whole Brain Technology as a Solution to Today's
   Business Problems 81

7. Whole Brain Marketing, Sales, and Advertising 86

8. Whole Brain Products for a Whole Brain World 90

9. Approaches and Styles of Management 98

10. Communication 115

11. Teams: Maximizing Results Through Mental Diversity 123

12. Productivity and Job Design 131

13. Supervision, Delegation, and Followership 140

14. Whole Brain Training and Development 150

PART III
Whole Brain Leadership

15. The CEO's Key Leadership Issues 163
16. Managing Financial Crisis 171
17. Ways to Make Reengineering Work 175
18. CEOs Around the World 179
19. Strategic Thinking Must Precede Strategic Planning 192
20. Organizational Change 197

PART IV
Whole Brain Creativity and Innovation

21. Applying Creativity and Innovation in Organizations 203
22. The Brain Is the Source of Creativity 214
23. Managing Creativity Through Multiple Processes 225
24. Going Creative 230

PART V
Whole Brain Personal Development

25. Creativity for the Businessperson 251
26. "Outside the Box" Thinking 256
27. Reclaiming Your Lost Creativity 265
28. Creative...Who ME? Tools and Techniques
    for Personal Creativity 276
29. How Decisions and Values Are Influenced
    by Your Thinking Styles 282
30. Entrepreneurship 291
31. M.B.A.s versus the Creatives 301
32. Breaking Down the Barriers to Whole Brain Growth 308
Afterword 315
Appendices 317
Reading List 327
Index 329

List of Figures and Tables

1-1. Preference Indicator Exercise 8

1-2. Roger Sperry's diagram of brain specialization 11

1-3. Clinical evidence of hemisphere specialization 12

1-4. Triune Brain Model 13

1-5. The hidden limbic system 14

1-6. The relationship of the Whole Brain Model to the theories of Sperry and MacLean 14

1-7. Herrmann's Whole Brain Model 15

1-8. Herrmann's Organizing Principle 16

2-1. The Four-Selves Model 21

2-2. The Four-Quadrant House. A metaphor for the four families of thinking preferences. 21

2-3. Universe-of-Thinking-Styles Model 23

2-4. The Turn-On Work Exercise 26

2-5. Four-Quadrant Locator Map of professional occupations 28

2-6. Three major elements of Whole Brain Technology; The Four-Selves Model, the HBDI Profile, and the Whole Brain Model 30

2-7. The relationship between brain dominance and competencies 30

2-8. Categories and pro forma HBDI profiles of occupations 31

2-9. Reading the HBDI Profile Grid 32

3-1. At Work Chart 36

3-2. At Home Chart 37

3-3. Situational Options Chart 39

3-4. Four views of an accident 40

4-1. Composite HBDI profiles of organizations from around the world 47

4-2. Composite HBDI profiles of freshmen entering the University of Toledo Engineering Program 48

4-3. Composite HBDI profiles of University of Toledo faculty (left) and entering seniors (right) 49

4-4. Composite average HBDI profiles for typical ethnic and cultural groups 50

4-5. Scattergram of male and female profiles from the HBDI database 52

4-6. Typical HBDI profiles of married and unmarried, living-together couples . 54

4-7. Male and Female Differences Chart . 55

4-8. Composite HBDI profile of a gender-balanced team 56

5-1. Pro forma HBDI profile of strategic finance and short-term operational finance. 59

5-2. Types of smartness of the four quadrants. 60

5-3. Composite HBDI profile of a family with one member falling outside of the predominant mental preferences. 61

5-4. Seating participants according to their mental preferences, using their HBDI scores. 64

5-5. HBDI profiles of a President/COO and a Chairman/CEO compared. 65

5-6. Pro forma HBDI profiles of Olympic Skiiers Hilary and Picabo. 69

5-7. How brain dominance influences the playing styles of golf pros 70

5-8. How brain dominance influences work styles. 71

5-9. HBDI profiles of different types of engineers 73

5-10. HBDI profiles of several common positions in finance. 73

5-12. HBDI profiles of B-quadrant-oriented professionals 74

5-13. HBDI profiles of typically limbic professionals. 74

5-11. *HBDI* profiles of business managers, showing differences between males and females. 74

5-14. *HBDI* profile examples of C-quadrant professionals 75

5-15. *HBDI* profiles of C- and D-quadrant professionals 76

5-16. *HBDI* profiles of D-quadrant professionals 76

5-17. *HBDI* profiles of cerebral-oriented professionals 76

5-18. *HBDI* profile examples of professionals preferring all four quadrants (1-1-1-1 profile) 77

6-1. The Earth from Space 82

6-2. Examples of different types of pro forma *HBDI* profiles. 83

6-3. A multidominant customer service team 84

7-1. Correlations between car types and mental preferences 87

7-2. A Four-Quadrant Model of advertisement types 88

8-1. Pro forma *HBDI* profiles of two companies' annual reports 93

8-2. An example of a Rube Goldberg-type invention 96

9-1. A composite *HBDI* profile of a U.S. corporate staff 101

9-2. A-quadrant management 103

9-3. B-quadrant management 105

9-4. A/B-quadrants management 106

9-5. C-quadrant management 106

9-6. D-quadrant management 107

9-7. C/D-quadrants management 108

9-8. Management styles and *HBDI* gender norms 109

9-9. The cerebral and the limbic management styles and male/female trends 109

9-10. National Inventors Hall of Fame: A composite *HBDI* profile 110

9-11. A female-preferred management style 111

9-12. The Whole Brain management style 111

9-13. Management Style Matrix. 113

10-1. Communication continuum 116

10-2. Average *HBDI* profiles of men and women 117

10-3. Typical processing modes for each quadrant 118

10-4. Communication Walk-Around Exercise 119

10-5. Differing expectations of listeners in terms of the four quadrants 121

11-1. Examples of homogenous team *HBDI* profile composites 124

11-2. Going from homogenous to Whole Brain heterogeneous teams 126

11-3. Process Storming Model. 129

12-1 *HBDI* profile of an employee. 133

12-2. Matching *HBDI* job pro formas to an employee's preferences 134

12-3. Atypical *HBDI* profiles for nurse, pathologist, and IRS agent 137

12-4. Typical *HBDI* profiles for nurse, pathologist, and IRS agent 138

13-1. *HBDI* profiles of 12 members of a Benefits Department 141

13-2. The Whole-Brain Delegation Walk-Around Model. 146

14-1. A Whole Brain Learning Design compared with a delivery that addresses only left-mode styles 153

14-2. The Learning-Style Model. 154

14-3. The Whole Brain Teaching and Learning Model 155

14-4. A comparison of a CEO's *HBDI* profile to that of the corporate culture 158

14-5. The adjustments of a CEO's thinking styles to accommodate an evolving and changing corporate culture 159

15-1. *HBDI* pro forma profiles of some key leadership issues of a U.S. corporation 164

15-2. *HBDI* pro forma profiles of a company's mission statement and corporate values. 166

15-3. Composite *HBDI* pro forma profile of a company's mission, values, and management culture 167

17-1. National Inventors Hall of Fame: A pro forma composite of the 84 members 176

18-1. Distributing traits in the Whole Brain Model. 180

18-2. The Hays Study: North American and Asian-Pacific CEOs 182

18-3. European versus North American CEOs' mentality 183

18-4. Hoestede Model of cultural patterns in Europe 184

18-5. Average *HBDI* profiles of 697 CEOs from around the world 185

18-6. Weighted average *HBDI* profiles of male and female CEOs and rate of differentiation. 188

18-7. Average *HBDI* profile of female CEOs in three countries 188

18-8. *HBDI* profile norms for entire *HBDI* computer database. 190

18-9. The top four *HBDI* work elements of CEOs organized by quadrant compared to the bottom six. 191

19-1. Strategic thinking versus strategic planning pro forma *HBDI*. 193

19-2. Two visual metaphors representing the idea of car 195

20-1. Going Creative Change Model. 198

20-2. Creative Process Chart. 199

21-1. The consequences of unleashing creativity list 209

22-1. Four key brain waves common to all human beings. 215

22-2. Creative process correlation with Four-Quadrant Model. 217

22-3. Whole Brain Creativity and Innovation Model. 218

22-4. The Creative Selves Model. 223

23-1. 77 creative processes 227

25-1. A comparison of a pro forma *HBDI* profile of work and that of creative individuals 253

25-2. Pro forma *HBDI* profiles of work and noncreative individuals. 254

26-1. Pro forma *HBDI* profile of Bill Cronkite, maverick 259

26-2. Pro forma *HBDI* profiles of four mavericks 263

27-1. Claiming Your Creative Space Exercise 272

27-2. How the author expanded his creative space in order to write this book. . 274

28-1. The Creative Space Certificate 278

29-1. The profile of a decision maker with a 1-1-2-2 *HBDI* profile 283

29-2. The decision maker with a 2-2-1-1 HBDI profile 283

29-3. An *HBDI* profile of a 2-1-2-1 decision maker 284

29-4. The 1-2-1-2 *HBDI* profile of a decision maker. 284

29-5. The Decision-Making Walk-Around Model. 285

30-1. Composite *HBDI* profile averages of male and female nontechnical entrepreneurs. 292

30-2. An atypical *HBDI* profile for an entrepreneur: 2-1-2-2 292

30-3. An entrepreneur with a strong C-quadrant orientation 293

30-4. An A-quadrant entrepreneur with a 1-2-2-2 *HBDI* profile. 293

30-5. The classic *HBDI* profile for a nontechnical entrepreneur. 295

31-1. Diversity game cards 303

31-2. The composite average *HBDI* profile of M.B.A.s compared to that of a group of art directors and advertising directors 304

31-3. A right mode shift of the Franklin University's composite M.B.A. average *HBDI* profile due to an Artist-in-Residence Program 307

32-1. Examples of what influences permanent and temporary changes to an individual's *HBDI* profile 312

Tables

18-1. Work elements reprinted from the *HBDI Survey* Form 185

18-2. Rank-ordered work elements most preferred by male CEOs in study .. 186

18-3. Rank-ordered work elements of 697 male CEOs listed by country 187

18-4. Rank-ordered work elements most preferred by the 76 female CEOs involved in study 189

18-5. Women's rank ordering of work elements in relation to men 189

18-6. Rank ordering of the top four *HBDI* work elements 190

18-7. Rank ordering of the bottom four *HBDI* work elements 190

Preface

The Whole Brain Concept upon which this book is based was developed in the late 1970s while I was Manager of Management Education at General Electric's Management Development Institute at Crotonville, New York. My inspiration came from my obsession with the nature and source of creativity, and my initial applications of the emerging technology were focused on GE managers. After "graduating" from GE in early 1982, my application base expanded rapidly to include: IBM, Caterpillar, Shell, DuPont, Goodyear, Coca-Cola, AT&T, Ciba Geigy, Tenneco, and ultimately hundreds of smaller companies. This expanded business base has provided the application experience reported in this book.

International interest in Whole Brain Technology, particularly in the *Herrmann Brain Dominance Instrument (HBDI)*, outpaced domestic interest, with Scandinavian countries taking the lead. Today, a decade later, the Ned Herrmann Group has active affiliates in Germany, France, England (northern and southern), Turkey, Mexico, Argentina, Australia, and New Zealand. This global activity provides a steady flow of international business application experiences and *HBDI* data to integrate with a flourishing domestic business. In writing this book, I have tried to interpret this rich business input from the perspective of decades of big company management experience (GE) and over a decade of experience as an entrepreneurial founder, owner, and leader of a small business (The Ned Herrmann Group). I feel that readers will benefit from my 48-year multiple-application perspective of domestic/international, Fortune 50/1000, and corporate manager/independent entrepreneur business experience. It was great to live through and fun to write about.

Acknowledgments

I was first approached to write this book by Richard Narramore who had recently joined McGraw-Hill. He had carried a knowledge of my work with him to his new editorial position and, were it not for his strong interest and confidence in a business book based on Whole Brain Technology, this book would not have been written. I thank him for his initiative. When the book proposal was accepted by McGraw-Hill, I asked my daughter, Laura Herrmann, to serve as project manager and designer for the new book. She had played a similar role for my two previous books—*The Creative Brain* and *What Will I Be When I Grow Up?* To undertake this new book project in full knowledge of the magnitude of the task was an expression not only of commitment but also of love for the work and love for me, her father. Her contribution to this book is an enormous gift, not only to me but to every reader.

Word processing of my dictated manuscript was performed by Anna Jo O'Brien. When revisions are factored in, this became a 1,200-page book, but you would never know it. She performed impressively and enthusiastically from start to finish. The young lady is my age!

Special recognition and thanks go to M.A. Nehdi for creating many of the profiles, models, and graphics for the book. Since much of my work is expressed visually, Nehdi's contribution to the book's effectiveness is central.

My thanks and appreciation go to the staff of The Ned Herrmann Group, our senior associates and international affiliates. I want to particularly recognize Ann Herrmann-Nehdi, CEO of NHG, Inc., Bob Geyer, Manager of Information Systems, Carol Whaley, Secretary, and Linda Powell, Business Manager. Their interest and support throughout the writing of this book has helped make its completion possible.

Senior associates who contributed to the book include Ted Coulson, Alison Strickland, Manny Elkind, and Ayn Fox. I thank them, as well as key representatives of international affiliates who contributed to the CEO study: Lionel Vuillemin, France; Roland Spinola, Frank Peschanel, Germany; Sally Cartwright-Bishop, UK; Dennis Martin, UK North; Mike Morgan, Australia and New Zealand; Savas Tumis, Turkey; Juan Carlos Folino, Latin American operations.

I want to specially acknowledge and personally thank my superb medical team for keeping me healthy and productive during the writing of this book. As chance would have it, their skills were needed on numerous occasions. Without their individual and collective expertise, I would not have been able to complete this book.

William Burch, MD - Personal Physician and Team Leader
J. Michael Bobbitt, MD
Alan Friedman, MD
Stuart Glassman, MD
Peter Goodfield, MD
J. Battle Haslam, MD
Duff Rardin, MD

PART I

Introduction to the Whole Brain Concept

Introduction

Have you ever asked any of these questions:

- Why is my business development stagnant?
- Why aren't my employees productive?
- Why isn't my organization creative?
- Why am I able to attract new clients but unable to maintain relationships with current ones?
- Why are my staff members constantly at odds with one another?
- What is blocking my organization from implementing creative change?
- Why aren't my employees turned on by their work?
- Why am I not turned on by my work?

This book offers answers to all these questions and a multitude of others, covering more than 100 high-priority business topics that range from diversity to creativity, from supervision to executive leadership, from understanding the self to understanding others.

The purpose of this book is to provide you with a fresh new understanding of familiar business processes, issues, and critical events. The Whole Brain approach, an organizing principle of mental processes, presents a unique new method of diagnosing business situations and provides an understanding of key business and leadership issues that have resisted meaningful measurement until now.

The applications of brain research and development in this book have been meeting the needs of business leaders, managers, and professionals at all levels of the organization since I first introduced them in 1977. They demonstrate how the mental preferences of employees, managers, and executives affect their work styles and productivity levels, which ultimately translate into bottom-line results.

All the data and examples cited, the experiences described, and the conclusions reached are based on actual working relationships with hundreds of organizations, both foreign and US-based, including 17 of the Fortune 50. The mental preferences of individuals and organizations cited have been selected from our active database of well over 110,000 individuals who have completed the *Herrmann Brain Dominance Instrument (HBDI)*, an assessment tool I developed in 1981 at General Electric. This strongly validated tool is in use in seven languages and has been applied internationally for over a decade with great success. Detailed information about the *HBDI* is included in Appendix B.

What Will You Gain from the Information in This Book?

♦ You will begin to understand how the brain works, so you can deal more effectively with everyday business situations.

♦ You will understand your mentality and that of your family members, friends, and colleagues. What turns you on, and why you do things the way you do them, will become crystal clear.

♦ You will see key leadership issues, such as productivity, motivation, job design and placement, creativity, and strategic thinking, from a unique new multiple perspective.

♦ You will question common assumptions about human resource assets in organizations and develop a new, broader paradigm.

♦ You will find groundbreaking career development advice and direction.

How to Read This Book

This book is aimed at business readers and is designed to be user-friendly. The Table of Contents provides an overview of the book's topics by part and by chapter. After reading PART I, which contains the premise upon which the book is based, and completing the Preference Indicator Exercise on pages 8 and 9 and the Turn-On Work Exercise on page 26, you can then read the remainder of the book in whole or in part, in sequence or out of sequence, depending on your interest and priorities. Many of the individual chapters can be read as relatively independent "articles" that are freestanding but still in context.

Each chapter begins with a series of bulleted statements describing the essence of its contents. Each chapter ends with a section called "So what?" which is a summary of its business-related meaning. These features enable you both to skim the contents for initial interest and to recall a chapter's essence easily.

The Appendix contains the answers to frequently asked questions about Whole Brain Technology, the *Herrmann Brain Dominance Instrument*, and reference material about brain dominance measurement and validation, as well as *HBDI* profile norms for selected occupations.

"The greatest thing by far is to be a master of the metaphor."

—

Aristotle

The Organizing Principle: A Four-Quadrant Model of the Brain

Chapter Headlines

♦ A powerful level of self-understanding can be attained through the diagnostic power of brain dominance.

♦ The Whole Brain Model identifies four quadrants of thinking styles directly related to the specialized thinking structures of the brain.

♦ Brain Dominance is the key to applying new knowledge of the brain to business.

At the core of Whole Brain Technology is a metaphor of how I believe the brain works. It is founded on my brain-based research and on observable evidence that thinking styles can be best described as a coalition of four different thinking selves. In the Whole Brain Model, these selves are characterized as follows:

♦ **The A-quadrant Analyzer:**
Logical thinking, analysis of facts, processing numbers

♦ **The B-quadrant Organizer:**
Planning approaches, organizing facts, detailed review

♦ **The C-quadrant Personalizer:**
Interpersonal, intuitive, expressive

♦ **The D-quadrant Visualizer:**
Imaginative, big picture thinking, conceptualizing

The *Herrmann Brain Dominance Instrument (HBDI)*, an assessment tool I developed in 1977 and finalized in 1981 during my career at General Electric, quantifies the degree of a person's preference for each of these four styles. Individual profiles resulting from the *HBDI* assessment provide the data upon which the conclusions of this book are based.

People who have been exposed to the Whole Brain Model and *HBDI* assessment through our workshops and seminars often come up with creative ways of explaining why it is so revealing to understand the inner workings of the brain, and to grasp the notion of preferring some styles of thinking more than others. Metaphors can often express what a direct approach cannot. The following explanation, by Janice Beer of Chevron Corporation, shines a new light on the subject:

> Do you tune in your favorite radio station when you're in your car by twirling the dial or by programming your favorite stations so you can get them by simply pushing a button?
>
> In some ways the way we use our brain is a little like the car radio. We can twirl the dial to get any station we like. But we also have favorite stations that we program in—the ones we prefer to listen to more often.
>
> Some people, like my husband, have only rock stations programmed. Other people, like my Mom, are more eclectic and have a combination of easy listening music and radio talk shows. Other people don't have a strong preference and are always fiddling with the dial or reprogramming the stations!
>
> Herrmann's four-quadrant model of how the brain works helps us get a read on what "stations" we may have preference for in our ways of thinking. Some of us have a strong preference in one quadrant while others of us have a preference in two, three, or even four quadrants. It's not right, it's not wrong, it's just different!
>
> Each of us can and does tune into any station we like. If we don't listen to a given station very often we may get some static and it may take some work to tune it in, but it's there for us to access.

"The empires of the future are empires of the mind."

—

Winston Churchill

You can sample the "stations" tuned to your thinking and work preferences by completing this five-minute Whole Brain Exercise in figure 1-1, located on the following pages.

This mini-assessment is designed to give you an approximation of your preferences. As you think about the distribu-

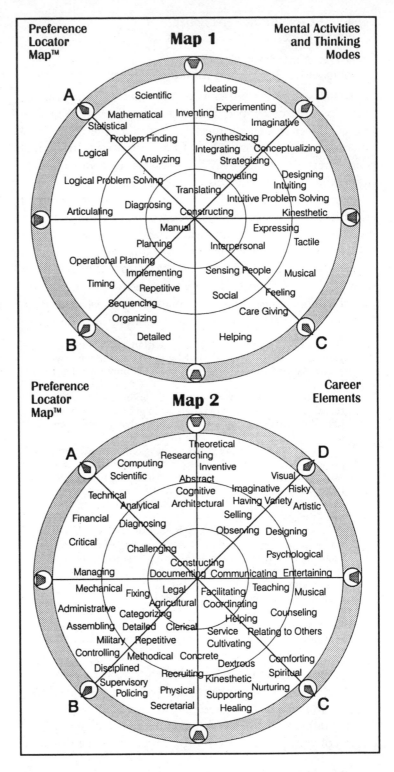

Figure 1-1.
Preference Indicator Exercise. Three preference locator maps reprinted from the author's book, *What Will I Be When I Grow Up?* and a special Accumulator Map designed for this exercise.
Instructions: Circle the eight elements you most strongly prefer on Map 1. Then move to Map 2 and circle the eight elements most important to your career long-term. On Map 3, circle the eight requirements you feel must be a part of your ideal job.

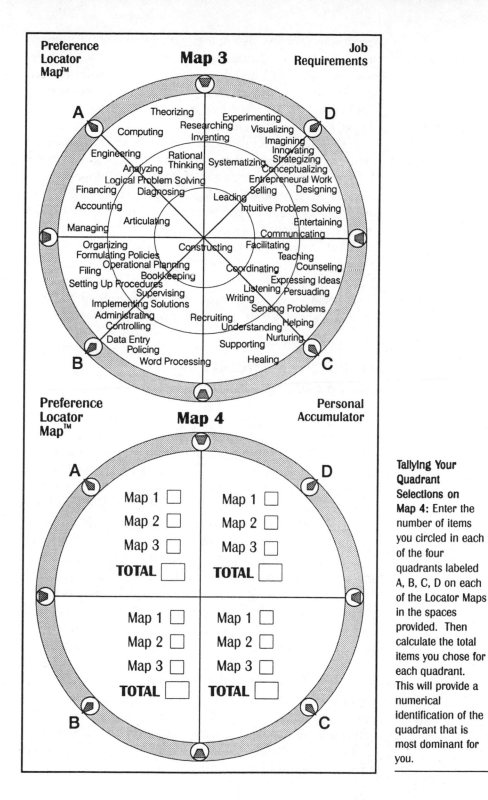

Tallying Your Quadrant Selections on Map 4: Enter the number of items you circled in each of the four quadrants labeled A, B, C, D on each of the Locator Maps in the spaces provided. Then calculate the total items you chose for each quadrant. This will provide a numerical identification of the quadrant that is most dominant for you.

tion of your thinking preferences, remember that the numerical values do not indicate *competence*—only thinking *preferences*. As you read through PART I, you may want to turn back to this exercise and review the results of this exercise. This is not a test with right or wrong answers. In this exercise, all scores are right answers if they ring true for you.

In this chapter and the next, I will trace the history of the brain-oriented research that led up to the development of the *HBDI*, the organizing principle of how the brain works, and the metaphoric Whole Brain Model I have developed. These three separate elements are the prime ingredients that make up the comprehensive Whole Brain Technology presented in this book. As you read through the following chapters, think about how the events of your life have been influenced by your thinking preferences and the thinking preferences of those around you. The following anecdote about my own self-discovery may help to jog your memory.

"Nobody realizes that some people expend tremendous energy merely to be normal."

—

Albert Camus

Research on Creativity Led Me to the Brain

A traumatic midlife illness put an end to the performing and singing I had done since my college years. This unfortunate reality had a silver lining; while I was recovering, I was able to unleash my latent artistic creativity. Though I had always aspired to draw and paint, I could never get past my feelings of inadequacy and self-doubt. Finally I reached the point where my self-imposed barriers no longer made sense. I bought an inexpensive paint set, selected a scene, and started. Then another, and another. Suddenly I was able to draw and paint, and ultimately to sculpt. Over the years I produced many hundreds of paintings and sculptures, won numerous awards, and sold most of my work. I was employed full time by GE as Manager of Management Education, but painting and sculpting had become my second occupation.

My newly discovered talent motivated me to research and understand the nature and source of the creativity that had presented itself. In 1976 I had the perfect opportunity to pursue this interest. I was asked to moderate a panel on the nature and source of creativity sponsored by the Stamford, Connecticut, Art Association, of which I was president at the time. As a result of my reading, I discovered how the brain

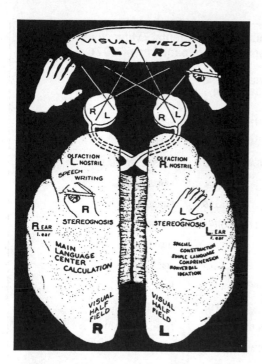

Figure 1-2.
Roger Sperry's diagram of brain specialization. Scheme of functional lateralization demonstrated by separate testing of right and left hemispheres after section of forebrain commissures. Diagram created by Sperry in 1970 is taken from Karl Pribram, *Languages of the Brain* (Brooks/Cole Publishers, 1971), fig. 19-9.

"One is not born a genius; one becomes a genius."

—

Simone de Beauvoir

plays the central role in our ability to be creative. While this concept may seem obvious today, the revelation was like a thunderclap of instant understanding at the time. Creativity was mental, and our ability to control our creative flow came through understanding the brain. This personal AHA! was shortly followed by a second: If there was something to be learned from the brain about creativity, then clearly there was important information about our learning process as well. Again, these conclusions that seem so obvious in 1996 were considered to be breakthrough concepts in 1976.

My continued research about the brain and its connection to creativity and learning led quickly to the work of Roger Sperry, who had shown through his experiments that the brain was divided into two hemispheres that were specialized in function, as shown in figure 1-2.

If you look at the human brain, it is easy to see two half brains connected by some specialized connecting tissue (called the *corpus callosum*). This is the tissue that was separated in the famous "split brain" operations carried out in the 1970s by Roger Sperry, Joseph Bogen, and Michael Gazzanaga. (These operations were a last-ditch effort to resolve what was considered intractable epilepsy.)

Figure 1-3.
Clinical evidence of
hemisphere
specialization.
(*Science News*
Volume 109, #14,
p. 219, issued on
April 3,1976.)

Clinical and Experimental Evidence of Hemispheric Dominance as of 1976

LEFT HEMISPHERE (RIGHT SIDE OF BODY)	RIGHT HEMISPHERE (LEFT SIDE OF BODY)
SPEECH/VERBAL	SPATIAL/MUSICAL
LOGICAL, MATHEMATICAL	HOLISTIC
LINEAR, DETAILED	ARTISTIC, SYMBOLIC
SEQUENTIAL	SIMULTANEOUS
CONTROLLED	EMOTIONAL
INTELLECTUAL	INTUITIVE, CREATIVE
DOMINANT	MINOR (QUIET)
WORLDLY	SPIRITUAL
ACTIVE	RECEPTIVE
ANALYTIC	SYNTHETIC, GESTALT
READING, WRITING, NAMING	FACIAL RECOGNITION
SEQUENTIAL ORDERING	SIMULTANEOUS COMPREHENSION
PERCEPTION OF SIGNIFICANT ORDER	PERCEPTION OF ABSTRACT PATTERNS
COMPLEX MOTOR SEQUENCES	RECOGNITION OF COMPLEX FIGURES

During this period, Robert Ornstein was writing about the psychology of consciousness in terms of the specialized brain. Numerous experiments carried out by these researchers and others provided convincing evidence that the brain was indeed specialized and the differences in specialization were located in each half brain. Doctors, the experimenters, and the popular press all picked up on the idea that the brain was made up of only two specialized hemispheres. Thus, the stage was set for the popularization of the left brain/right brain dichotomy.

Why the Left Brain/ Right Brain Model Falls Short

The world, it seems, has had a long love affair with dichotomies. Right/wrong, good/bad, sweet/sour, up/down, and left/right. Separating anything into just two categories is a simple, easy, and apparently satisfying approach to categorizing differences. The problem is, most often the simple dichotomy

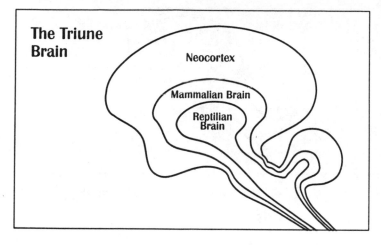

Figure 1-4.
Triune Brain Model
(as developed in the
1970s by Paul
MacLean, a
neuroscientist
working out of the
National Institutes of
Health). This is a
view of the brain
from the side.

falls short of accurately describing the differences involved. I believe this is certainly the case when considering differences in brain function.

In the mid-1970s, Paul MacLean, of the National Institutes of Health, developed the Triune Brain Model that allocated the specialized functions of the brain based on human evolution: that is, the human brain developed sequentially as a reptilian brain, then the mammalian brain, which in turn was finally capped by the neocortex, as shown in figure 1-4.

Despite the emergence of this new theory, throughout the 1970s and 1980s the popular press continued to report developments in brain research with an almost exclusive focus on left and right hemisphere issues. In most cases the limbic system was not mentioned at all, and if it was, the reference was limited to its well-known role in emotional processing.

There Is More to the Brain Than You Think

The role of the limbic system was basically overlooked or ignored at the time. The limbic part of the brain is a relatively small, complicated structure, divided into two interconnected halves nestled within each of the cerebral hemispheres. When you look at an actual brain you can't see it. When a brain has been split open you *still* can't see it. It is only apparent when the brain is dissected. It is essentially hidden from view. Today, computer modeling techniques provide dramatic visual confirmation of the limbic system as a separate brain structure

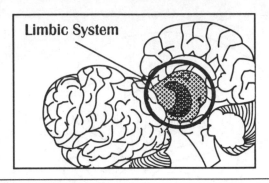

Limbic System

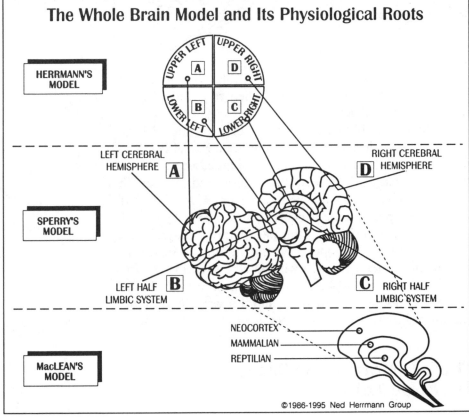

The Whole Brain Model and Its Physiological Roots

HERRMANN'S MODEL

UPPER LEFT | UPPER RIGHT
A | D
B | C
LOWER LEFT | LOWER RIGHT

LEFT CEREBRAL HEMISPHERE **A**

RIGHT CEREBRAL **D** HEMISPHERE

SPERRY'S MODEL

LEFT HALF **B** LIMBIC SYSTEM

C RIGHT HALF LIMBIC SYSTEM

NEOCORTEX
MAMMALIAN
REPTILIAN

MacLEAN'S MODEL

©1986-1995 Ned Herrmann Group

nestled within the lower portion of the two hemispheres.

While somewhat primitive compared to the neocortex of the cerebral hemispheres, the limbic cortex is neural, synaptic, and therefore capable of thinking in the same way as its cerebral cousin. However, up until recently, there hasn't been a reliable way of analyzing the mental processes of the limbic system.

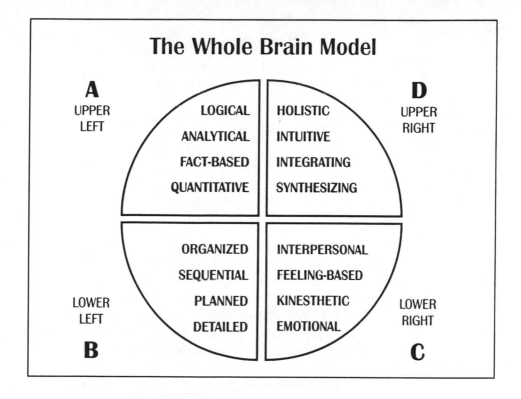

The Whole Brain Model

A
UPPER
LEFT

LOGICAL

ANALYTICAL

FACT-BASED

QUANTITATIVE

HOLISTIC

INTUITIVE

INTEGRATING

SYNTHESIZING

D
UPPER
RIGHT

ORGANIZED

SEQUENTIAL

PLANNED

DETAILED

INTERPERSONAL

FEELING-BASED

KINESTHETIC

EMOTIONAL

LOWER
LEFT

B

LOWER
RIGHT

C

Figure 1-7.
Herrmann's Whole Brain Model. The A, B, C, D four-quadrant model with descriptors for each mode symbolizing those identified by Roger Sperry and Paul MacLean.

I was convinced MacLean's model added a significant piece to my understanding of the thinking parts of the brain. My own experimentation and analysis of MacLean's and Sperry's work lead me to combine elements of the two separate theories into a four-part model representing the whole *thinking* brain. This four-quadrant model serves as an organizing principle of how the brain works: four thinking styles metaphorically representing the two halves of the cerebral cortex (Sperry) and two halves of the limbic system (MacLean).

Here's a metaphor of how all the thinking parts of the brain interact to create a whole network of thinking capabilities. Visualize these thinking parts of the brain as represented by four small chessboards with the bishops on one board, the knights on a second, rooks on a third, and king and queen on a fourth. The pawns are equally divided among the boards. The cortices of the two cerebral hemispheres represent one pair of chessboards, and the cortices of the two halves of the limbic system represent the other. Since each of the four cortices is specialized in a different way, the chess pieces are distributed on the basis of the four specialized domains that

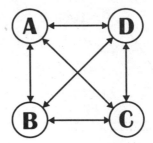

The Organizing Principle

Four interconnected clusters of
specialized mental processing modes,

that function together situationally and iteratively,
making up a whole brain in which one or
more parts becomes naturally dominant.

make up the Whole Brain Model. To play chess you need all the pieces from all the boards. Through hundreds of millions of interconnections, the working brain provides pathways for specialized activities to take place.

Of course the four thinking parts of the brain functioning together are infinitely more complex than any man-made game. But by focusing on both sets of paired thinking structures in the brain, we can quantify their relationships to each other in the form of this four-quadrant model. I believe this model to be a complete metaphor of the entire thinking brain. It is a coalition of an individual's thinking preferences.

The Concept of Brain Dominance

"The brain is as strong as its weakest think."

—

Eleanor Doan

Why *brain dominance?* Dominance provides the basis for measurement of differences. Let me explain. The human body is seemingly symmetrical but actually significantly asymmetrical. That is, there are differences between paired structures throughout the body system. Our hands, feet, eyes, ears, and even the sides of our face, while seemingly the same, are actually quite different. Because of the differences between our right hand and arm and our left hand and arm, nature has provided a physical characteristic that we call dominance. This is the basis for the differentiated development of these body parts. The more dominant hand and arm develop to a higher level because this limb is used more frequently. This results in most of the world's population exhibiting a dominant hand and arm, of which approximately 90 percent are right hand and arm dominant.

This same concept of dominance can be applied to the paired structures of the brain. One member of the pair, through increased use due to preference, develops to a higher level than the nondominant one.

The principle thinking structures in the brain exhibit the same duality characteristic of the other paired structures of the body. Whole Brain Technology is based on the physiology of the *thinking* brain. In order to think, the brain must have a cortex, because it is only within a cortex that neural, synaptic activity takes place. In the entire brain there are only four cortices capable of thinking: the two halves of the cerebral hemispheres and the two halves of the limbic system. These two sets of paired structures are quite different from each other. The left hemisphere is different in size, shape, and specific gravity than the right; the left and right halves of the limbic system are similarly differentiated. These sets of paired cortices are just as asymmetrical as our pairs of hands, feet, or eyes. As dominance of one structure over its partner develops through life's experiences, the degree of that dominance becomes evident from the mental preferences the person exhibits.

"Every man is, in certain respects:
A...
like all men,
B...
like some other men,
C...
like no other man."

—

C. Kluckholm and H. Murry

Measuring Degrees of Dominance

The Whole Brain Model is the product of numerous studies using electroencephalographic (EEG) data from the brains of several dozen test subjects responding to a battery of psychological tests. The electrical activity that takes place in the cerebral hemispheres can be measured by placing electrodes around the scalp. However, this technique could not be used to measure the electrical output from the limbic system, which is located too far below the surface. (It was not until 1983 that positron emission tomography, popularly known as PET scanning, first gave researchers a chance to see the inner structures of the brain at work.) Despite this measurement limitation, the results of these studies still provided enough information for me to build a scaffolding of the thinking style clusters, the architecture of the organizing principle just described. Though some of these experiments were carried out in the lecture halls of GE's Management Development Institute, it became very clear early on that wiring up GE managers and executives with EEG apparatus was not a practical method of gathering data for the development of my model. What was needed was a *metaphoric* model, one that would emulate the specialized structure of the human brain to allow for quantification of an individual's relative preferences for specialized thinking. By this I mean the degree of dominance of one or more of the four quadrant parts of the model. Thus was born the *Herrmann Brain Dominance Instrument*. The date was August 1979. The place was GE's Management Development Institute, where I hosted the first Whole Brain Symposium.

Because this is a metaphorical model and not a clinical one, it permits us to make selected applications while a precise clinical model is still decades from perfection. The metaphoric Whole Brain Model provides a useful and valid basis for determining thinking style preferences lacking a location-specific, precise physiological construct.

What We Know About the Brain Today

> *"In the head the all-baffling brain; in it and below it the makings of heroes."*
>
> —
>
> Walt Whitman

In 1989, Congress passed Public Law 101-58, which established the 1990s as the Decade of the Brain. Ironically, the focus of the popular press coverage of recent brain research has shifted to the limbic system. Previously, press coverage was limited to a few scientific magazines. Now every major news and business magazine runs stories on the brain, and in almost every case has included a significant reference to the limbic system. The limbic system was traditionally mentioned only for its role in emotional processing. Now, the limbic system's central role in processing short-term memory and memory transformation into long-term memory has been recognized. This establishes the limbic system's essential role in learning. The limbic system's critical interface between sensory input and cerebral processing has also been addressed. Crucial roles of the thalamus and hypothalamus in managing the brain's overall activities have been cited. These specific elements of the limbic system serve as the brain's brain.

In spite of 2,500 years of continuous research on the brain, there is a lot we still don't know. It is often reported that our knowledge of the brain doubles every ten years. Considering the complexity of the brain, it's not likely we will ever know everything about it, but those of us living during this decade are fortunate because I believe our knowledge about the brain has much more than doubled due to the national attention being given to brain research during this decade of the brain.

So What?

- Creating a metaphoric model of the four thinking styles of the brain facilitates application of current knowledge of the brain function even though clinical evidence is still in development.

- The left brain/right brain dichotomy popularized by the press is too simplistic and incomplete to serve as a model on which to base a reliable and valid brain dominance assessment.

- The major theories of how the brain is specialized (Sperry's left brain/right brain theory and MacLean's triune brain theory) are integrated into a new comprehensive model that serves as an organizing principle.

- Whole Brain Technology evolved from a personal experience with creativity, which helps make it reality-based rather than another psychological construct.

- The natural phenomenon of dominance between paired structures of the body applies equally to the brain, and is the basis of the theory of brain dominance.

2

The Link Between Brain Dominance and Thinking Preferences

Chapter Headlines

♦ Mental preferences can lead to "turn-on" work and avoidances to "turn-off" work.

♦ A preference and lack of preference are of equal importance to an individual.

♦ The Turn-On Work exercise provides readers with a quick understanding of their mental preferences.

♦ The *HBDI* is a metaphor of how the brain works and serves as an assessment tool that profiles thinking styles in an easy-to-understand four-quadrant model.

The *HBDI* and other diagnostic tools of this technology do not actually measure brainwave activity in the thinking structures; however, they do provide useful measurements of mental preferences, which in turn can be easily interpreted and translated into quite predictable behavioral outcomes in the workplace.

For the purposes of understanding the Whole Brain Model, our degree of preference for each of the four thinking modes can be determined by our relative attraction to or aversion for each of the mode descriptors, which can be loosely defined as families of mental processes that have some commonality. Let me introduce you to each of the families.

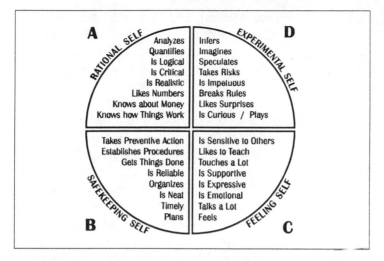

Figure 2-1.
The Four-Selves Model characterizes specialized modes of the Whole Brain Model in the form of selves we act out in response to everyday situations.

Think of a four-family house that represents the specialized brain (as seen from the rear). The upper left apartment is occupied by the Rational family, the lower left by the Organized family. The Feeling family lives in the lower right, and the family known as Experimental lives in the upper right apartment. Logical, Analytic, Quantitative, and Factual (quadrant-A processes) are the "children" of Mr. and Mrs. Rational. Sequential, Structured, Detailed, and Linear (quadrant-B processes) are the offspring of Mr. and Mrs. Organized. The children of Mr. and Mrs. Feeling in the C quadrant are Inter-

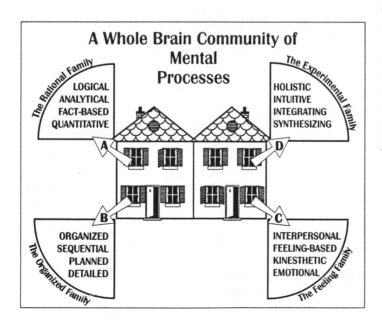

Figure 2-2.
The Four-Quadrant House. A metaphor for the four families of thinking preferences and their relationship to the architecture of the brain.

personal, Emotional, Musical, and Spiritual. Mr. and Mrs. Experimental of the D quadrant have a handful with Imaginative, Synthesizing, Artistic, and Conceptualizing. The four thinking families taken together form a whole brain community of mental processes available to everyone.

When the four families get together for an event, there is no advance discussion about the roles and responsibilities of the individual families. They fall into place naturally and predictably. A while ago the Feeling family suggested that it was time for a group party similar to last year's barbecue. Mr. and Mrs. Organized responded first by saying, "It's been 11.5 months, and if we wait two weeks it will be exactly a year since the last one. A Saturday afternoon would be perfect, with preparations starting at 4:00, dinner at 6:00, and a dessert finale at 8:00." Mr. and Mrs. Feeling said, "That would be great. It allows enough time for other family members to get here." Mrs. Organized said, "What other family members and how many?" "Oh, just some of our first cousins," they responded.

When Mr. Rational overheard the conversation, he said, "Great. This is an opportunity to use my new remote controlled, high-tech stainless steel barbecue grill setup. It's got everything, including a thermostatically controlled gas burner, teflon-coated grills, minifridge, wet bar, and even a state-of-the-art surround-sound entertainment system! It's absolutely the best item in the *Sharper Image* catalogue. The only thing it lacks is a phone, but I'll bring my cellular."

> *"To different minds, the same world is hell, and a heaven."*
>
> —
>
> *Ralph Waldo Emerson*

The Experimental family suggested an earlier starting time for a round-robin badminton game and wondered about expanding the menu to include veggieburgers, smoked turkey, seafood-stuffed sausages, and the seven-grain buns that had just become available. They also thought kite flying would be fun. The Feeling family agreed, but Mrs. Organized said, "I think we should do it exactly the way we did it last year with no changes at all, excepting reducing the number of barbequed ribs, since we had too many left over last year." Mr. Rational proposed a party budget increase of 3 percent in order to take care of cost increases in food over the past 12 months, and that the cost be split equally among the four families. Whereupon Mr. Organized said, "Exactly how many first cousins are you going to invite?"

Well, you get the idea. Each family settles into a role that is consistent with its mental preferences and, taken together,

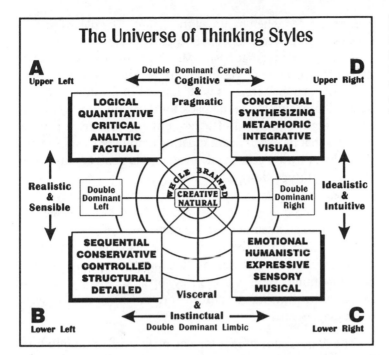

Figure 2-3.
Universe-of-Thinking-Styles Model puts the characteristics of each quadrant in stylistic terms.

they will cover all the necessary behavioral bases as they prepare for and carry out the annual barbecue party.

If we now change the scene to the workplace and translate their barbecue party behavior into styles of management, we'll be able to see the business implications of brain dominance. Consider this scenario. Ms. Rational is manager of finance at the local manufacturing plant. She is courteous and polite but is always focused on business and tends toward the more directive side of management. The Human Resource staff often get complaints that her style is too hard, with an emphasis on the facts and less attention to individual's feelings. Mr. Organized, on the other hand, is the plant manager and in charge of production. Efficiency is paramount. His department follows a comprehensive manual of procedures that he himself developed and for which he won a managerial award. No deviation is permitted. Making sure all runs according to plan, safely, and on time is everything to him, and so he tends to be impatient with ideas and methods that deviate from the norm.

Mrs. Feelings operates a daycare center that has the reputation of being the nicest and most pleasant children's facility in the area. The kids love it and the parents couldn't be happier, not only with their kids' reactions but also with the way they are treated when they visit the center. The place is called Lots of Love Daycare Center, and parents are encouraged to participate on a regular basis. Mr. Experimental is a creativity course developer. He functions as a manager of a small group of corporate trainers who develop innovation and creativity programs. He has a knack for thinking up very imaginative, almost-unheard-of ideas, but the real reason he is leader is that he excels at anticipating employee development needs by at least a year in advance, and is good at conceptualizing prototype designs.

These managers give you an idea of managerial styles for each separate quadrant of the Whole Brain Model. Keep in mind that in an attempt to define purely A, B, C, and D styles, they are extremes of the norm. Most managers would be a combination of these styles, as most people prefer more than one quadrant. Here is a brief synopsis of the styles illustrated in the previous scenarios. Turn to Chapter 9 for more on management styles.

> *"Such as are your habitual thoughts, such also will be the character of your mind; for the soul is dyed by the thoughts."*
>
> —
>
> *Marcus Aurelius*

The A-quadrant style is logical, analytical, and often bottom-line tough. No decision is made without the facts and reality is *now*. In the extreme, the A style can be hardnosed, with a great emphasis on success at any cost, if the numbers look right. An A quadrant would require his/her staff to be well versed in the facts and to use logic rather than intuition or gut feelings to make decisions.

The B style is very detailed, structured, and solid, down-to-earth with no equivocation and ambiguity. Things are done according to procedure and on time, and delivered as promised. Neatness and protocol count, and time costs money. The average B-quadrant manager values following orders, getting the project in on time, a well-organized office, and accurate documentation.

The C-quadrant style is highly participative and team-oriented, and people are considered to be the most important asset. Human values and feelings are paramount and, if push comes to shove, people come first. To the C-quadrant manager, the workplace should be friendly and condone open communication. Outside the organization, people are just as important. The customer isn't a mail drop; the customer is a real person that needs undivided attention. The door of a C-quadrant manager is always open and if something doesn't seem right, standard procedure is to address the problem in a sensitive way.

The D style is intuitive, holistic, adventurous, and risk taking. In contrast to its diametrically opposed B-quadrant neighbor, its credo is, " If there is a better way, let's try it out," as opposed to "If it ain't broke, don't fix it." Experimentation is highly valued. And it is normal for a D-quadrant manager to try out several approaches at once. The style is a very open one, with very little structure. Seeing into the future and avoiding shortsighted solutions is a common trait.

Preferences Lead to Competencies: What's Your Turn-On Work?

Dominance leads to the development of preferences, which in turn establish our interests, lead to our development of competencies, and influence our career choices and ultimately the work that we do.

In the Preference Indicator Exercise on pages 8 and 9, you learned about the location of the various areas of brain specialization where you prefer to live. To add to that information, the following example uses the families of thinking styles metaphor to define where you prefer to live at work in particular. Afterwards you'll get a chance to see what additional information can be gained through the *HBDI*.

The Whole Brain Model has already been described as a four-family house occupied by the families of Mr. and Mrs. Rational, Mr. and Mrs. Organized, Mr. and Mrs. Feelings, and that interesting couple, Mr. and Mrs. Experimental. Imagine now that there is a large room in each of the four sections of this big house filled with things from The Sharper Image, Circuit City, Bloomingdales, Sears and Roebuck, F. A. O. Schwartz, and Star Magic. This is the ultimate array of "stuff" that could turn anybody on. But instead of being randomly distributed, all these items have been carefully selected to appeal to the differing mental preferences of each of the four families. The members of each family are all having a great time. But when they visit the rooms of the other families, they are not nearly so turned on and, in some cases, are totally turned off by what they find there.

"If you love what you do, you will never work another day in your life."

—

Confucious

Now, move from "turn-on" products to "turn-on" work. Each of the four rooms in the four parts of the house displays turn-on work opportunities for the inhabitants. By *turn-on work*, I mean activity that is so interesting, so stimulating, so pleasurable to do that you would select it for these special attributes over other work that was offered to you. It may not be the easiest work to perform, but in all cases, it is more satisfying and fulfilling and, therefore, if given a choice, this is what you would select. And finally, it is the kind of work that doesn't require constant external rewards because the doing of the work is rewarding in itself.

Let me move from metaphor to example. The exercise in figure 2-4 demonstrates the power of the whole brain idea as an organizing principle and shows how self-understanding

Figure 2-4.
The Turn-On Work Exercise. An array of work elements that correspond to each quadrant. Follow the instructions to identify which ones turn you on or turn you off.

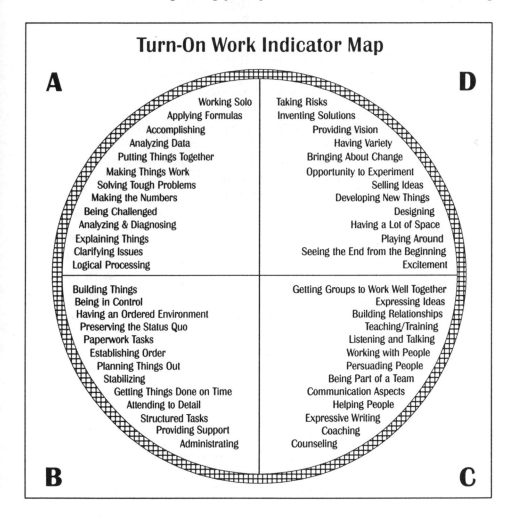

Turn-On Work Indicator Map

A

Working Solo
Applying Formulas
Accomplishing
Analyzing Data
Putting Things Together
Making Things Work
Solving Tough Problems
Making the Numbers
Being Challenged
Analyzing & Diagnosing
Explaining Things
Clarifying Issues
Logical Processing

D

Taking Risks
Inventing Solutions
Providing Vision
Having Variety
Bringing About Change
Opportunity to Experiment
Selling Ideas
Developing New Things
Designing
Having a Lot of Space
Playing Around
Seeing the End from the Beginning
Excitement

B

Building Things
Being in Control
Having an Ordered Environment
Preserving the Status Quo
Paperwork Tasks
Establishing Order
Planning Things Out
Stabilizing
Getting Things Done on Time
Attending to Detail
Structured Tasks
Providing Support
Administrating

C

Getting Groups to Work Well Together
Expressing Ideas
Building Relationships
Teaching/Training
Listening and Talking
Working with People
Persuading People
Being Part of a Team
Communication Aspects
Helping People
Expressive Writing
Coaching
Counseling

of our mental preferences can help define our turn-on work.

You can get an idea which family you are a member of by selecting the eight elements from all four quadrants that *most turn you on*. Visit each quadrant-shaped room (A,B,C,D) to make your selections. Circle the ones you choose in pencil so that you have a record of the distribution of your choices.

As you made your eight selections, you probably found several work items that *turned you off* rather than turned you on. Select two of these turn-offs and underline them.

Now look at your results. Is there one room in this four-quadrant indicator house that has most of the things that turn you on, or are your eight items fairly equally divided between just two of those quadrants? Or three, maybe even four quadrants? Are the underlined turn-off items opposite the quadrant's that turn you on?

This simple exercise will add to your personal data on your mental preferences. There are no right or wrong answers. It's just that you are more energized by certain kinds of work and drained by others. The things that turn you on are usually in strong alignment with your thinking preferences. In addition to several descriptors, each quadrant has its own color and our clients often prefer to refer to them that way. The following explanation of the work-related quadrant descriptors also include the quadrant colors as they appear on the front cover.

If you have four or five circled items in the rational, *blue* quadrant, then it is likely that you prefer to think in logical, analytical, fact-based terms. If this is the case then you probably have one or two additional turn-ons in the organized *green* quadrant or the experimental *yellow* quadrant, and perhaps your turn-offs are in the *red*, interpersonal quadrant.

Another possibility for business managers is for your eight turn-on choices to be fairly equally divided between the rational blue and organized green quadrants of this model, with your turn-offs in the red feeling and yellow experimental quadrants. The reverse might be true for those of you who are entrepreneurial or human resource–oriented, who are highly turned on by experimental kinds of work or a combination of experimental and feeling work elements, and turned off by organized or analytical work elements.

The more scientific among you would select your items from the A and the D quadrants, while those of you who are interested in manufacturing things, selling real estate, or do-

"To be succcessful, the first thing to do is fall in love with your work."

—

Sister Mary Lauretta

ing social work would likely choose descriptors from the bottom half of this model, i.e., the B and C quadrants.

And then there will be a few of you who have selected one or more turn-on items in each of the four quadrants. This more distributed selection of turn-on work is typical of CEOs, general managers, and executive secretaries, to name a few, whose jobs demand a broader understanding of the wide world of thinking preferences.

Figure 2-5.
Locator Map showing the distribution of Professional Occupations in the Whole Brain Model.

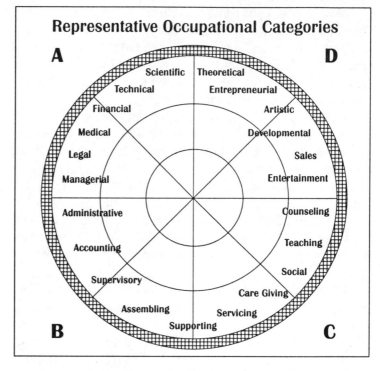

Figure 2-5 contains a distribution of over 30 occupations in the four quadrants and four modes of the Whole Brain Model.

Before you leave this exercise, circle the quadrant letter(s) (A, B, C, D) that identify your preferences and underline the one that represents your least preferred mental activity. Now follow the same procedure for indicating the turn-on work and turn-off work of your close business friends and family members by thinking about the clues provided by their visible behavior. In addition, I encourage you to photocopy an unmarked version of this exercise for your business friends and family and measure how your perception of their preferences matches their self-analysis.

This very simple exercise does not attempt to provide a sophisticated and validated assessment, such as the *HBDI* provides. However, it will reveal the *general trend and direction* of your preferences. You can still benefit from what the *HBDI* measures and the multitude of thinking preference norms cited in this book. The data from the *HBDI* will expand the understanding you have already gained from the Preference and Turn-On Work Indicators. The following section provides an overview so that you'll be able to interpret the *HBDI* references throughout the book and therefore easily apply this new information to your own unique situation.

Understanding Thinking Preferences Measured by the Herrmann Brain Dominance Instrument (HBDI)

In order to grasp the meaning of all the thinking style trends and patterns, you should know what the *HBDI* is, what it indicates, and how to interpret the examples of *HBDI* profiles that are a major part of this book and the application of this work. However, it is not necessary for you to have use of the *HBDI* to understand or apply Whole Brain concepts. Many people have found the *HBDI* profile grid to be an effective method of displaying the degrees of preference for the quadrants. And so I elected to illustrate the trends and norms in the form that I feel communicates this information most effectively.

"No one who learns to know himself remains just what he was before."

—

Thomas Mann

The *Herrmann Brain Dominance Instrument* (*HBDI*) charts your location in the world of thinking style preferences and is a metaphor for how I believe the brain works. Originally developed in the context of the business needs of GE, the *HBDI* takes into account the work preferences of individuals as well as other aspects of their lives: education, hobbies, and in general, self-assessment.

The *HBDI*, a survey of 120 items, can be thought of as an assessment tool that profiles thinking style preferences. The resulting profiles are displayed on a four-quadrant grid that emulates the four principle thinking structures in the brain. In the east/west positions are those preferences that are commonly referred to as left brain/right brain ways of thinking.

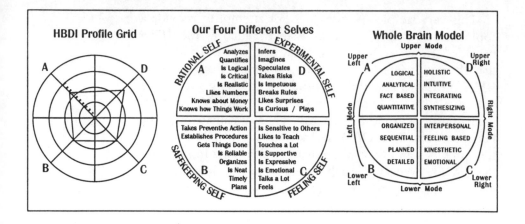

Figure 2-6.
Three major elements of Whole Brain Technology; The Four-Selves Model, the *HBDI* Profile, and the Whole Brain Model.

In the north/south positions are those ways of thinking that are referred to as cerebral in the north, and limbic in the south. Cerebral modes consist of "cognitive and intellectual" ways of thinking, and the limbic mode encompasses "visceral, structured, and instinctive" ways of thinking.

The four-quadrant display on the left of figure 2-6 is an example of a typical profile, labeled "John Doe." The model in the middle is the Four-Selves Model, which describes the coalition of our thinking selves in a more behavioral way. The model on the right is the Whole Brain Model, which is the conceptual and structural basis of the profile grid.

Remember, the *HBDI* displays mental preferences, not abilities or competencies. However, there is a strong relationship between preferences and competencies in that typically one leads to the other (figure 2-7).

Figure 2-7.
Relationship between brain dominance and competencies and all the phases in-between.

BRAIN DOMINANCE
↓
INTEREST
↓
PREFERENCES
↓
weak ← **MOTIVATION** → strong
↓ ↓ ↓
Low COMPETENCE High

It is also important to know that a preference for a particular thinking style and an avoidance of another style are of equal consequence to an individual. A preference, particularly a very strong preference, will lead to turn-on work. The turn-on work exercise in the previous section was designed to give you an approximation of your degree of preference for work elements in each of the four quadrants. In contrast, a lack of preference or an actual avoidance in a quadrant results in being turned off to the mentality of the work elements in that particular quadrant. Being turned on is highly motivational and often represents a state of self-actualization. Being turned off is highly demotivational. For these reasons, the *HBDI* profile is quite predictive of a person's acquisition of competencies and engagement in work. Figure 2-8 is a partial universe of profiles and likely occupations.

Since examples of visual profiles and numerical profile codes are used throughout this book, it is necessary to know

"I've got a great ambition to die of exhaustion rather than boredom."

—

Angus Grossart and Noble Grossart

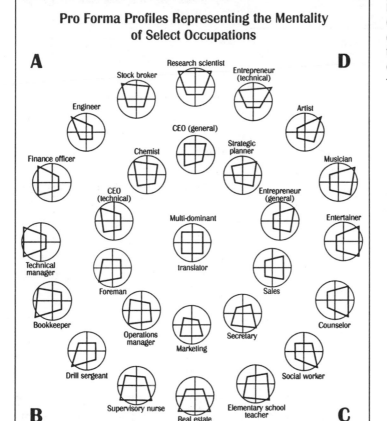

Figure 2-8.
Categories of occupations and pro forma profiles of each.

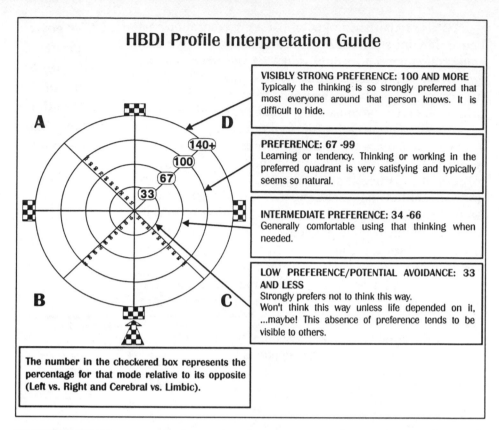

HBDI Profile Interpretation Guide

A   D

VISIBLY STRONG PREFERENCE: 100 AND MORE
Typically the thinking is so strongly preferred that most everyone around that person knows. It is difficult to hide.

PREFERENCE: 67 -99
Learning or tendency. Thinking or working in the preferred quadrant is very satisfying and typically seems so natural.

INTERMEDIATE PREFERENCE: 34 -66
Generally comfortable using that thinking when needed.

LOW PREFERENCE/POTENTIAL AVOIDANCE: 33 AND LESS
Strongly prefers not to think this way.
Won't think this way unless life depended on it, ...maybe! This absence of preference tends to be visible to others.

B   C

The number in the checkered box represents the percentage for that mode relative to its opposite (Left vs. Right and Cerebral vs. Limbic).

Figure 2-9.
Key to reading the *HBDI* Profile Grid (*HBDI* Interpretation Package).

enough about what they mean in order to interpret these references in the remaining chapters. Refer to the key in figure 2-9 as you read through the following list of tips.

Some Tips for Understanding HBDI Profiles

1. Look at the shape of the profile and identify the quadrant with the most prominent preference. Under normal everyday circumstances this quadrant would be the direction of that person or group's preferred mode of thinking.

2. Look for the second-most preferred quadrant of the profile. The combination of the most and second-most preferred quadrants results in a dominant mode—such as left, right, cerebral, or limbic.

3. Look for the least preferred quadrant. Often the lack of preference for a particular thinking style is just as im-

portant as the strong preference. The strong preference indicates the likelihood of a person being turned on to a particular style and the absence of preference, particularly if it is a score of 33 or less, indicates the possibility of an individual being turned off. In many cases, both of these conditions are visible to family, colleagues, and friends.

4. Look for strong preferences in opposing quadrants, such as B/D and A/C. These profiles often represent internal conflicts as individuals make decisions or react to everyday situations. For example, in the case of the B/D profile, a person could be on the one hand imaginative, holistic, and risk taking and at the same time status quo, detailed, and traditional or organized. In other words, such a person has one foot on the accelerator and the other foot on the brake.

5. Look for profiles that are very balanced, with relatively equal scores in all four quadrants. This profile represents a relatively equal distribution of preferences and therefore a balanced distribution of interests, skills, abilities, and competencies. This is extremely rare. Only 2.5 percent of our database of individuals has a primary preference in all four quadrants.

6. In all cases, the profiles displayed represent actual data, whether it is that of an individual or a group average. When profiles are labeled "pro forma" the data is inferred by applying a diagnostic technique based on Whole Brain Technology.

"Nothing about ourselves can be changed until it is first accepted."

—

Sheldon Kopp

So What?

■   The *HBDI* is a metaphoric assessment tool that emulates the brain.

■   The *HBDI* profiles an individual's mental preferences in a four-quadrant model.

■   There is a strong relationship between preferences and acquired competencies.

■   Hundreds of business occupations have been profiled and norms for those profiles are available.

3

Measuring Thinking Styles the Whole Brain Way

Chapter Headlines

♦ How thinking style preferences develop and how they can change.

♦ *Situational* wholeness is the answer to Whole Brain aspirations.

♦ Knowing your mental preferences and your mental options is essential to achieving full development of self.

♦ How to get the most out of this book by learning how to interpret the *HBDI* profiles used as relevant examples.

How Do Your Preferences Develop and How Permanent Are They?

Are we on a genetically programmed path that is determined by our genes and chromosomes? The answer is "No, but—." We are, I believe, a product of both nature and nurture. And for most of us, it is the nurture aspect that predominates in who we are and who we can become. That is a message of hope! Because if we were limited to only our genetic inheritance there would be no opportunity for us to develop into our own unique person. Little, if any, of the learning that takes place during our maturing process would have any effect. We would be the product of our inheritance and nothing else. I don't think there is a person alive who would accept that as an accurate description of who they are. It's not nature OR nurture. It's nature AND nurture. The basic building block of our adult self is the DNA of our inherited genes and chromosomes. But that's only the beginning. From that foundation we can become the architects of the unique emerging human being.

My research into the brain leads me to believe firmly that the grand design is to be whole; that the normal, ordinary, everyday brain is specialized and interconnected in ways that position it to develop as a balanced, multidominant brain capable of accessing and using all of its mental options. However, my data on hundreds of thousands of individuals suggests that few, if any, end up being that exquisitely balanced. In the more typical case, as we mature mentally we develop preferences for particular modes of processing. These preferences emerge from our latent brain dominance characteristics that begin very subtly, but are reinforced and grow stronger through daily use.

During the early stages of this maturing process we really don't know any better. By the time we are able to understand the consequences of this strengthening dominance, the thinking pattern has already been established. In the typical case, by the time we become conscious of our mental preferences we have already reinforced them many times over, so that they have now developed sufficient strength to become a mind of their own. We have already done this with our right hand or left hand, and after a few million physical movements based on that preference, we have developed a lifetime of handedness preference and skill. In a different but analogous sense we have developed some of our mental dominances into such strong preferences that they have led to competencies in particular ways of thinking. We have become very good at language; or we have developed impressive math skills; or we are exceedingly organized; or we can accurately sense the feelings of others; or we are always coming up with new ideas. These early competencies arising out of preferences that grew out of dominance characteristics can lead to entire mental processing families of development.

Change and growth can follow the pursuit of our interests. As interests develop and expand they can result in enormous change in an individual's mental capacity and range of

"I believe the grand design is to be whole."

—

Ned Herrmann

"At Work" Activities to Help You Access and Develop Your Less Preferred Modes

Activities for right-mode dominant people to engage in and learn to conquer:	Activities for left-mode dominant people to engage in and learn to enjoy:
A **Upper Left Activities**	**Upper Right Activities** **D**
♦ Analyze and solve a technical problem. ♦ Read and understand a budget or financial report. ♦ Calculate your salary per minute/second. ♦ Learn a new computer program that would enhance your job performance. ♦ Clearly define work goals for next quarter. ♦ Learn to use a spreadsheet and develop a budget report for your department. ♦ Conduct a statistical analysis. ♦ Use logic in your decision making.	♦ Set aside time for idea generation and think of at least one "crazy" idea per day. ♦ In your "mind's eye" (with eyes closed) imagine your organization ten years from now. ♦ (Re-) decorate your office; add creative toys and/or posters to the decor. ♦ Design a "logo" for your job. ♦ Instigate a brainstorming session on an important issue. ♦ Illustrate a memo to a colleague. ♦ Make a decision based on intuition. ♦ Conceptualize a new program or product for your organization.
♦ Use a "time log" to record your daily activities with precision. ♦ (Re-) organize your filing system; your desk. ♦ Create a "things-to-do" list and check off items when done. ♦ Plan out a project in detail and follow thru with it. ♦ Arrive on time at work or for appointments all day. ♦ Create a highly detailed job description. ♦ Read the policy manual and keep it accessible for reference. ♦ Be conservative and safekeeping in your decision making.	♦ Spontaneously recognize another employee in a way that is personal and meaningful for them. ♦ Be aware of your nonverbal communication and make it friendlier; e.g., smile, be relaxed. ♦ Motivate others to have a fun, "people" event. ♦ Volunteer to assist a coworker on a company project. ♦ Try playing a "music" radio station in the background while you work. ♦ Spend at least 15 minutes per day getting to know others personally. ♦ Make a decision using team concensus.
B **Lower Left Activities**	**Lower Right Activities** **C**

Figure 3-1.
At Work Chart. Suggestions for exercising each quadrant with work-related activities.

thinking. If we assume that the whole spectrum of mental options is preloaded into the developing brain, then the opportunities for growth and change are limitless.

The life experiences that produce change can also build walls that prevent change from happening. Learning environments that limit rather than stimulate, or parents that disallow the pursuit of the child's interests, not only thwart development but also erect barriers that foreclose on whole domains of thinking; teachers who present information in

"At Home" Activities to Help You Access and Develop Your Less Preferred Modes

Activities for right-mode dominant people to engage in and learn to conquer:	Activities for left-mode dominant people to engage in and learn to enjoy:
A **Upper Left Activities**	**Upper Right Activities** **D**
◆ Predict what will happen tomorrow based on what you know about today.	◆ Fly a kite the way it is meant to be flown.
◆ Find out how a frequently used machine actually works.	◆ Invent a gourmet dish and then prepare it.
◆ Take a current problem situation and analyze it into its main parts.	◆ Play with clay and discover its inner meaning.
◆ Review a recent impulsive decision and identify its rational aspects.	◆ Take a 15 minute "theta break" (a relaxed brain wave state) before getting out of bed.
◆ Convert your retirement dreams into a quantitative formula.	◆ Drive to "nowhere" without feeling guilty.
◆ Join an investment club.	◆ Run, don't jog.
◆ Engage in some logic games.	◆ Take "500" photographs without worrying about the cost.
	◆ Create a personal logo or mandalla.
	◆ Go dancing in your own style.
	◆ Allow yourself to daydream.
	◆ Imagine yourself in the year 2020.
◆ Assemble a model kit by the instructions.	◆ Play with children the way they want to play.
◆ Develop a personal budget.	◆ "Dance" without moving your feet.
◆ Prepare a personal property list.	◆ Take a 10 minute "feeling break" every morning, afternoon, and evening.
◆ Jog, monitoring your stride and/or heartrate.	◆ "Love" a pine cone or any other natural thing.
◆ Organize your CDs, videos, or audio tapes in sequence according to categories.	◆ Play the music you like when you want to hear it.
◆ Prepare a family tree.	◆ Allow tears to come to your eyes without feelings of shame or guilt.
◆ Go ballroom, square, or line dancing.	◆ Experience your own spirituality in a non-religious way.
◆ Find a mistake in your bank statement.	◆ Discover things children have taught you, and find ways to thank them.
◆ Organize your home and garden tools.	
◆ Be exactly on time all day.	
◆ Organize your picture files.	
B **Lower Left Activities**	**Lower Right Activities** **C**

Figure 3-2. At Home Chart. Suggestions for exercising the four quadrants in nonwork activities.

ways that serve their own learning style deny learning to others who learn differently. Suffice it to say that the normal person has built into his or her brain a full set of mental processing options that can be accessed and applied if life's circumstances don't get in the way. We are wired to be whole and we can become more so by taking more complete charge of our own development. Figures 3-1 and 3-2 contain exercises to widen your comfort zone of mental preferences at work and at home.

On Being Whole Brained

Should you aspire to a whole brain profile, that is, a profile with four strong primaries, one in each quadrant? Should your goal be a perfectly balanced 1-1-1-1? The answer is a clear "NO." The world would be a dull place indeed, if everyone faced life's variable situations and every decision with such an equally distributed array of mental preferences.

What should be everybody's objective is to be as *situationally* whole brained as possible. This means that you continue to have the advantage of a dominant preference that provides you with a leading response to everyday situations, but that you are not limited by that dominance. You have available to you a much broader spectrum of mental options that can be accessed because you know of the existence of your situational capabilities, and you have practiced using these options to the extent that these secondary modes represent competencies you can count on.

To reiterate, there is an advantage to having strong, dominant preferences. Because of these preferences you have developed interests that have led you to competencies, which represent your mental strengths. In a given situation, that's where you look first for an answer or an appropriate response. In most cases, you don't have to stop and think about everything you do. You go ahead and do it. Those few people who are truly ambidextrous often have to stop and think, "Which hand shall I use this time?" For the vast majority of the world's population this is not an issue. We reach out with our dominant hand automatically. However, we could use our nondominant hand if we needed to. I believe this analogy holds true for our mental activity as well as our physical, particularly if we are open to it and have practiced it. For me, the truly whole-brained person is the person who has optimized the use of his or her established competencies and, through understanding that other mental options are available, is prepared to be open to them and to apply them situationally.

As a case in point, over the years I have developed an uncanny ability for long-range planning. I have been able to conceptualize 5-, 10-, and 15-year goals and make them come true. It is less natural for me to think of and fit short-term goals and develop detailed plans to achieve them. However,

"The people who get on in this world are the people who get up and look for the circumstances they want, and, if they can't find them, make them."

—
George Bernard Shaw

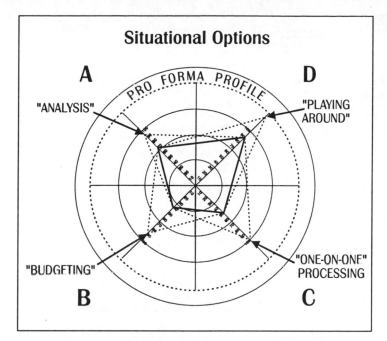

Figure 3-3.
Situational Options
Chart. Use of each
specialized mode is
available to us
situationally.

because I have become keenly aware of this difference in
mental preferences, I have developed a competence and discipline around short-term planning that I use whenever I have
to. In earlier times, I would concentrate on the long-range
thinking that came naturally. Now that I know I have an
available option, I am able to access and apply short-term
planning competencies, including dealing with excruciating
detail. I do it when I have to because it's useful to me. I *don't*
do it when I *don't* have to because it doesn't turn me on and
tends to be boring. The point is, I am able to be much more
situationally whole now that I know what my mental options
are. Knowing your preferences and your mental options
positions you to supplement your existing competencies with
needed situational competencies.

Everyone Has a
Least Preferred Quadrant

It is in the nature of things that since we as individuals are a
coalition of four different selves, we prefer to use one or more
of those selves compared to the others. All profiles are made
up of most preferred and least preferred thinking modes.

UPPER LEFT **A** FACTS "Once again...forensic science using the undeniable facts of blood type, fingerprints, and spectrographic analysis of paint fragments proves beyond a doubt..."	FUTURES **D** **UPPER RIGHT** "This accident demonstrates the lethal combination of drunk driving and faulty car design. These two issues are national in scope and deserve urgent Congressional attention if future generations are to be adequately protected..."

**Examples of Four Reporters' Views
of the Same Accident**

"At 3:30 pm, Thursday, April 9th, on Route 9, 15 miles north of Columbus, a black 1978 Plymouth, 4-door sedan traveling at 75 miles per hour in a 35 mph school zone..." **B** FORM **LOWER LEFT**	"Tearful, screaming mother attacks the cowering suspect as irate police officers hold off an angry mob at the terrifying scene of a tangled school bus and the accident's bloody victims." FEELINGS **C** **LOWER RIGHT**

Figure 3-4.
Four reporters' views of an accident, each one representing a different quadrant viewpoint.

These combinations of preferences are sometimes extreme. By that I mean that one or two preferences are so prominent that their consequences are visible in our behavior. And the corollary is also true, that an *absence* of preference can also have visible behavioral consequences. The chances are good that we will do the things that we prefer to do as a result of our thinking style and we will not do those things that we don't prefer to do.

It is interesting to group people together on the basis of their most preferred and least preferred thinking preferences. In the case of most preferred, the group can typically reach an easy consensus in subjects that fall into the domain of their thinking preferences. However, this is not the case when dealing with least preferred thinking modes. When grouped together on the basis of their least preferred quadrants, the group is *heterogeneous* in terms of preferences and *homogeneous* in terms of nonpreferences. Unless you give them a special assignment in their common area of least preferred thinking, they will exhibit the behaviors of a diverse group and therefore have difficulty in achieving consensus. Since there is a shared lack of preference in a particular mental domain, there is an opportunity for group learning to take place. For example, using communication as the theme for an assignment, we will group people together on the basis of their least preferred quadrants and then ask them to play the role of reporters at an accident scene (figure 3-4).

They are asked to interpret the accident through the stereotypical perceptions of reporters who don't like to use a particular quadrant in their perceiving and writing about an event. Let's take the C quadrant as an example. If we group four or five people together who don't prefer to think and write in C-quadrant language, but require them to do so for this assignment, they will typically develop an extreme stereotypical version of a C-quadrant newspaper story. It will be filled with emotion and people issues. They will enjoy doing it and it will be a hilarious experience. But the important outcome is that they will learn a bit about how to perceive an event in C-quadrant terms and how to write about it using C-quadrant language.

The exercise in "least preferred" thinking quickly reveals that the stereotype in the C quadrant is *emotionality*. In the A quadrant it is *facts*. In the B quadrant it is *details*. And in the D quadrant it is *off-the-wall fantasy*. Even though the stereotypes are ridiculous in the extreme, the assignment provides practice in thinking and writing in ways that these individuals *almost* never use and typically disregard when other people, who *prefer* to use these modes, do so in a business situation. Walking in the moccasins of those who prefer the things we least prefer provides an instant wake-up call to the need to pay more attention to what others are saying, and to have more respect for the way they are saying it. Since we are living in a composite whole brain world, and the reality of any multifunctional group is the diversity of its thinking and therefore its perceptions and language, it is essential from a communications standpoint to increase our tolerance of and understanding of what people are saying who are different from us.

The Consequences of
Lack of Preference

Given that we all prefer to think in some ways more than others, what do we do about our lack of preference?

Our strong primaries often represent work activities that turn us on, and our tertiary scores almost always represent work activities that turn us off. When people are turned off they drop out of the game. They become selectively blind and deaf to the discussions and activities that take place in their areas of avoidance. If a person has avoidance in one of the quadrants, and a large percentage of the work he or she has to do falls into that quadrant, then the likelihood of job success is enormously reduced.

Occupational mismatch, in which a person is assigned to work that does not fall into his or her area of preference, can produce very poor results. Take, for example, a financial manager who has a super-primary in the A quadrant, and a score so low in the C quadrant that it is clearly an avoidance. Because much of the mentality of financial work falls in the A quadrant, this person will perform well on all of the logical, analytical, quantitative aspects of the work but will be selectively blind and deaf to the people aspects of his financial assignment. This person would probably be described as a "cold, heartless number cruncher" as a consequence of that avoidance. The finance job would typically require much more than just the ability to deal effectively with numbers. Therefore, this person's avoidance in the C quadrant would seriously limit his or her ability to perform high-level finance work because, in most instances, that requires interest and competence in dealing with human resource issues.

Check this out yourself. Think about your coalition of preferences. Are they equally distributed or do you have some very strong turn-ons and possibly a few turn-offs? Go back to Chapter 2, and review the Turn-On Work Exercise. This time, instead of just underlining one turn-off, underline all the work activities that turn you off and reflect on their consequences for the work you do and the way you do it. There are several action steps that you might consider. The first is to eliminate as many of these turn-offs from your work assignment as you can by delegating them or discussing reassigning them to a more appropriate person. The second is to

"To know what you prefer, instead of humbly saying 'Amen' to what the world tells you you ought to prefer, is to have kept your soul alive."

—

Robert Louis Stevenson

begin to make friends with those things that currently turn you off. Now that you have a better appreciation of the consequences on your work and career, you may well decide to change your attitude about those work elements.

So What?

- Who we are, what we do, and how we do it are the result both of nature and nurture.

- In most cases nurture is the primary influence. This is a message of hope. We can change if we want to.

- If a person's environment and work remain stable, it is likely that their preferences will remain the same.

- Interesting work that turns us on is the most powerful influence on our mental preferences.

- Knowing your preferences and your mental options positions you to supplement your existing competencies with needed situational competencies.

- Our natural asymmetry leads to both most preferred and least preferred mental modes.

- A person's *lack of preference* can be as important to his or her job performance as the strong preferences that qualified them for the job.

4

How Your Brain Gets Along with Other People's Brains

"For my thoughts are not your thoughts, neither are your ways my ways."

—

Isaiah

Chapter Headlines

♦ Hard data supports the finding that the world's population is equally distributed in the four-quadrant model.

♦ Leaders of composite whole brain companies typically *do not* lead on the basis of their diverse workforce.

♦ Contrary to commonly held opinion, all ethnic groups, on the average, comprise a balanced composite whole brain.

♦ Brain dominance leads to preference, which leads to interest and ultimately to the acquisition of competencies.

♦ Profiles of married couples are typically contrasting, while profiles of unmarried, living-together couples are typically very similar.

Same-Thinking-Style Competitiveness

Individuals with strikingly different thinking styles often have difficulty understanding each other. In contrast, individuals with very similar thinking styles often become competitive with each other. What is happening here is that while the thinking styles are nominally very similar, there are some minor differences in preference that could be just enough to give Person #1 a slightly different perception of a given situation compared to Person #2. This somewhat different perception could lead to "We both have pretty much the same understanding, but my way is better than your way."

Let me be a bit more specific. Take two individuals whose thinking styles are strongly rational. Two of the defining characteristics of rational thinkers are logical processing and analytic processing. In this example, Person #1 prefers both but is more logical than analytical. Person #2 also prefers both but is more analytical than logical. They team up to work on the same problem, with one tilting toward analysis and the other tilting toward logic. They are both clearly on a rational track, but through their differentiated preference, have developed higher-order preferences and, therefore, skills in these two quite similar but different thinking modes.

These two individuals are developing a strategy around this year's sales plan for one of their industrial customers. Person #1, the sales engineer, says the customer has purchased 500 of the same motor every year for the past three years, and therefore we should project a minimum of 500 for this year.

Person #2, the inside sales support engineer, says yes, but his analysis shows that the orders came in distinct cycles, with the majority in the second and fourth quarters, and this affects the manufacturing cycle. And what if they don't order in the fourth quarter? This could adversely affect year-end results. Person #1 counters with the logic of a three-year track record. Person #2 argues that analysis has uncovered a buying pattern that could affect future business. They struggle to reach agreement on an issue where they are both partly right.

This form of thinking style competition seems to favor the left mode but can also take place in the cerebral mode. In this next case you have two individuals, both with double dominant preferences in the rational A quadrant and the experimental D quadrant, but the mix is different. Person #1 favors rational thinking a bit more than experimental, and Person #2 favors experimental a bit more than rational. They are clearly on the same track but one sees a faster route to the finish line than the other. This kind of competition can occur in scientific research or in an R&D lab.

Two R&D physicists who share an A/D profile are working together to design a flatter television screen. The one with rational preferences proposes a research study of all the

"Everything that irritates us about others can lead us to an understanding about ourselves."

—

Carl Jung

known screen designs as the first step. That would be the obvious logical thing to do. In contrast, the physicist with experimental preferences would much rather play around with different combinations of existing screens to determine which criteria contribute most to flatness. That would be the more interesting and creative way to start the task. They argue about which approach will produce quicker results. Again, both are partly right, but each feels strongly that his approach is best.

As they work through their individual solutions to a problem, I can visualize them becoming quite competitive about which approach is best. It is likely that either the logical or experimental approach would ultimately produce a solution, but because they are aware of both but favor one, they are often inclined to be quite competitive about the one they prefer.

> *"The central question is whether the wonderfully diverse and gifted assemblage of human beings on this earth knows how to run a civilization."*
>
> —
>
> *Adlai Stevenson*

The right mode and limbic mode quadrants are less susceptible to competition because people favoring these quadrants seem to compete with themselves rather than others. They are also inclined to be softer in their approach and more attentive to their relationships. In contrast, the more cognitive-oriented thinking styles are more sharp-edged and assertive and less concerned with interpersonal relationships. Damn the torpedoes—full steam ahead!

It is not my purpose, by citing these examples, to suggest that competition in thinking styles is bad. In fact, competitive approaches can lead to better decisions and better solutions. My purpose is to suggest that there are consequences to pairing people with similar profiles. Most people would assume that, since their thinking styles are so similar, they will be entirely compatible in a team situation. With these observations, I'm suggesting that the assumption of compatibility might be premature and that, in some cases, similar but not precisely the same thinking styles could lead to vigorous competition. The leadership challenge would be to have this competition be healthy and synergistic rather than hostile and combative. It would be up to the manager to establish a climate that fostered interaction between members of an organization on the basis of creative added value.

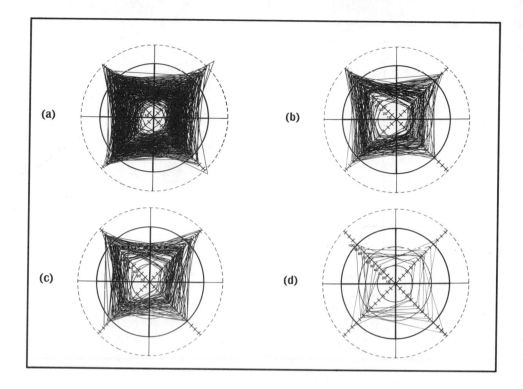

The World Is a Composite Whole Brain

Figure 4-1.
Composite profiles of organizations from around the world: (a) U.S. chemical company; (b) Asian financial institute; (c) Singapore Manager's Seminar; (d) Canadian Broadcasting Company.

The reason I can say that the world is a composite whole brain is that hard data from around the world demonstrates that finding conclusively. Management studies conducted in the United States and by affiliates and independent professional practitioners in many countries have a common theme. If the sample size is large enough—for instance, 250, 500, or 1,000—the composite of individual profiles represents a highly diverse, but well balanced, distribution across the four quadrants of the Whole Brain Model. This is true in all parts of the world. Figure 4-1 shows some sample composite profiles.

CEOs are always surprised by the balanced data representing the composite of their employees. We have not asked all the CEOs, presidents, or leaders, because the list is too long, but all of those we have asked have held a different assumption about the aggregate mentality of their employees. They all think that their organizations have a tilt to the left mode. For this reason, none of them have managed their

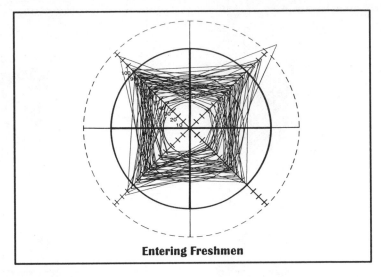

Entering Freshmen

companies on the basis of the composite whole brain reality of their organizations. Their leadership and communication styles have been either tilted in one direction, or too confined, for the global nature of the thinking and learning styles of their employees.

I estimate the costs of business leaders holding wrong assumptions about the mentality of their human asset at hundreds of millions of dollars in lost profits due to the misalignment in jobs, training, communication, and leadership.

Can you imagine the difference in performance that would result from companies being managed in a style that is in alignment with their human resource asset? If we now widen the lens to include not only their own organization but also their customers and the general public, the implications become even more profound. Leaders must now rethink their external assumptions as well as their internal practices, particularly if they are in consumer-oriented businesses. Think of publishers of newspapers, books, and magazines addressed to the general public. How could the editing be modified to optimize readership? Widening the lens even further includes the composite whole brain reality in educational institutions. It stands to reason that if the student body is a composite whole brain, then that should also be the case for the faculty and the curriculum. In contrast to the data on the students, we have not yet found a learning institution that has either a composite whole brain faculty or a composite whole brain curriculum.

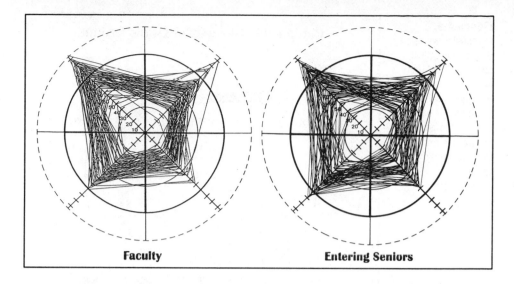

| Faculty | Entering Seniors |

A striking example is the freshman class of a large Mid-western university. The composites shown here represent approximately 500 entering freshmen in the School of Engineering.

This extraordinarily well-balanced composite was a shock to everybody with the exception of the Dean of Engineering, who intuitively knew that there was a mismatch between the faculty and the students and that this condition would lead to extremely adverse consequences. Shown in figure 4-3 is the faculty of the School of Engineering, alongside the composite of the graduating seniors four years later.

As you can see from figure 4-3, the composite of the graduating seniors emulates that of the faculty. Missing from the graduating senior composite are all those who failed to make the grade, or transferred to another school, or dropped out because of unsolvable frustration.

I think this example of an engineering school could be duplicated in most of the colleges and universities around the world. To compound the tragedy, even when those responsible know that they have been holding the wrong assumptions about their students or employees, they do not commit themselves to change what they are doing and the way they are doing it. There are some exceptions, and these are champions of human resource development that the world will some day recognize by their achievements.

Our worldwide database is so far-ranging that readers could pick their own categories and the answer would be

Figure 4-3.
Composite profile of University of Toledo faculty and entering seniors.

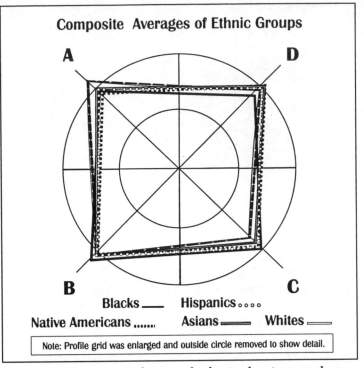

Figure 4-4.
Composite average profiles for typical ethnic and cultural groups. Scores of individuals are averaged for each quadrant to generate an average profile for each ethnic group.

Composite Averages of Ethnic Groups

A   D

B   C

Blacks ____ Hispanics ....
Native Americans .... Asians ==== Whites ____

Note: Profile grid was enlarged and outside circle removed to show detail.

essentially the same. What are the brain dominance characteristics of a particular ethnic group, for example? When separate composite profiles are diagnosed for each identifiable ethnic group, on the average, they produce a composite whole brain: there is essentially no *difference* in brain dominance preference between populations of Whites, Blacks, Hispanics, Native Americans, and Asians.

Brain dominance preferences, of course, do not equal intelligence. Brain dominance preferences describe the overall coalition of an individual's mental preferences in each quadrant. There are an infinite number of discrete profiles for the world as a whole, or for each ethnic group. The findings I am reporting here show that when those individual profiles are assembled into a composite whole, and averaged, the result is a 1-1-1-1 balanced profile. The composite profiles for the different ethnic groups and the world in general are shown in figure 4-4.

While these profiles are not a measure of intelligence, they are a measure of potential competency. The composite whole brain distribution for all ethnic groups taken together suggests that the distribution of potential competencies is similar within each ethnic group.

"My theology, briefly, is that the universe was dictated but not signed."

—

Christopher Morley

I believe that in each ethnic group there is an equal potential for such occupational aspirations as airline pilots, medical doctors, nurses, schoolteachers, social workers, scientists, financiers, engineers, police officers, musicians, entrepreneurs, psychologists, and managers. These are, of course, only samples because in reality I could fill the book with examples of specific occupations.

From a business perspective it is important to note that occupational choices cross country and cultural boundaries. The *HBDI* profiles of airline pilots are approximately the same no matter what the ethnic or cultural background is. The reason is that the work requirements are the same for airline pilots from India, China, Japan, Germany, France, Mexico, Brazil, Australia, and the United States. The same is true for nurses; the same would be true for pathologists or engineers. The more rigorous the professional requirements, the more likely it is that the profiles of occupational colleagues would be similar. The reason, again, is that the work requirements are approximately the same regardless of the culture or the ethnic population. Remarkably, the same is true for CEOs, as described in detail in Chapter 18 on pages 186-191.

In the idealized, and I believe attainable, world of the future, businesses will be able to find every capability they need in the composite of candidates representing all ethnic groups, cultures, and genders. Acquiring competence will be up to the individual regardless of which group he or she is from. Designing jobs to take advantage of available competencies and aligning workers with those jobs is up to the managers of the business.

> *"Women and men in the crowd meet and mingle, yet with itself every soul standeth single."*
>
> —
>
> *Alice Cary*

Adam and Eve in the Workplace

Suppose you found a spot, out in the wide open spaces, where you could create a profile grid a quarter of a mile in diameter, and you were near enough to a big city to invite 2,500 businessmen and 2,500 businesswomen to attend a whole brain barbecue in the middle of this profile grid. All they would have to do to get free ribs would be to position themselves on the grid based on their *HBDI* profiles.

Now suppose that after they had positioned themselves, you rented a small plane and flew over the grid. As soon as the plane started circling over the barbecue area, all the men

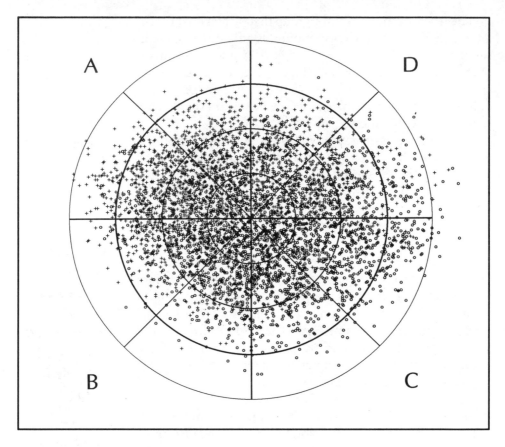

A

D

B

C

Figure 4-5.
Scattergram of male and female profiles from the *HBDI* database. Profile scores are reduced to a single point for a population of 2,500 males and 2,500 females. (Number in group was reduced for better quality reproduction.) Graph shows the favoring of the A quadrant by men ('+' symbol) and the C quadrant by women ('o' symbol).

put on the blue baseball caps with male symbols, and all the women put on red berets with female symbols. WOW! You knew men and women were different, but you couldn't really believe this!

You didn't know exactly what to expect, but the pattern created by these 5,000 businesspeople was extraordinarily well balanced except in the A and C quadrants. There were a lot more baseball caps in the A quadrant and a lot more berets in the C quadrant. It was hard to be very precise, but it looked as if there were an equal number of caps and berets in both the B and D quadrants and this was also true of the center of the grid. There was a big cluster of people, maybe three hundred deep, around the barbecue pits in the center that were speckled with caps and berets in equal distribution. Another WOW!

Looking at the pattern from a mile high, it was clear, for this 5,000-person group, that the most preferred quadrant for males was the A quadrant and the most preferred quadrant for females was the C quadrant. It was equally evident that there were far fewer caps in the C quadrant; and far fewer berets in the A quadrant.

The 5,000 people that accepted this barbecue invitation came from 20 companies within the metropolitan area. That's about 250 from each company. Do you think if we had 20 separate barbecues that the patterns would be the same? Well, maybe not so exquisitely balanced, but the answer is, Yes!

It's common knowledge that men and women are different. But, in terms of their mental preferences, there hasn't been a statistically valid way of measuring this difference until the *HBDI* became available. OK, so there's a mental tilt in the direction of the A quadrant for males and the C quadrant for females, so what? What are the implications and consequences of this in the workplace?

In terms of work that turns people on, there is a pretty even distribution across the occupational options, with the exception of those jobs that require strong competencies in technical, numerical, logical, analytical, diagnostic work. The majority of women find this work boring or just too nitpicky, analytical, or technical. In contrast, the kind of work with a heavy C-quadrant orientation is primarily relationship-based, involving people as individuals or teams or communities. This is work that requires competency in understanding feelings and interpersonal transactions. Men are often turned off by the sensitivity and patience required in these kinds of jobs or are actually incompetent in performing them. But, there are women who "think like men" and men who "think like women" and that's why there are berets in the A quadrant and baseball caps in the C quadrant. The reality is, given any kind of career options, men and women will sort themselves out in jobs as the caps and berets have indicated.

It would be interesting to speculate on what happens when these 5,000 people go home at night. About 70 percent of them would be married so you would have another set of patterns to consider. Generally speaking, most of the baseball caps would have wives from a different quadrant than theirs and, similarly, most of the berets would have husbands from a different quadrant than theirs, thus confirming that opposites attract. In stark contrast, most of the single people, either male or female, who, while unmarried, were living with someone, would have a "most significant other" typically in the same quadrant that they occupy.

"Nobody expects a man and a woman to reach the same corner at the same time."

—

Marta Lynch

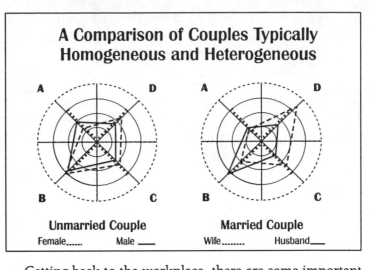

A Comparison of Couples Typically
Homogeneous and Heterogeneous

Unmarried Couple
Female...... Male ____

Married Couple
Wife......... Husband___

Getting back to the workplace, there are some important
consequences and implications of these facts. In terms of
mental requirements and turn-on characteristics, the majority of jobs could be performed equally by men and women.
Since this distribution isn't the case in our culture, that means
that norms have evolved that classify too many jobs as primarily male or female occupations. There is evidence that
this is slowly changing, but far too slowly to achieve any
kind of level playing field. Even so, there are a number of
professional occupations where women are prominently involved. These include medical doctors, lawyers, stockbro-
kers, scientists, chief executive officers, and business owners. At the other end of the spectrum are roles most business
travelers will recognize in the form of sharply increased numbers of women in baggage handling jobs at the airports. Not
too long ago, this was exclusively a male occupation, but it's
obvious that women can do this work, just as they can function as UPS drivers. In the health care field, you now see
more male nurses than ever before. This was once an exclusively female occupation but it is obvious males can do this
work. There are now many more female truck drivers, cab
drivers, airline pilots, and construction workers. There are
male secretaries, travel agents, and house husbands.

The implications for team selection are profound because
there are important differences in male and female thinking
preferences that would argue for gender-balanced teams as
the most effective in general and particularly when creative
problem solving is involved.

*"Women
speak two
languages,
one of which
is verbal."*

—

*Steve
Reubenstein*

Male/Female Differences
(Resulting from Various Scientific Studies)

MALE ↔	FEMALE
Mathematics Ability ↔	Reading Ability
Mechanical Aptitude ↔	Foreign Language Mastery
Seeing Patterns, Abstract Relations ↔	Hearing More Acute
Spatial Ability ↔	Verbal Ability
Better at Things & Theories ↔	Intuitive and Sensory Superiority
Using More Probing Questions ↔	Using More Evocative Questions
More Analytic ↔	More Contextual
Seeing Things More Linearly ↔	Seeing Things Globally/Holistically
Better at Problem Solutions ↔	Better at Problem Understanding
More Understanding of Facts ↔	More Understanding of Process
Forming Task Teams ↔	Forming Groups/Communities
Approach to Creativity likely to be technical, hardware, "thing" oriented ↔	Approach to Creativity Likely to be Intuitive and Relational

Figure 4-7.
Male and Female Differences Chart. Mental preferences for men and women are listed for comparison.

Examining the characteristics that typify male thinking and female thinking can only lead to one conclusion, and that is that a creative team leader wants both. It has been demonstrated over and over that teams made up of diverse thinking styles produce more creative solutions than homogenous teams. To be direct, I can say flatly that it is not possible to create the optimum whole brain team with only one gender involved. The differences are both subtle and profound. You cannot get to where you want to be mentally without both males and females involved in the process.

Over the years my organization has had many opportunities to test out these conclusions. In all the workshops that we offer, there are opportunities for team interaction, and although it is our objective to build gender-balanced, heterogeneous teams, sometimes the logistics of a particular workshop don't allow for that ideal combination. Therefore we have the opportunity to observe relatively homogeneous teams, both in thinking style and gender, as they undertake creative workshop assignments. The homogeneous teams of either gender tend to reach early consensus and settle too quickly on what prove to be mediocre conclusions. In comparison, gender-balanced, heterogeneous teams not only con-

"Once, power was considered a masculine attribute. In fact, power has no sex."

—

Katherine Graham

Figure 4-8.

Teams benefit from
a good mix of
preferences. Sample
composite of a
gender-balanced,
and therefore
mentally-balanced,
team.

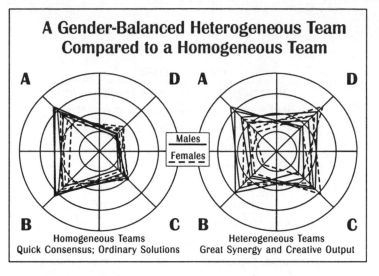

A Gender-Balanced Heterogeneous Team Compared to a Homogeneous Team

Males
Females

Homogeneous Teams
Quick Consensus; Ordinary Solutions

Heterogeneous Teams
Great Synergy and Creative Output

sume all the time allowed, but also ask for additional time and almost invariably produce the highest, most imaginative, creative results.

When I ask each team to describe their team process, the homogeneous teams of either gender talk about the smoothness of the team interaction, the relative speed with which they decided what to do, and the ease with which the team roles were assigned and carried out. The heterogeneous teams of either gender talked about the difficulties of team interaction, highlighting the struggle they had in deciding on a plan of action—e.g., the independent carrying out of the roles and the difficulty of putting those roles together to make a unified presentation of the results. The gender-balanced, heterogeneous teams experienced similar difficulties in time management and independent role development, but in most cases had such a superior grasp of the team's conclusions that the team members could contribute independently yet synergistically.

Some business cultures, particularly those that are technically oriented, claim that they don't have the necessary balance of genders to be able to form gender-balanced, heterogeneous teams. One of the reasons that they don't feel that they have the correct balance is that they are overlooking a large number of female employees whom they don't feel qualify as potential team members. Many who hold this view are missing the point. It is not the organizational level of a potential team member that qualifies him or her, but rather the quality and style of the person's thinking. Since most organizations are, in fact, a composite whole brain, most do in fact have the balance of genders and styles to form all the teams they would ever need.

Adam and Eve in the workplace should be partners, collaborators, and creativity generators.

So What?

- Hard data from many companies, organizations, universities, schools, conventions, etc., from around the world clearly demonstrate that the world in general, and the business world in particular, is a composite whole brain.

- Different preferences within the same-thinking style can lead to competitive ways of accomplishing the same work task, which can add value if managed appropriately.

- Managers who form teams of same-thinking individuals have an opportunity to establish a climate open to constructive, creative interaction that will produce synergistic rather than hostile outcomes.

- Most organizations have a sufficient balance in genders to provide appropriate candidates for gender-balanced, heterogeneous teams. Organizational level is not the criterion for team selection; rather it is the style and quality of thinking that should be the determining factors.

"In terms of game theory, we might say the universe is constituted as to maximize the play."

—

George Leonard

"Most of us assume that we are seeing the world the way it really is."

—

Ned
Herrmann

Identifying Brain Dominance Characteristics with the Whole Brain Model

Chapter Headlines

♦ Since our perception is influenced by our dominance, having good eyesight and hearing doesn't guarantee that you actually hear and understand what is intended.

♦ Mental preferences lead to interests, which lead to motivation to learn, which result in developing competencies, which qualify a person for work that leads to satisfaction and fulfillment.

♦ Different occupations have unique mental requirements, which result in specific occupational norms.

Most of us with reasonably good eyesight would assume that we are seeing the world the way it really is. If our hearing is as good as our eyesight, we are also convinced that we hear everything as it is intended to be heard. In fact, the accuracy of our senses is sometimes imperfect. It is much more likely that we are seeing and hearing based upon our perceptions, which are biased by our thinking preferences, which result in turn from our brain dominance.

Figure 5-1.
Pro forma profile which illustrates how different the mentality of strategic finance is from short-term operational finance.

How many of us have wondered about a course we took, a job, a relationship, or an event that turned out in ways we couldn't quite understand, because we just didn't seem to "get it"? On frequent occasions, we've overheard people say, after understanding their thinking preferences, "Oh! I see. Now I understand why I flunked algebra." Or one married partner, upon seeing the couple's profiles plotted together, will say, "Oh! You think differently from me. Gee, I thought

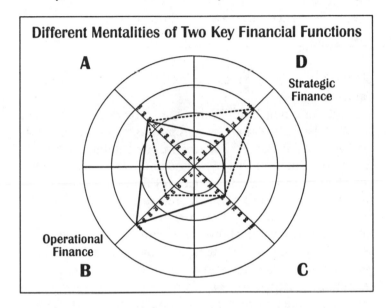

you were being contrary on purpose." Or a parent writes in and says, "It's amazing. My son is not crazy. He's just different." In fact, we are all unique, and that is why each of us is normal. This discovery process is a frequent outcome of individuals understanding their thinking styles by means of the four-quadrant metaphor.

Relative Smartness

In 1976, Henry Mintzberg, Ph.D., a management professor at McGill University, wrote a classic article in the July issue of the *Harvard Business Review*, in which he raised several questions. The first of them was "How can some people be so smart and dull at the same time? How can they be so capable

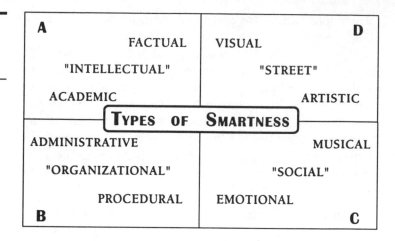

Figure 5-2.
Types of smartness of the four quadrants.

A		
FACTUAL	VISUAL	**D**
"INTELLECTUAL"	"STREET"	
ACADEMIC	ARTISTIC	

TYPES OF SMARTNESS

ADMINISTRATIVE	MUSICAL	
"ORGANIZATIONAL"	"SOCIAL"	
PROCEDURAL	EMOTIONAL	
B		**C**

of certain mental activities and at the same time be so incapable of others?"

I believe Whole Brain Technology provides the answer to Dr. Mintzberg's question. By reason of our brain dominance we have established preferences in our thinking, which in turn lead to interests that, when pursued, can establish competencies in that discrete domain of thinking, while at the same time a neighboring domain remains relatively dull. For example, an individual whose preferences and interests lead to comprehension and ability in algebra, which is linear processing, may be relatively incapable of understanding solid geometry, which is visual and spatially-oriented. I chose this example to illustrate how two forms of math can involve two completely different methods or thought processes. This is true of other disciplines as well—chemistry versus physics, painting versus sculpture, bookkeeping versus financial analysis. The reason is that these are two separate mental activities in which a person can have highly varying competencies.

Look at the model of smartness in figure 5-2 and find those areas where you either excel or fall short.

In my experience, I have found that there are enormous numbers of people who don't understand why they are smart and dumb at the same time, or why they are seemingly blind and deaf to certain information and demonstrate 20/20 vision and acute hearing of information. My classic example of this phenomena involves a friend who confessed that he didn't understand his son John and had given up trying to parent him. He was frustrated by John's behavior, didn't like John's friends, was embarrassed by the way John appeared,

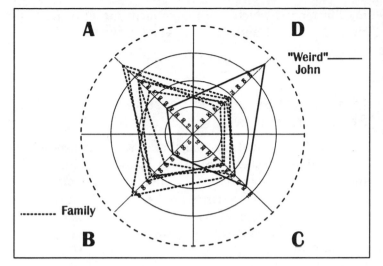

Figure 5-3. Composite profile of a family with one member (Weird John) falling outside of the predominant mental preferences of the family culture.

and was depressed about John's poor performance in school and his apparent lack of any career direction. He further stated that it wasn't just him—the entire family reacted about the same way to John's appearance and behavior.

My friend, who was very familiar with my work, asked if I could administer *HBDI* profiles to his entire family. First, I processed the individual *HBDIs* for each of them. Then, to compare the shape of each family member's profile to another, I generated a composite of all the family member's profiles printed on one sheet. This printout revealed that John had the exact opposite thinking preferences from the rest of his family members. The contrast of the predominant "smartness and dullness" of the family with John's was dramatically apparent to everyone. My friend finally realized that John wasn't abnormal, stupid, or a problem child, he was simply *different* from the rest of his family. As a matter of fact, from John's perspective, it was the family that was weird, not him.

When he saw the profiles, the father said, "Oh, my God, what have I done?" At that point he realized he had been critical of John for not having the same interests as the rest of the family. When the family gathered around the kitchen table, looking at each other's profiles, one of John's brothers looked at him as if he were meeting John for the first time.

A year or so after this incident, John married his girlfriend, of whom the family had approved throughout their relationship. Guess what? The bride's profile matched the family composite, and thus was started a new cycle of understanding differences, which is a requirement for all of relationships to avoid misunderstandings and to be successful.

Intellectual Smartness versus Street Smartness

Note that "intellectual smartness" and "street smartness" occur in different places as shown in figure 5-2. Intellectual smartness is the category that IQ attempts to measure. There is no measure of street smartness other than experiential success. Organized business tends to hire on the basis of intellectual smartness, whereas independent, informal business frequently thrives on the basis of street smarts. If organized business had a good way of hiring and applying street-smart people, the chances are high that those businesses would be more successful. But street-smart people appear to be dumb when scrutinized through the bureaucratic filters of the typical business hiring process. They usually have no résumé or logical series of work experiences. As a result they are out of the business mainstream and are not logical candidates for high-level jobs. On the other hand, many entrepreneurs are street smart and extremely successful in an informal business setting. I have a personal problem with IQ tests because by their very nature, they attempt to measure only a very narrow spectrum of what I am referring to as "smartness." The standard IQ tests that I've seen focus on language, mathematics, and spatial manipulation. While those are possible indicators, they don't represent the full spectrum of mental smartness, and the results, I feel, are very misleading no matter whether they are high or low.

"If a cluttered desk is the sign of a cluttered mind, what is the significance of a clean desk?

—

Tom Wolfe

I recall that the armed services routinely tests for IQ and apparently provides the results to branches of the service that are interested. In my own case I had signed up for flight training but was wooed by the quartermaster corps because they had latched on to my IQ scores and felt that I could be a bigger success in dealing with war material, such as uniforms and shoes, than in being a fighter pilot. Flying turned me on; messing with a warehouse turned me off. So I ended up in India with the lowest rank possible—an unassigned (but highly trained electronics expert) private. When my contingent arrived at the remote camp that was our final destination we were lined up for a welcome by the commanding officer—a regular Army captain. His first words were, "Can any of you boneheads fix a radio?" Every one of us was smart enough to know that you didn't volunteer. After a minute of total silence, the Captain said, "Can any one of you fix *my* radio?" After another minute of silence, I raised my hand and said, "Yes, sir. I can." And the Captain said, "Step forward, Sergeant." For my initiative I was rewarded a promotion on the spot. Thus began an impromptu but award-winning career in the Army Airways Communication System.

Based on close to 50 years of business experience, I would have to say that most of us need to change our assumptions about smartness, dumbness, and intelligence. I have made it plain from the outset that the *Herrmann Brain Dominance Instrument* does not measure intelligence, but as a predictor of thinking and learning styles it can provide clues of likely behavior and related competencies.

Brain Dominance in Action

I was first alerted to these brain dominance clues more than 50 years ago while a student at Cornell. I noted that the Engineering students had crew cuts, carried slide rules, and talked in technical terms. They wore mostly sweaters and windbreakers. Meanwhile, across the quadrangle, students in the Arts and Sciences College had longer hair, wore sports jackets with leather patches on the elbows, and talked about literature and economics. There were many more women on this side of the campus. The music department was even more obviously different. Here there were more women than men. The clothes were loose and comfortable and often colorful. The students lounged around and sang or listened to music, and the buildings were converted Victorian houses. There were ivy-covered buildings on the Arts quadrangle and steel, concrete, and glass buildings in the Engineering area. Those early observations, made so long ago, continue to hold true today. Brain dominance continues to be a consistent basis of human behavior.

Hardly a day goes by when there isn't an excellent example of brain dominance evident in the behavior of characters on television, in the movies, or better yet, in real life. Brain dominance examples from real life are not nearly so funny but are just as revealing.

Figure 5-4.
Typical layout for a
presentation where
participants are
seated according to
their mental
preferences, using
their *HBDI* scores.

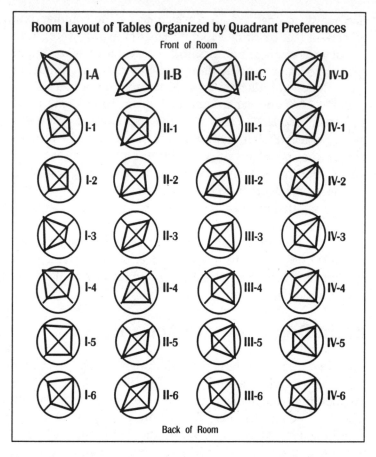

Room Layout of Tables Organized by Quadrant Preferences

The Chairman and a Company President Discover Their Differences

The sponsor of my management presentation in Seattle some years ago invited me to have breakfast with the chairman and president of a local company important to him. During a lively breakfast conversation I could see that these two men had sharply different views of any given topic, and their non-verbal reactions provided exclamation points to their words. Their eyes literally flashed as they interjected opposing views.

These two men, along with the 100 others who attended the meeting, had been profiled on the basis of their mental preferences and assigned seats based on their *HBDI* profiles. In fact, the first tables in each of the four rows represented the extremes in each quadrant and therefore served as demonstration tables for my workshop. I knew what the chairman and president did not: that they had opposing profiles

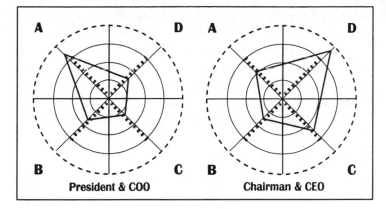

Figure 5-5.
Profiles of two
corporate officers:
President/COO and
the Chairman/CEO.

A | D | A | D

President & COO | Chairman & CEO

B | C | B | C

and had been assigned to the A- and D-quadrant demonstration tables.

I excused myself early from breakfast in order to get ready for the presentation, and therefore I was in a position to observe these two men as they entered the room and were directed to the opposite front-row tables. I watched them as they proceeded to their tables and, before sitting down, looked at each other and conveyed by their expressions some understanding of what was going to happen. They had been at each other's throats for 15 years and maybe they were about to find out why. Early into my presentation I conducted an exercise in which individuals revealed their work preferences. The exercise was similar to the Turn-On Work Exercise in Chapter 2. Each of the 35 tables seated three participants with very similar profiles. As the individuals determined their work preferences and then shared them with others at the same table, they discovered that these were highly homogeneous groups. I then had the four front-row demonstration tables reveal what work turned them on.

As it turned out, the chairman and the president were the spokesmen for their tables. The president, who was the chief operating officer, represented the logical, rational, analytic A table. The chairman, who was the founder and CEO, represented the holistic, intuitive, risk-taking D-quadrant table. As each made his diametrically opposite comments, they were looking at each other, and I had the distinct feeling that the source of their 15 years of arguments and differences of opinion and frustration was being revealed.

Later they approached me and admitted that they had really missed the boat. They had not taken advantage of their differences of opinion in terms of creative alternatives, but rather had frustrated each other during almost their entire relationship. They both had been adding value, but they could have been very much more effective as CEO and COO if they had taken advantage of their mental diversity. For me, and for the workshop participants, it was a memorable public demonstration of the consequences of brain dominance. For the two men, it was the beginning of a true partnership.

The "Number Cruncher"

Allen Greenspan, Chairman of the Federal Reserve Board, was described in the February 5, 1995, *Charlotte Observer* as "a lover of numbers and dry statistics"; however, his past reveals another side. He toured with a swing band in his youth. But today he's considered to be nothing more than a bespectacled "nerdy" economist who is a conservative Republican, the kind touted by Ayn Rand in *The Glory of Capitalism*. David Jones, the economist, describes Greenspan as follows: "He's the ultimate numbers cruncher. I walk into his office and he won't say, 'David, good morning' or 'how are you?' but, he will undoubtedly say, 'David, do you have any numbers on inventories of imported goods?' or something like that..." Greenspan's father was a stockbroker. In his youth, Allen showed an early talent for math and an impressive recall of major league batting averages. I believe a profile of Greenspan would show a very strong A-quadrant preference. Greenspan gives evidence of being "all business, no chat," which is common for A-quadrant-dominant individuals.

Two Preferences Are Better Than One

In the same paper, the Charlotte Hornets President, Spencer Stolpen, and team owner, George Shinn, were described as "working very well together, even though they are strikingly different." The article went on to say, Shinn is "impulsive and emotional with a tendency to rush to judgment." Stolpen, on the other hand, was described as "more deliberate, measuring what he says and does to fit a specific purpose." George Shinn is the business entrepreneur who had a vision of an NBA franchise and managed to pull it off. Meanwhile, Stolpen, the president, does not have a basketball background. His primary role is masterminding the Hornets' compliance with the NBA salary cap and dealing with the collective bargaining agreement. In terms of the quadrants, Shinn is a D-quadrant, visionary entrepreneur and Stolpen is a deliberate, step-by-step, organized, and detailed B-quadrant manager. Together, working as a team, they are building a successful and valuable franchise.

Scripts That Fit the Quadrants

Often scriptwriters create characters of a certain type to make a point. These are often consistent with extreme quadrant preference. For example, Mr. Spock in the *Star Trek* series was so rational that he was established as a nonhuman from another planet in our universe. Spock's mentality was contrasted with that of Dr. McCoy, a medical doctor who was so empathic, caring, and nurturing that he was too good to be true in the real world. Spock is an example of someone with extreme A-quadrant dominance. What he needed to do, he did well. Dr. McCoy exemplifies the strong interpersonal and caring qualities of the C quadrant.

Characters who have diametrically opposed preferences (for example, quadrants that are diagonally opposite each other on the Whole Brain Model) often make the most obvious displays of typical quadrant traits. A good example are the characters in *The Odd Couple*. The playwright Neil Simon creates Felix, a superneat, straightlaced character consistent with B-quadrant characteristics, offset by Oscar, a devil-may-care, sloppy, irresponsible, unpredictable photographer, an example of D-quadrant tendencies in the extreme. They epitomize not only this classic struggle of differing preferences, but also the avoidances that go with them.

In Ann Tyler's *The Accidental Tourist* the leading character's sister puts the canned goods in her kitchen cupboard in alphabetical order and chides the other characters when they hand them to her out of order. This character is an example of how important preferences for organization and structure are to a B-quadrant individual.

Those of you who have seen *Mrs. Doubtfire* can appreciate how the screenwriter has juxtaposed a playful and spontaneous D-quadrant character with a no-nonsense B-quadrant wife who has a great need for planning and consistency. There are a lot of dynamics in combining a B-quadrant-orientation with a D-quadrant one. They can balance each other or continuously be at odds if their preferences are at the extreme level.

Mental Preferences of Sports Figures

In February 1995, there was a cover story in *USA Today* on the two best women skiers in the United States. The story reports that the team coaches try to reward their best athletes with single rooms on their stops along the World Cup racing tour. No one is sure what would happen if the nation's best women skiers, potentially the best two women downhill skiers in U.S. skiing history, had to share four walls for a night. Hilary Lindh isn't anxious to find out. "We're noninteractive. We don't deal with each other if we don't have to." And Picabo Street isn't eager to find out either. "There is a lack of genuine affection, a lot of negative energy," she says.

Their differences start with personalities that are poles apart. Hilary, 25, of Juneau, Alaska, is reserved, stern, and individualistic. The media have stereotyped her as being "as cold and distant as her native state." In contrast, Picabo goes out of her way to accommodate the media and generally charms them off their feet. She is engaging, warm, bubbly, thoughtful, and articulate. She considers it important to promote her sport and it bothers her that Hilary doesn't make more of an effort. "I guess she's too shy or something, but she just doesn't express herself in that way."

If Hilary keeps her feelings to herself, Picabo rents billboards to express hers—at least that's the way Hilary sees it. "I'm glad we are as different as we are. In fact, I'm proud of it," Hilary says. "Like the fact that I don't have to announce whatever I'm feeling to everybody in the world. I just don't think that's necessary." She continues by saying, "I don't think I'm cold and distant. . . . not to family and friends, anyway. Maybe I'm the strong, silent type. I don't like the comparisons because the two of us look like such extremes."

Nothing illustrates their differences better than the incident which resulted in a big misunderstanding.

In preseason training camp in 1993, when Hilary was coming back from major knee injury, she and Picabo were in a group session with a team psychologist. Picabo, as usual, was doing most of the talking and stunned Hilary by saying that she felt so sad about Hilary's injury the previous year that she cried for her.

Hilary, not sure how to respond, laughed.

"She laughed at me," says Picabo. "I just shut her off. . .

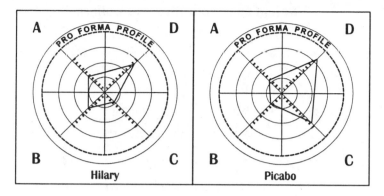

Figure 5-6.
Pro forma Profiles
of Olympic Skiiers
Hilary and Picabo.

put a wall up." Says Hilary, "I did laugh, but it was a nervous reaction. It's not that I didn't believe her, I was just embarrassed. I wasn't laughing at her, but I can see how that could have been the beginning of the end. She hardly talked to me at all after that."

That incident is "classic Hilary and Picabo," says Paul Major, U.S. Skiing's Alpine Director. "I can just see that Hilary reacted with nervous laughter, and Picabo had her feelings hurt tremendously. That just shows you how they think, or don't think, when it comes to each other."

Here are two young people who are both competing to be the best, but who don't really understand themselves or each other. It is clear to me that they have very different mental preferences and that these differences are getting in the way of their understanding each other. So far their relationship has been an uphill struggle all the way. Based on this news story, I have prepared the following pro forma profiles of Hilary and Picabo in figure 5-6.

What do you think would happen if they knew about their own and each other's thinking preferences? Based upon my experience with thousands of satisfied individuals who have sought me out for help with conflict resolution, I think there's a good chance that both Hilary and Picabo would see their differences in a new light.

How many of you who have watched golf tournaments on television have ever noticed the different styles of professional golfers? Particularly visible are the antics of Lee Trevino and Fuzzy Zoeller as they crack jokes, whistle as they walk, and relate to the gallery. Their open, loose, gregarious style

"Wit consists in seeing the resemblance between things which differ, and the difference between things which are alike."

—

Madame de Stael

Figure 5-7.
Pro forma
distribution of golf
pros' styles in terms
of the four
quadrants.

Different Quadrant Styles of Golfers

A QUADRANT

D QUADRANT

Jack Nicklaus

Tom Watson

Ray Floyd

John Daley

Fuzzy Zoeller

Payne Stewart

Gary Player

Tom Weiskopf

Nick Faldo

Arnold Palmer

Chi Chi Rodriquez

Lee Trevino

QUADRANT **B**

QUADRANT **C**

is in sharp contrast to golfers like Gary Player, Tom Weiskopf, and Jack Nicklaus. These golfers are dead serious, highly self-critical, and very deliberate in preparing for each shot. In contrast, Lee Trevino will be cracking jokes with the gallery and then typically walk up to his ball, take one practice swing and fire away. Gary Player will be meticulous in his preparation, excruciatingly slow in finding a comfortable position, taking numerous practice swings, and then finally executing the actual shot. This routine also describes Jack Nicklaus. He can consume several minutes in preparation before addressing the ball for the actual shot, and when the ball misses his intended target by as much as ten feet, he will become visibly upset and take a few more practice swings to correct the error of his ways. In contrast, Fuzzy Zoeller, whistling a happy tune, will jauntily approach his ball and within the span of a few seconds, hit his ball and continue to whistle his way to the next shot without a sign of remorse over landing in a trap.

These professional golfers are all playing the same game but their approach is highly differentiated by their mental preferences. Figure 5-7 shows how 12 prominent professional golfers' styles correlate with the four-quadrant model, based upon their behaviors during televised golf tournaments.

Figure 5-8.
The picture on the left depicts a staff member with a very loose, unstructured work style. The one on the right illustrates someone who prefers working at a clean, orderly desk.

Signs of Dominance in the Workplace

I encourage you to seek out examples of brain dominance in action in your own workplace. Take a break and wander around the office area and notice the differences in the different work spaces. As you do so, think about the individual who owns that work space and assess the degree of alignment between how that work space looks and the everyday behavior of its occupant. For example, here is Mary's desk and it's neat as a pin. Mary is the administrative assistant who prides herself on being highly organized and punctual. She is fastidious in her dress and appearance. Her work space is just outside Bill's office, which is layered in paper. The surface of his desk is not visible. The windowsill has become a bookcase and the guest chair is stacked with reports, as is the top of the filing cabinet. Mary tries to keep Bill's desk neat and orderly, but Bill complains about his papers being somewhere other than where he put them and so she has given up on trying to logically categorize his work. Both Mary and Bill are very good at what they do, but it's clear that their preferences influence their priorities. Mary cannot tolerate her desk being messy and Bill is far more interested in the project he is working on than in how his office appears. Contrary to popular belief, Bill has his own system that works for him. The brain dominance profiles of Mary and Bill are in good alignment with the appearance of their work spaces. Mary's profile has a strong lower left B-quadrant preference. Her need for order and to work only on the project on her desk is quite visible. In contrast, Bill's profile is heading in the opposite direction, toward the upper right D quadrant. Bill works on several projects at a time and therefore needs to have all his materials out in front of him. He has no need to clean off his desk at the end of the day.

If you venture into the finance area, you will see a high percentage of desks that are neat and orderly, even though there are papers and reports on most of them. If you look closely at the reports, you will see that the writing is quite legible, with small, precisely formed letters and numbers. The need for unquestionable accuracy in this area of the company is obvious in the work styles of the staff members.

Whenever you encounter an office with lots of paper on the desks and numerous surfaces, it likely belongs to people whose job requires simultaneity, creative thinking, and a nonstructured environment. Cleaning up and being neat is less important than addressing the task at hand. Sometimes cleaning up gets in the way of their work because it doesn't come easy to them. People are working just as hard, but differently.

There is a lot of common sense involved in these clues of brain dominance preference. It is rare to find a major discontinuity between a person's work space and his or her brain dominance profile. This is true not only of individuals but of functions such as finance, sales, marketing, R&D, legal, advertising, engineering, manufacturing, and human resources.

Occupational Norms: N = 113,000

There is a strong relationship between our preferences and the kind of work that turns us on. In this section, I will report on the distribution of high-frequency occupational profiles of general interest.

In looking at over 113,000 *HBDI* profiles and sorting them into occupational choices, it became clear that there are norms around mental preference and occupational choice. For example, the engineering profession (figure 5-9) has a distinct tilt toward the A quadrant. The degree of tilt is determined by the type of engineering; chemical engineering is the most strongly A-quadrant-preferred occupation within the broad engineering profession.

The finance profession (figure 5-10) also has a strong A-quadrant tilt and the actuarial occupation is the most strongly A-quadrant-oriented within the finance function.

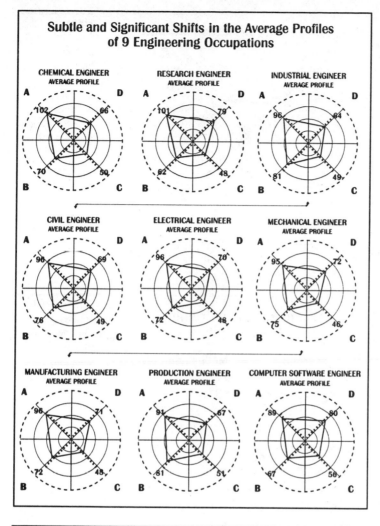

Figure 5-9.

A continuum of engineering profiles. Composite average profile norms for nine types of engineers, displayed in a continuum from most A-quadrant, to most B-, C-, then D-quadrant preferences.

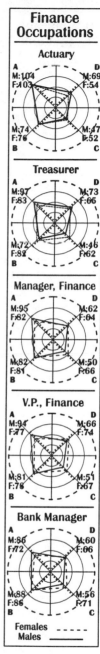

Finance Occupations

Figure 5-10.

A continuum of profiles of financial positions.

Business managers as a whole represent a multidominant occupation for both males and females (figure 5-11).

Foremen in the manufacturing function represent a strong B-quadrant preference, as do finance clerks, bank tellers, and record keepers (figure 5-12).

Moving next to double-dominant limbic profiles, we have secretaries as the most common occupation preferring this

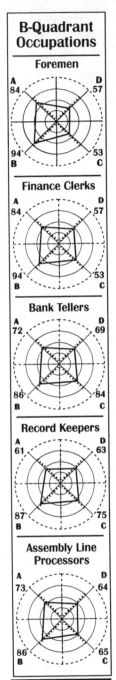

B-Quadrant Occupations

Foremen

A 84 · D 57 · B 94 · C 53

Finance Clerks

A 84 · D 57 · B 94 · C 53

Bank Tellers

A 72 · D 69 · B 86 · C 84

Record Keepers

A 61 · D 63 · B 87 · C 75

Assembly Line Processors

A 73 · D 64 · B 86 · C 65

Figure 5-12.
Examples of B-quadrant-oriented professionals

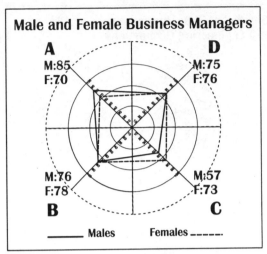

Male and Female Business Managers

A — M:85 F:70
D — M:75 F:76
B — M:76 F:78
C — M:57 F:73

_____ Males   Females _____

Figure 5-11.
A continuum of profiles of business managers, showing differences between males and females.

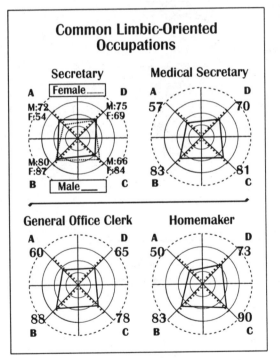

Common Limbic-Oriented Occupations

Secretary

Female ....
A — M:72 F:54
D — M:75 F:69
B — M:80 F:87
C — M:66 F:84
Male ____

Medical Secretary

A 57 · D 70 · B 83 · C 81

General Office Clerk

A 60 · D 65 · B 88 · C 78

Homemaker

A 50 · D 73 · B 83 · C 90

Figure 5-13.
Profiles of typically limbic (B and C quadrant) professionals in continuum format.

duality. General office clerks are also in this group. Homemakers share this strong dual B- and C-quadrant preference (figure 5-13).

The database norms clearly identify the nursing profession as a very C-quadrant-oriented occupational group. So-

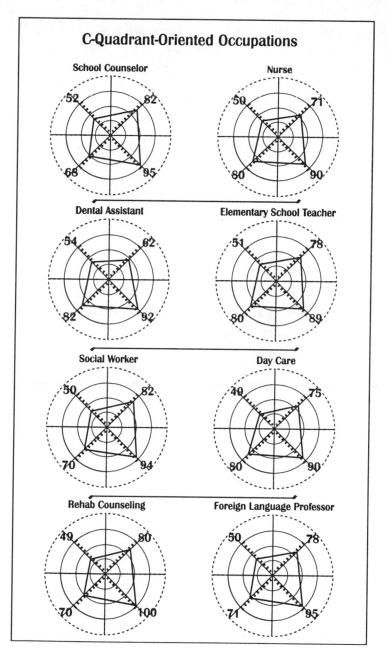

Figure 5-14.
Examples of C-quadrant professionals.

cial workers, professional volunteers, and teachers share in this preference, particularly elementary school teachers and school counselors (figure 5-14).

As we continue in a counterclockwise manner to identify occupational preferences, we come to the double-dominant

Figure 5-15.
Profiles of C- and D-
quadrant
professionals

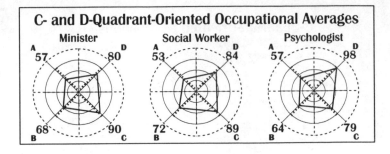
C- and D-Quadrant-Oriented Occupational Averages

Figure 5-16.
Profiles of D-
quadrant
professionals.

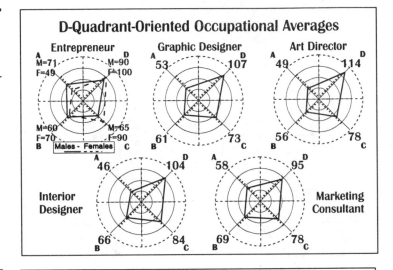
D-Quadrant-Oriented Occupational Averages

Figure 5-17.
Examples of
cerebral-oriented (A-
and D-quadrant)
professionals.

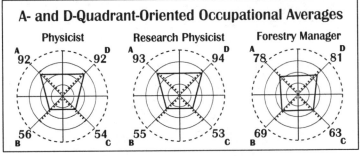
A- and D-Quadrant-Oriented Occupational Averages

C/D-quadrant right mode. Here we have many ministers, counselors, psychologists, and social workers (figure 5-15).

In the D quadrant, there are artists, graphic and interior designers, art directors, and entrepreneurs (figure 5-16).

With the double-dominant cerebral profile, we find scientific occupations, such as research and development, and particularly members of the physics profession (figure 5-17).

This brings us to the multidominant profiles with three primaries, or even four primaries (figure 5-18). Chief

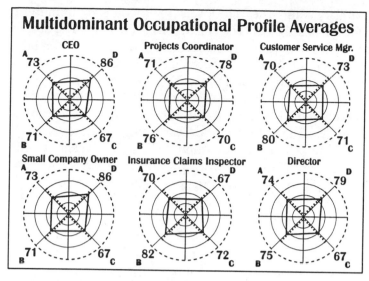

Figure 5-18. Examples of professionals preferring all four quadrants A,B,C,D (1-1-1-1 profile).

executive officer is a prominent occupational category. Other four-quadrant occupations include: projects coordinators, directors, and managers of customer service. The number of occupations is small, since only 3 percent of the total database is quadruple-dominant profiles.

It must be understood that part of the occupational norm data in the database is influenced by people who occupy positions that are not in strong alignment with their preferences. Therefore there will be engineers who don't share the A-quadrant-oriented norm, but are still survivors in the engineering profession. And there will be artists who don't share the strong D-quadrant preference. But our experience in working with these people is clear: those who engage in this occupation work *differently* than those who constitute the norm and those who are in strong alignment with the mentality of the work. It is also clear that those who are not in alignment with the job norm have a significantly lower level of satisfaction and fulfillment in performing the work. They are, in many cases, individuals who are trapped in work that is not entirely suited to them but, since they can perform that work with reasonably satisfactory results, they continue to occupy that position and receive the economic rewards even though it is not the ideal work for them to do.

Generally speaking, when we look at the database, we find that the highest satisfaction comes from those who have a strong alignment between their mental preferences and the mentality of the work that they are assigned to do; and the corollary is also true. The lowest satisfactions are from those who are misaligned. The conclusion is obvious. The best of all worlds both from the perspective of the company and the employee, is to have the closest alignment that can be achieved between the worker and the work.

I would encourage you to ponder this issue for yourself. There is enough material in this book to give you clues about yourself and about your work. Diagnosing the degree of alignment will help answer questions you may have about your own career. Does your work provide the basis for turning you on? If not, what adjustments can be made in your work package to improve the turn-on work potential? In the worst case, what other jobs are there to which you can aspire, that would have the alignment characteristics that would lead to job satisfaction and fulfillment? In the final analysis, work should be satisfying and fulfilling. It's never too late to make the necessary career changes to achieve that end.

So What?

- The closer the alignment between an individual's mental preference and the mental requirements of the job, the more likely that job success and satisfaction will be achieved.

- Nonalignment of job candidates with those occupational norms will significantly reduce the likelihood of them achieving full job satisfaction and fulfillment.

- The best of all worlds for the company and the employee is to have the closest alignment that can be achieved between the worker and the work.

PART II

The Whole Brain Organization

Whole Brain Technology as a Solution to Today's Business Problems

---

Chapter Headlines

♦ Using pro forma techniques as a diagnostic tool provides new ways of seeing business problems clearly and, by clarifying problem issues, can improve overall competitiveness.

♦ Productivity problems are often the result of a mismatch between employees' mental preferences and the mental requirements of the work to which they are assigned.

♦ Aligning employees to their work improves their chances to be smart, productive, and satisfied.

♦ Customer service goals can be met by understanding the C-quadrant focus of this business activity and adjusting styles and approaches accordingly.

> *"In thousands of years there has been no advance in public morals, in philosophy, in religion, or in politics, but the advance in business has been the greatest miracle the world has ever known."*
>
> —
>
> *Wallis E. Howe*

The spectacular photograph of the earth reproduced in figure 6-1 is actually a composite of many. Over 400 satellite pictures were seamlessly combined to show the earth in a way that not even a space traveler would be able to see it. It's a favorite metaphor of mine because it states visually one of the objectives of applying Whole Brain Technology to a particular problem situation. The earth is typically obscured by

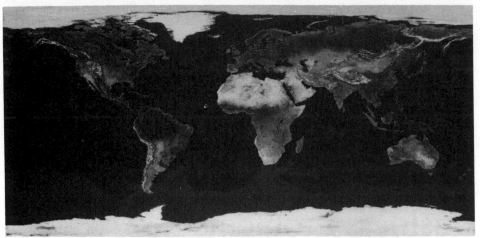

Figure 6-1.
The Earth seen from space. A Satellite composite view of the earth. This image of the world is a mosaic of over 400 images revealing the Earth, in natural color, unobstructed by clouds for the first time.

"The manager of the future will simply be a learning guide."

—

Peter Drucker

clouds, so you never see it in its entirety. Whole Brain Technology provides opportunities not only for seeing, but also for understanding business problems that are usually hidden by obscuring clouds. If we think of Whole Brain Technology less as a theory or concept, and more as a tool or technique, much like the way the Hubble telescope is used to view the earth in a cloudless environment, we can come closer to understanding the advantage it brings to solving business problems.

A key problem-solving technique of Whole Brain Technology is the *pro forma process*. This is a diagnostic process in which the thinking required to perform a task, carry out a complete job, or the elements of a document are analyzed in terms of the four quadrant strengths. The profiles that result from this process are called *pro forma* to distinguish them from the *HBDI* profiles.

Application examples include pro forma profiles of: organization culture, documents such as an annual report or a vision statement, the direction of an individual's lifework such as that of Einstein or Plato, a concept such as metaphoric thinking, or a philosophy such as participative management (see figure 6-2 for examples).

Imagine for a moment a company whose business has dramatically dropped off but that has never given any thought to understanding the mentality of its products, corporate image, management style, or employees. Then, suddenly its leaders are able to see its corporate problem from all angles,

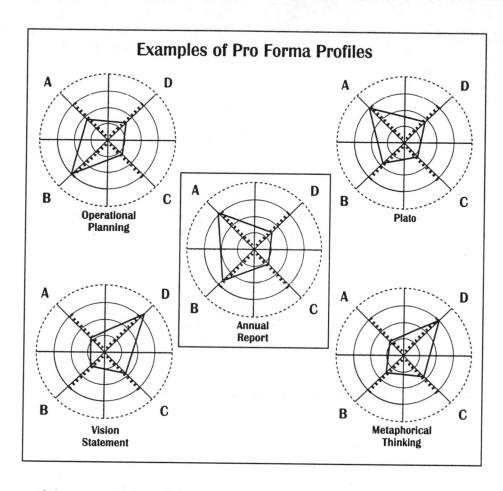

Figure 6-2.
Examples of pro forma profiles.

as if they were looking down on it on a cloudless day. The pro forma process can be applied to almost anything you are trying to diagnose or problem solve and is especially useful when comparing one element of a business to another and checking the alignment of these elements. Styles of management, leadership, production, communication, and teamwork can all be understood clearly through this process. All the chapters in PART II apply the pro forma technique as a means of expressing the mentality of many aspects of business. The following section demonstrates how the pro forma process can expose potentially damaging misalignments. Chapter 15 discusses in detail how the pro forma process is used to address key leadership issues.

Figure 6-3.
A multidominant
customer service
team. Each function
of the customer
service is operated
by someone in
alignment with the
mentality of the
function.

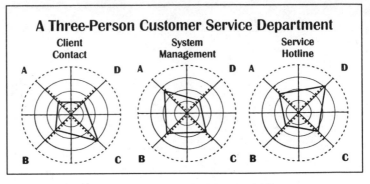

A Three-Person Customer Service Department

Client Contact	System Management	Service Hotline

Expanding the Mentality of Customer Service with Pro Formas

Customer service has been a major buzz word of the late 1980s and 1990s. From a work mentality perspective, customer service primarily requires the discipline of the B-quadrant and the interpersonal skills of the C-quadrant activity. If you assign individuals to the task who have no strong preference for that kind of work and therefore little motivation to perform it, then you will not solve the customer service problem, you will create it.

Can you imagine an individual who has an avoidance in the interpersonal C quadrant processing customer complaints, or being an effective and friendly waitress? What if, in addition to their distaste for working with people, they prefer the rational A or experimental D quadrants? An A-quadrant customer service representative would probably love analyzing all the data in your customer tracking software but would dread the interpersonal aspects. An A/D-quadrant-dominant service provider might lose all track of time while talking to customers on the phone or go off on tangents that engage an imaginative mind. Here again, good alignment between the individual and the requirements of the work is key to a successful customer service program.

If you only had three people in your department, you would want the person most comfortable with and turned on to personalizing your company's approach to have direct contact with the client/customer, in other words, a C-quadrant-dominant person. In today's world, this person would also need to feel comfortable with computers. You may want to have an A/B-dominant person maintaining the system and making sure that common solutions to problems are readily available to the customer service rep or the customer. This person would focus on the need for consistent and accurate data on each customer and would be a resource for analyzing a situation and providing a logical solution. A person with some D-quadrant imagination would be helpful in devising new ways of approaching a problem when "just the facts" won't do the job. This creativity would be especially helpful for software technical support people. If the customer encounters an undocumented problem, you'd need someone who's comfortable with "outside the box" thinking to come up with the illogical yet highly plausible solution. As in many functions of business, having access to all thinking modes will greatly enhance the quality of the service you can provide.

Competitiveness has always been a major ingredient of business success. If you can't compete, you will not survive. High-quality, low-cost, customer-driven companies are by definition competitive. They are smart in the way they design and produce their products, deploy their resources, and acquire and retain customers. By removing the obscuring clouds from these key business issues, Whole Brain Technology can make a significant contribution to a company's competitiveness. Its Hubble telescope capabilities allow management to see the needs of the marketplace with an increase in clarity so that they are able to make smarter decisions. The pro forma technique provides a way of diagnosing customers' needs more precisely by their mental preferences.

> *"Making unseen business issues visible is like discovering that stars also shine in the day time."*
>
> —
>
> *Ned Herrmann*

So What?

- Whole Brain Technology can serve as a diagnostic tool to aid in seeing business situations more clearly by revealing the participants' mental preferences.

- Professor Mintzberg wondered why people are smart and dull at the same time. Realigning employees so they are smart in the work they do will improve both business results and employee satisfaction.

Whole Brain Marketing, Sales, and Advertising

Chapter Headlines

"Marketing is simply sales with a college education."

—

Anonymous

♦   Consumers represent a balanced array of mental preferences, and when given a choice, they will buy products that are aligned with those preferences.

♦   Products have a "mentality" and so do buyers.

♦   Magazine ads have a particular "mentality" and so do readers.

♦   Studies show a strong alignment between the mentality of the buyer, the mentality of the ad that attracts them, and the product they purchase.

If you are a business manager attempting to reach a consumer market, the owner of a car dealership, the publisher of a newspaper in a metropolitan area, or the superintendent of schools in a city, you will have to base your decisions on the assumption that the people who create, market, and buy your products are in fact a highly diverse group that in the aggregate represents a balanced array of mental preferences and thinking-style options.

If your product is a highly specialized niche product or service like a security system, travel services, video rentals, or plumbing, understand the mentality of your selected clientele. Happy-go-lucky, carefree, risk-oriented people will not seek out and purchase a security system. There are, how-

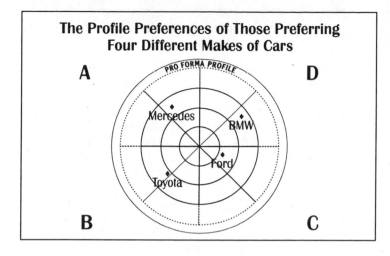

The Profile Preferences of Those Preferring Four Different Makes of Cars

ever, as many as 25 percent of a given metropolitan population who would be potential buyers. These are people who are constantly security-minded. They feel that laws should be strictly enforced and place a high priority on protective services and devices. They are customers for alarm systems for both home and car. Out of the total population they are the segment that would take the initiative to acquire these devices. Since this audience is basically conservative, somewhat skeptical of flamboyant claims, and generally "from Missouri," the advertising would have to be aligned with this set of consumer characteristics. It would have to be straightforward, documented with specific, realistic examples, conservative in language, black and white, properly sized and formatted, *and placed* in the part of the paper or the magazine that security-minded people would be likely to read.

Products can be diagnosed to reveal the mentality of their design. Take automobiles, for instance. There are people who buy Dodge Reliants, Mercedes Sedans, Chrysler Minivans, Ford Explorers, and Chevrolet Corvettes. Each of these buyers is expressing mental preferences in the type of purchase he or she makes. The person who aspires to the BMW is not going to read the ad for the Dodge Reliant or stop at the Dodge Reliant showroom. He or she is looking for different things. The person who aspires to the Mercedes is simply not a prospective buyer for the other models that I have cited. The Mercedes buyer is a person interested in elegance and engineering performance. The BMW buyer is looking for a different kind of performance. The BMW is not a family

Figure 7-2.
A four-quadrant
model of
advertisement types.

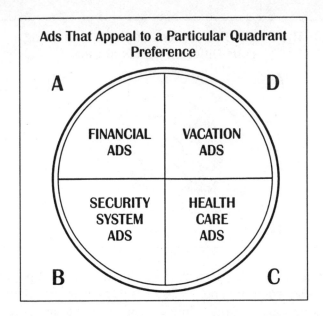

Ads That Appeal to a Particular Quadrant Preference

A

FINANCIAL
ADS

D

VACATION
ADS

SECURITY
SYSTEM
ADS

HEALTH
CARE
ADS

B

C

car, but the Chrysler Minivan may well be the ideal car for a family that loves camping or family excursions to the beach.

Studies by our French affiliate show the extremely high degree of alignment between individuals who have strong preferences in each of the quadrants, the kind of products they buy, and the sorts of commercials that appeal to them. For example, a strong B-quadrant viewer will turn off a "futuristic" commercial promoting a bank. The concept and style of the commercial doesn't compute in the conservative, orderly, B-quadrant mind.

Studies of magazine ads that I have conducted reveal that they run the entire gamut of mental options for each quadrant and each mode of the Whole Brain Model. The studies also show that they tend to cluster in terms of style and format and location in the magazine, based on the product or service being advertised. For example, ads dealing with financial investments are almost always black and white, very straightforward, crowded with numbers and percentages, and generally in the beginning pages of a magazine like *Forbes* or *Business Week*. Ads for vacations are dramatically different. These are almost always four-color, with exotic scenes provocatively displayed and often curvaceous females or hot air balloons, or sunsets in the background. Family health care ads are often soft-focus photos of caring parents and smiling children, designed to pull at our heartstrings. Automobile ads, particularly those in automobile magazines, are often multiple-page foldouts in full color, ranging across all four quadrants in order to appeal to every potential facet of a prospective buyer's fantasies.

These ads are prepared by professionals who have diagnosed the market with costly research, including special interviews and focus groups. The objective is to align the product with the market segment likely to purchase. On the average, this seems to work; but my feeling is that advertising agencies frequently fall far short of their goal because they do not take into account the rather predictable mental preferences of the target population. The same is, I believe, true of marketing and sales departments, of manufacturers, or service deliverers. All too frequently they are employing antiquated concepts in developing their marketing plans and sales strategies. The Whole Brain Technology provides a whole new world of opportunity for the marketing, sales, and advertising fraternities.

So What?

- Whole Brain Technology offers an improved approach to marketing, sales, and advertising.

- Products can be diagnosed to reveal the "mentality" of their design.

- Ads can be created to match the "mentality" of the products they advertise and the consumers they are trying to reach.

- Products can be designed or redesigned to be mentally aligned with specific markets and strategically advertised to attract specific buyers with definable preferences.

Whole Brain Products for a Whole Brain World

"There are three kinds of people who are anachro-nisms in business today: those who think the world is flat, those who don't believe in gravity, and those who think you can depend on mass markets."

—

Amal Johnson

Chapter Headlines

◆ User-friendliness of products is determined by brain dominance alignment with the user.

◆ Products can become more user-friendly by including the customers in the design.

◆ New Boeing 777 Airliner design approach expands the user-friendly concept to include not only passengers, but also the crew and the airline carrier.

◆ Whole Brain Technology, through its diagnostic power and its design direction, offers vast entrepreneurial opportunities.

User-friendly is a term that means something different to each of us. What might be user-friendly to one person could be user-unfriendly to another, and often the reason is the difference in brain dominance characteristics. The first example that comes to mind is the digital watch. I remember getting one more than 40 years ago because I was curious. The face of the wristwatch had a small window that illuminated in red digits when you pressed a button. The intrigue didn't last very long. In the first place, you had to press a button to see the time, and, in the second place, I didn't find the digital display very satisfying. My life had been based on a watch with hands. All of a sudden I was faced with numbers that were less meaningful than the position of the hands. I found myself mentally converting the digital readout into the hands of an analog watch. When the battery wore out, I was too busy to get it replaced and so I simply put my old wristwatch back on my wrist. A truer test of my preference occurred a few years later when I was given a slick new electronic watch that had both digital and analog readout. This was supposed to be useful when traveling to different time zones, but I typically left both modes on the same setting. It didn't take long for me to discover that I ignored the digital readout and looked almost exclusively at the analog readout. For *me*, the hands were more meaningful than the numbers.

The next time this became an issue was when I rented a car that had a digital readout speedometer. I found it interesting for the first few miles. Then, the constant change in numbers up and down, as I worked my way through traffic, began to drive me nuts! I found my eyes going to the digital readout and I was becoming irritated by the constant change. I found it annoying rather than helpful. For me, it was not user-friendly, but rather an irritating distraction. The next time I rented a car, I specifically asked if the car had a digital speedometer; if it did, I asked for another model.

Our mental preferences have a great deal to do with how we interact with the everyday aspects of life. Take a strip map, for example. People who have a good sense of direction and who are reasonably skilled at map reading are frequently uncomfortable using a strip map. The reason is that their mental preference is to see the world as it really is. North is north and west is west. A strip map disregards the compass and arranges the routing based on a linear display of the roads regardless of their direction. The purpose of the strip map is to be user-friendly and for some it might be; however, not for all people. In both these simple examples, the intention of the designers was to provide something that was user-friendly but, in so doing, they disregarded the fact that the world is made up of individuals with unique thinking preferences.

Instruction book writing is an example of a brain dominance-oriented activity that cries out for significant improvement. Most instruction books that I have seen are so user-unfriendly that they seem to advertise the C-quadrant deficit. The way the instructions are written is so inadequate that they are largely ignored, particularly by individuals who are C- and D-quadrant oriented. Many C-quadrant-preferred individuals are so turned off by highly technical or overly detailed and sequential instructions that they don't read past the first few lines. They become exasperated and either give up or ask for help.

D-quadrant-preferred people try to "wing it" by using the picture on the box as their primary source of information, and then experiment with various ways of putting the product together, often ending up with something that doesn't *quite* work and a handful of leftover parts.

The manufacturers who try to minimize shipping complications, costs, and inventory by packaging their products in ways that "require some assembly" have, I feel, a responsibility to make that whole process more user-friendly for the consumer. In contrast, some kit designs are marvels of creativity and the instructions to put them together are so well thought through that they are fail-safe. This is a form of creative design that I greatly admire, and it serves as an example of what this chapter is all about: how to creatively improve the human interface with the manufactured product. The other side of the coin is that far too many kit products are designed for the benefit of the manufacturer rather than the user and this means that they are ignoring the C-quadrant aspects of their whole brain leadership opportunities and responsibilities.

Why haven't those of us who live in the United States adopted the metric system? It isn't because the engineers and scientists among us don't already use the metric system; it's because more than half the population doesn't understand it even though it has a significantly clearer logic behind its design than do inches, feet, and yards. For people who are not oriented to quantitative, logical processing, the metric system is baffling. I recall a specific nationwide campaign some 50 years ago that had as its objective to convert to the metric system before year-end. The campaign was entirely A- quadrant-oriented and as a result was a total failure. Wrong strategy! The campaign was preaching to the choir.

A classic example of the impact of brain dominance on product design is the radical difference between IBM's PC and Apple's MAC computer. During the early stages of the product introduction, computer users sorted themselves out based on their personal mental preferences. People with right mode profiles bought the MAC and people with left mode profiles bought the PC. As a matter of fact, the two companies could accurately be described on the basis of the architecture of their products. IBM was a left mode company; Apple was a right mode company. The impression was that Apple devoted a great deal of attention to the user-friendliness of its line of MacIntosh computers. By contrast, IBM's approach seemed to be "This is it. Take it or leave it."

In 1985 I obtained copies of the annual reports of IBM and Apple and diagnosed their "mentality" in the Whole Brain Model in order to create pro forma profiles of the two annual reports. Here is the result of my diagnosis:

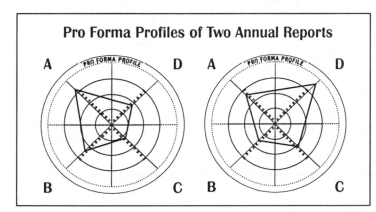

Figure 8-1.
Pro forma profiles characterizing the contrasting dominant styles of two computer manufacturers' annual reports, which also reflects the differences in the corporate cultures.

Which one do you think is IBM? Apple?

In seminars conducted around the world in the past ten years, attended in total by as many as 20,000 people, I have asked the audiences to identify which large computer manufacturer's annual report was represented by A and B. *Every* audience in *every country* got the correct answer—A was IBM and B was Apple.

I then asked whether there was a relationship between the mentality of the annual report and the leadership of the company. After a moment of hesitation, the audience responded yes. I then asked whether there was any relationship between the leadership of the company and the architecture of the computers they manufactured. Again the audience response was yes. The final question had to do with the relationship between the architecture of the computer and its user-friendliness. The audience response this time was a *resounding* yes! Keep in mind that these responses were consistent regardless of the country or culture.

I believe it is impossible to count the number of potential applications of brain dominance technology to products and services used by human beings. Mental preferences are distributed across a wide and predictable array of possibilities. Since these preferences are knowable, describable, and diagnosable, there is an opportunity for designers and suppliers to align their products with the mental preferences that exist in the general public. An example of an attempt to do this is the strategy of manufacturers and distributors who offer specialized products for left-handed people. Some products like scissors, ladles, and can openers are obviously user-friendly only for right-handed people. Ten percent of the world's population is left-handed. Statistically, that represents hundreds of millions of people who struggle every day to make use of these standard products. This clearly represents a marketing opportunity as well as a human relations need. If you consider the full potential provided by Whole Brain Technology, the opportunities are unlimited: personal organizers, computer keyboards, automobile instrument panels, appliances, toys, calculators, furniture, ballpoint pens, cameras, travel clocks—all would be more user-friendly if redesigned to meet the mental needs of vast numbers of people who think in particular ways. Whole Brain Technology makes these particular ways of thinking totally predictable. Entrepreneurs who are turned on by making the product/human interface more user-friendly should have a field day meeting these marketing needs.

In May of 1995, the new Boeing 777 Airliner was introduced to the public, perhaps the first whole brain user-friendly airliner ever designed and produced. It redefines user-friendliness because it is deliberately designed to be friendly not only to passengers, but also to the flight crew and the airline itself.

Instead of being designed in secret as is usually the case, it was designed with the full involvement of the initial purchaser—United Airlines. Boeing and United conceived a "working together" design concept that involved the designers and the users throughout the design process from the nose to the tail. The results are a breakthrough in user-friendly design. Here are some examples of over 300 features responding to the needs and desires of passengers, crew, and airline carrier:

Passengers	Crew	Airline
Personal entertainment center	Easy to fly	Economy of operation
Wider seats	Computerized cabin management control	Consistency of crew training
Wider aisles		
More shoulder room		
6'4" standing room	Ability of crew to control air temperature	Larger cargo compartments
Center seats a "tad" wider		
Larger overhead bins	Individual heating systems in doorways	Range of 4,350 miles
Video telephones	Increased size of push buttons so maintenance crews in cold climates won't have to remove their gloves. Design can accommodate to both shrink and stretch version	More seats
Communication systems between passengers		User-friendly, functional, aesthetically pleasing deck. Designed to achieve world flight approval
Quiet cabin		
		Flat cabin aisle floors

By factoring human considerations into the design process with the active involvement of the users, manufacturers can make a quantum leap forward in user-friendliness. The diagnostic capabilities of Whole Brain Technology can contribute uniquely to the design process to the benefit of all.

Inventing the Impossible Solution

As a pool owner, I have often wished for a gadget that would clean a swimming pool automatically, including not only the bottom but the sides as well. The cleaner that came with the pool consisted of an array of plastic hoses that whipped around the bottom surface, propelled by water jets. What this did was stir up what was on the bottom surface so that the pool filtering system would carry away the dirt and debris. The problem was that the device got hung up at the corners of the pool, and even when it worked as designed, it really didn't work according to my need. Furthermore, it didn't clean the sides of the pool. In my frustration, I fantasized about a device that would solve the problem, but even in my wildest dreams I could not figure out how to clean the sides of the pool as well as the bottom. And then I discovered the Kreepy Krawly.

Many readers who are old enough will remember a cartoon that was popular in the 1930s and 1940s that featured bizarre solutions to everyday problems, like an automatic window closer. Rube Goldberg, the cartoonist, created a device with a small windmill that, when stirred by the breeze, would rotate a feather that would tickle a sleeping chipmunk, who would drop a nut from his mouth on to a miniature seesaw, which flipped up to release a hopper full of marbles, which filled a small bucket, the weight of which pulled a rope through a pulley that was connected to a stick that held the window up. When the stick was pulled loose, the window closed by gravity. Now that may seem outlandish, but when you examine the Kreepy Krawly you will be instantly reminded of Rube Goldberg.

Figure 8-2.
An example of a Rube Goldberg-type invention.

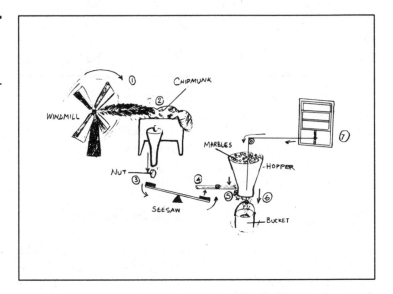

The working head of the machine looks like a robot with a circular flat bottom, connected by a long length of flexible tubing to the pool's skimmer system, which in turn is connected to the pool's pump. The machine is nothing short of a miracle of creative design. If there were a Rube Goldberg contest, Kreepy Krawly would win it hands down.

I am certain that after the basic concept of the pool cleaner had been demonstrated through a series of experiments, the inventor continued to innovate around the basic design in order for the device to move through a random pattern, across the bottom and up the sides of the pool and down again so as to sweep not only across the entire bottom and sides of the pool to loosen the dirt and debris, but then through the suction system to vacuum the pool's surface areas as it moved through its continuously random pattern. Within an hour or two the entire bottom and sides of the pool are cleaned. The evolutionary nature of the design was confirmed when I looked at the model numbers and dates of the main machine and its accessories. I can project that the design cycle of the Kreepy Krawly took at least five years and will last at least five more as various adjustments and additions are made to further perfect the operation of the machine. Not only is Kreepy Krawly a conversation piece, but it is, without a doubt, the best pool cleaner I am aware of.

Kreepy Krawly is a perfect example of applied creative and innovative thinking in a market where there are already existing products. It is an example of "building a better mousetrap," of finding a better way to do a job that's being inadequately performed by other devices. It is an example of having the courage of your convictions to hang in there until the design can be marketed, and then to keep improving the product through continuing research, experimentation, and development.

So What?

- *User-friendly* is in the eye of the beholder.

- Since the world is a composite whole brain in terms of preferences, there are many user-unfriendly products such as the "some assembly required" kits.

- New Boeing 777 Airliner design approach expands the user-friendly concept to include not only passengers, but also the crew and the airline carrier.

- Whole Brain Technology, through its diagnostic power and its design direction, offers vast entrepreneurial opportunities.

"The world of reality has its limits; the world of imagination is boundless."

—

Jean Jacques Rousseau

9

Approaches and Styles of Management

Chapter Headlines

♦ Mental diversity sheds new light on the ongoing challenges of managing diversity.

♦ How to manage its mentally diverse human asset is a company's greatest challenge.

♦ Management styles result from thinking preferences and avoidances that are based on brain dominance characteristics as shaped by life experiences.

♦ Most thinking styles are the result of combinations of preferences and therefore, management styles cover the entire range of thinking-style options.

Professor Henry Mintzberg of McGill University concluded that managers can be smart and dull at the same time. It was both a brilliant and courageous observation that all of us should take to heart. Whole Brain Technology through the *HBDI* and pro forma profiles provides diagnostic tools to help explain why some managers don't get it and why others do.

Think for a minute about areas where you are smart and areas where you are not very smart, and possibly even dull. I was smart in physics and dull in chemical engineering. Even if I had been able to graduate in chemical engineering, I never would have been very good at it or liked it. There are probably millions of people who are not very good at what they do but who could be smart, and even brilliant, in other kinds of work. Can you *imagine* a business where most of the people are smart at what they do because they are fully aligned to the mental requirements of their jobs? The human resource aspect of aligning work with employees' preferences is one of the major advantages of applying Whole Brain Technology. After all, a company's investment in its workers is probably one of the highest costs of doing business.

Managing Mental Diversity

In 1989, I did a national study of the top ten "hot button" issues in business and industry. The candidate list included such topics as: Quality, Service, Globalization, Change, Technology, and Creativity; but the hottest button of all was Diversity. What kind of diversity emerged as the winner?

As I investigated the subject in more detail, I discovered that the key aspects of diversity most commonly addressed were race, gender, age, and to a lesser degree, culture and disabilities. My sources included human resources professionals, operating managers, senior executives, and major publications. In my research, there was not a single mention of the aspect of diversity that I consider the most significant and the most positive of all—that is, mental diversity, the differences in thinking styles. In PART I, I reported that the business world is a composite whole brain. That means that organizations are comprised of an extraordinarily balanced array of thinking styles. Logic would tell us that this level of thinking-style diversity would occur in companies with over 10,000 employees; however, my data clearly establishes that this diversity is also true of business organizations with 100 employees and in many cases, with fewer than 50 employees. It is highly likely that your company's workforce is made up of a balanced distribution of thinking-style preferences. The question to ponder is whether this diverse workforce is managed to take advantage of its potential productivity.

In the hundreds of cases that I have studied, which includes 17 of the Fortune 50 and 200 of the Fortune 1000 lists, there has not been a single company that has managed on the basis of the organization's diversity potential. The mental composition of an organization's workforce has never even been considered.

"So much of what we call management consists of making it difficult to work."

—

Peter Drucker

Financial balance sheets list assets and liabilities as a way of understanding current business status. These are important measures and need to be taken into account; however, the typical balance sheet is incomplete. The vital asset of most businesses is not money, or bricks and mortar, or proprietary technology, or the products manufactured. It is the human resource: the current and future engine of the business. As many human resource executives can attest, the value of this resource base is often taken for granted.

The human resource is the vital asset that goes home every night and must come back in the morning if your business is to survive and grow. In most contemporary businesses, this asset is made up of knowledge workers and this is true even for those businesses that have a large manufacturing component. In these highly competitive times, production workers need to work smart; therefore, the mental demands of the work are greater than ever.

So how do we manage this vital asset? I believe we start by understanding the value of its diversity at a significantly high level of sophistication.

I once was asked, "What does the brain have to do with managing?" In the context of mental diversity, I can reframe the question as follows: "What does having a workforce with a balanced array of thinking-style preferences have to do with managing?" My answer is: "Everything." The characteristics and aspects of brain dominance discussed so far impact all of the following management responsibilities:

- Job design
- Job placement
- Management communications
- Team selection
- Organization design
- Manpower planning
- Rewards and recognition

Imagine trying to optimize the management of these issues with a style limited to only one or possibly two quadrants. Shown in figure 9-1 is the composite of an organization of approximately 800 employees. The issues that I have just listed are sure to be interpreted differently by each cluster of employees whose preferences are distributed around

> *"Power is given to you by others. It is not yours; it is in trust with you and it is a great responsibility. Power is to be used for the benefit of those whose trustee you are."*
>
> —
>
> *Mahatma Gandhi*

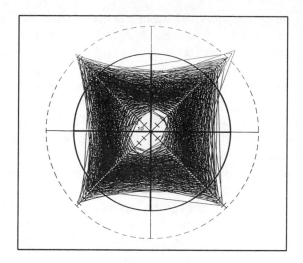

Figure 9-1.
Actual composite profile of a staff of people from a major U.S. corporation.

the four-quadrant model. If, on the other hand, management is interpreting and administering programs and processes from just one or two of the quadrants, typically the left mode, A/B quadrants, the productivity and overall effectiveness of the organization will be substantially discounted.

Let's take management communication as an example. There are at least four discreet processing modes, each one characteristic of a quadrant. A top management cadre whose group preferences are tilted primarily to one of the four quadrants, such as the A quadrant, and who communicates best in that mode, will miss connecting with three-fourths of the human resource assets. In the case of the company whose composite profile is shown in figure 9-1, I demonstrated this with 800 people seated on the basis of their mental preferences. I got responses from each of the four corners of the room to what work turned them on, what work turned them off, and how they reacted differently to the same questions.

The one-day program was scheduled as follows. The president had a total of 30 minutes; 15 minutes each at the beginning and at the end. I had the six and one-half hours in between. The president's initial segment was almost entirely made up of A-quadrant-style business facts and numbers. The exposition of Whole Brain Technology that followed had a major influence on his closing remarks. His delivery was largely spontaneous and accounted for the diverse audience by incorporating an element of each quadrant in his presentation. His audience loved it. This was a spectacular demonstration of conversion to the realities of mental diversity.

In many business situations creativity is the difference between success and failure. It is their competitive advantage. Creativity is mental and mental diversity is a key to the creative process. Business leaders who understand the significance of diversity in the creative process can take advantage of their organization's potential by forming teams that are made up of different thinking styles. As will be discussed in Chapter 11, heterogeneous teams are the ultimate weapon in the race toward creativity.

Taking full advantage of the mentally diverse human asset requires a quantum leap in management understanding and competence. It changes the management game. No longer is any single style, whether it be authoritarian or participative, good enough to optimize business results. Multiple styles, situationally applied, are required to take full advantage of the richness of the human resource. There is a glaring fact of life that all managements should understand. This highly diverse, high potential, vital asset is already in place. You don't have to recruit it. You just need to understand it in order to make more effective use of what's already there.

"The best leaders are apt to be found among those executives who have a strong component of unorthodoxy in their characters. Instead of resisting innovation, they symbolize it— and companies cannot grow without innovation."

— *David Ogilvy*

A Whole Brain Analysis of Management Styles

Just as our brain dominance characteristics influence our preferences, competencies, and "turn-on" work, they are also embedded in our management style. As we engage in work that is consistent with our mental preferences, we will gradually develop a personal style of working, visible to others. As I illustrated in the Brain Dominance in Action section on page 63, our mental preferences carry over into our daily work habits. This is also true for management styles, because we are viewing the world through the lenses of our personal mental preferences. For example, management tasks such as problem solving, determination of work assignments, interpersonal relationships, staff communications, and budget preparation, as well as other work elements, will be thought of and carried out on the basis of an individual's preferences *and* existing competencies. As this emerging style is affirmed by good results, the managerial behaviors are reinforced and can be difficult to change, especially if the style is in alignment with the surrounding management culture.

Management styles are not only influenced by what turns us on; they can also be recognized by what turns us off. It is not uncommon for our areas of "dullness" to be more obvious than our areas of smartness. So that you can best understand your areas of management smartness and dullness, I have described management styles by each quadrant of the Whole Brain Model and then in combinations of quadrants. Each description points out the strengths and the pitfalls of each style. Now I hasten to say that only 7 percent of our 113,000 active database have a thinking style confined to a single quadrant. In general, every person, even those with a strong preference, actually represents a coalition of preferences comprising each of the four quadrants. So as you read through the following descriptions, keep in mind that only a small percentage would actually exhibit a quadrant-specific style. Management style, like our personal preferences, can be enriched, broadened, or further focused. The goal is not to be a master of one or all styles but to gain an awareness of all the styles so that you can honor your strengths and cultivate situational smartness in your areas of dullness. The A-quadrant example that follows illustrates how easily our mental preferences can dictate our management style without any training or intervention to change that natural progression.

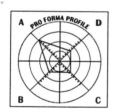

The A-quadrant style is typically authoritative, directive, and all-business.

Figure 9-2.
The A-quadrant management style pro forma profile.

An A-quadrant manager is focused on the task at hand, with an extreme comfort level with concrete, technical information, such as computer programming, equipment specs, stock market indexes, chemical formulas, medical terms, and legal briefs, to name a few. Typically he or she will gravitate toward the information side of the job (what is to be produced, created, or analyzed) as opposed to the "management of people" end of it. Managers of this type are often content working on problems where they can focus their energy on thinking, processing, and analyzing as opposed to talking through solutions to problems. If this person were a man in a technical profession, some people may say, "Oh, he's so analytical. He never shows any emotion whatsoever." This would not be an uncommon description of a strongly A-quadrant-oriented engineer. He is living in a rational, technical world where most things can be explained in logical, analytic terms. When this technical person is promoted to manager he continues to view the world through these same A-quadrant preferences and his style as a manager carries over his already strong factual orientation. Opinions, unless backed up with factual evidence, are not considered to be important. His interface with his staff would typically be restricted to technical discussions on engineering specs of projects and very short directives. The only time he enjoys talking with others is in the process of analyzing and defining the facts and in debates on the best equipment, methodology, and combination of people to produce the desired result. A technical manager, such as the one just described, might have a secondary preference in the B or D quadrants (depending upon the type of engineer or technical job), but it is rare to encounter one with a primary or secondary preference for the C quadrant. The C quadrant is in direct competition with the preferred rational, logical A quadrant. Unless there are frequent work-related needs for these other preferences to be applied, this manager's style will be largely characterized by the strong, active A-quadrant characteristics. Many will perceive him on the basis of those things that *turn him on*. They will also perceive him on the basis of those things that *turn him off*. If this manager has no preference for expressive, interpersonal, emotional, feeling-oriented modes, then this absence of preference will be a visible factor in his style. Taken a step further, if this manager has an active avoidance of those C-quadrant "interpersonal" preferences, this could become the predominant style characteristic. If this were the case, some would consider him to be a cold-hearted, nonfeeling sort who cares only about his technical equipment and proving his theories.

In the absence of feedback, a person's style begins to harden and become more and more unchangeable. When a person such as I have just described works for a senior manager who has the same style characteristics, they then tend to become additive and begin to form a management culture. Since it is a normal, human characteristic to seek out those who are like us, it is often the case that managers hire in their own image. This natural process tends to reinforce the manage-

> *"Every step we take—no matter how small—to understand the needs of the people we strive to serve will increase our bond with them and move us in the direction of a higher standard of leadership."*
>
> —
>
> *Mahatma Gandhi*

ment style of an organization whether it is good or bad. The A-quadrant style is often characterized as "authoritarian" or "directive" or "strictly business." But it doesn't have to be that way. The obvious virtues of A-quadrant preferences and competencies can be packaged in other combinations, particularly when there are no significant turn-offs that foreclose the active contributions from the other quadrants.

The B-quadrant style is typically traditional, conservative, and risk avoiding.

Figure 9-3.
The B-quadrant management style pro forma profile.

Managers who strongly prefer B-quadrant mental processes typically exhibit a highly traditional and conservative style. They strive for safety and stability and therefore tend to resist change. They excel at structure, following procedures and taking into account all the details necessary to meet deadlines. They like order and work best in an organization where the lines of authority are clear. Accountability is important to the B-quadrant manager, so he or she may want to follow the rules before adding a step to a process that may improve the product in the long run but would increase the risk of going past a deadline. They typically avoid risk and focus primarily on short-term results. There are certain areas of business that benefit from a management style that doesn't stray from the norm. Banking and finance managers, lab technicians and purchasing managers are all required to follow procedure. They don't like to experiment and are turned off by grandiose schemes and entrepreneurial adventures (you'd want this for a lab technician testing your blood, but what about a business development consultant?). An extreme version of the B-quadrant managerial style is frequently most visible in the manufacturing function. This is an area where work needs to be performed on the basis of documented procedures and strict schedules. It is in this function that programs like zero defects and total quality management are rigorously implemented. When carried to the extreme, this is a "nose to the grindstone," time-clock-driven managerial style. There is some human resource interest incorporated in this style, but it is productivity first and human resource concerns second.

Figure 9-4.
A combination of A and B styles in pro forma profile.

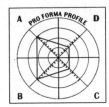

The A- & B-quadrant management style is practical and realistic.

The combination of the A- and B-quadrant managerial styles can be overwhelmingly powerful because the main characteristics of this left mode style are "hard" rather than "soft." The most frequently occurring male profile in business occupations is double-dominant left, which means a fairly equal distribution in terms of A- and B-quadrant preferences. Frequently, managers who have this double-dominance exhibit a combination of the two styles just described. (The popular press refers to this style as *Left Brain*.) Managers with this combination of preferences often have supplemented their competencies with an M.B.A. degree. This represents an overlay of financial measurement on top of other functional competencies such as engineering or manufacturing. This increases the relative "hardness" of the resulting style.

Figure 9-5.
C-quadrant management style pro forma profile.

The C-quadrant style is personable, interactive, and intuitive.

The C-quadrant style is highly participative and oriented to teams and communities. It is a style that considers the human resource as the primary asset of the business. C-quadrant style managers are concerned with the organizational climate, policies, and programs that affect employee relationships within the organization. They are also advocates of employee development, on-site training, and taking into account the design and safety characteristics of the employee working facilities. The C-quadrant style would likely advocate ombudsmen, employee counseling, on-site health care, and talking through employees' problems. This style would place a high priority on effective employee communication processes and feel comfortable with face-to-face interaction. Although the business world is a composite whole brain, the

C-quadrant management style is not prevalent. In fact, C-quadrant-oriented employees have a difficult time getting promoted to frontline management jobs. Their style is considered too soft to be fully competitive in a finance-driven business culture dominated by the A and B styles.

Since several important functions of the business are in themselves C-quadrant-oriented, such as human resource development, it is typical that managers within these functions exhibit the style characteristics that I've just described. However, since these characteristics are often not in good alignment with the principal managerial style of the total organization, these more C-quadrant managers are not in all cases equal partners in the management of the enterprise. They are often tolerated by the A- and B-oriented senior managers as a necessary part of the business, but certainly not where command decisions are made.

 *The D-quadrant style is holistic, risk-oriented, adventurous, and entrepreneurial.*

Figure 9-6.
D-quadrant management style pro forma profile.

D-quadrant preferences involving conceptual, holistic, imaginative, and integrative mental modes result in managerial styles that can be described as adventurous, risk-oriented, global, big picture, and visionary. This style is often in direct opposition to the prevailing culture. D-quadrant-oriented managers come up with last minute ideas that wreak havoc with production managers. This is the style of entrepreneurs, growth-oriented leaders who think far into the future, new-product developers, super salespeople, strategic thinkers, and brainstormers in the advertising industry. D-quadrant managers have an open, less-structured style than any other quadrant style. This style is wonderful for individuals who are independent and thrive under a system which trusts they will put in the time necessary to get the work done. However, for some, the lack of structure and specifics to carry out directives can be very uncomfortable. D-quadrant managers are the opposite of B-quadrant managers; they feel confined by conforming to procedures especially if it gets in the way of moving forward.

"The world will belong to passionate, driven leaders— people who not only have enormous amounts of energy, but who can energize those whom they lead."

—

Jack Welch

This managerial style would advocate the "skunk works" approach to product development, in which the work environment is designed around the needs of the work and those doing it, so that optimum results can be achieved. (For a full description, see Chapter 24.) This style would consider advertising an investment rather than an expense, and would be comfortable with "outside the box" strategies or ideas. Imaginative, hands-on involvement would characterize the D-quadrant style. For example, take the President of DialPage, David Garrison. One Christmas he and his staff, dressed as Santa Claus and his helpers, made surprise visits to all the company plants. The employees enjoyed it because this action fit the open, fun-loving culture that he had developed.

Fun and creative thinking are legitimized. This style considers "outside the box" thinking and work spirit to be as important as technical excellence. At Apple Computer for example, employee creativity, productivity, and quality performance are rewarded with such events as Halloween costume parades and parties.

Figure 9-7.
A combination of C and D styles in management.

The C- & D-quadrant style is open-minded, intuitive, and flexible.

Just as there is a combination left mode style of A and B quadrants, there is a combination right mode style of C and D. The profile 2-2-1-1 is among the most frequent in business and is seen in many organizations that are service-oriented rather than hardware-oriented. The C/D right mode style is people-oriented, open-minded, and inclined to be idealistic. It is strong on employee involvement, self-directed work teams, customer service, and a stimulating work climate. Employees who work under this managerial style are often more involved, and have more freedom than those who work under an A/B left mode style.

Our database clearly differentiates the left mode A/B style from the right mode C/D style on the basis of gender-oriented preference. The left mode A/B style has a strong alignment with male-oriented preferences (logical, analytic, rational,

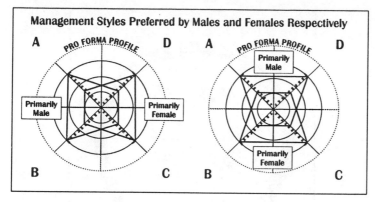

Management Styles Preferred by Males and Females Respectively

Figure 9-8.
Gender norms reflected in management style norms. Men are more A/B; women prefer the C and D quadrants.

structured, and organized) and the right mode C/D style has a strong alignment with female-oriented preferences (interpersonal, emotional, expressive, informal, and open). These two styles show the same dominance characteristics that exist in our Western culture—the left mode style dominates the right mode style. This is particularly true in the business setting.

There are two other combination styles that show distinct gender differentiation. The cerebral style made up of the A and D quadrants is strongly male-preferred. The limbic style, made up of B and C quadrants is strongly female-preferred.

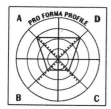

The cerebral style combines preferences for technical and experimental thinking.

Figure 9-9.
Two pro formas: the cerebral style, A/D, is strongly preferred by males; the limbic B/C style is more preferred by women.

The cerebral style is characterized by relatively equal preferences for both the A and D quadrants. These two quadrants represent strikingly different modes of thinking, with the A quadrant being strongly logical, analytic, and rational and the D quadrant being equally strongly conceptual, intuitive, and imaginative. This style combines technical and experimental thinking and is therefore the primary style for scientists, inventors, and research and development organizations.

A study of the members of the National Inventors Hall of Fame shows that A/D-dominant profile is clearly the preferred profile among its members, and the same has been shown to be true for 250 members of the Lawrence Livermore National

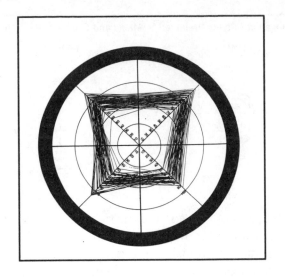

Figure 9-10.
National Inventors Hall of Fame: a pro forma composite of the 84 members showing the strong A/D cerebral mental preference of inventors.

Laboratory, which the public would recognize as the center of Star Wars research. The same double-dominant pattern describes the R&D departments of many major corporations, such as Polaroid. The technologists who design and develop computer chips share this same average profile and therefore function with the same style characteristics.

These populations of inventors, scientists, and technologists are strongly male-dominated. Well over 90 percent of all U. S. patents are held by males. Fifty years ago that percentage was over 97 percent male.

Like the left mode and right mode styles, the A/D style usually lies between the two quadrants that make it up. However, the cerebral style can be strongly tilted toward either A or D, and you can easily tell the difference. An A-oriented R&D operation would be scientific, serious, and strongly business-oriented. In comparison, a cerebral style with a strong D-quadrant orientation would be highly experimental, motivated, but loose and open.

People who exhibit the cerebral style often get "lost in their work." It's heady stuff, with frequent insights and technical, scientific breakthroughs. They get a lot of internal rewards from the work they do without always having to depend on rewards coming from the managerial bureaucracy. Often this style is recognizable by what it lacks—a groundedness in the security-minded and people-concerned qualities of the limbic quadrants.

"The question 'Who ought to be boss?' is like asking 'Who ought to be the tenor in the quartet?' Obviously, the man who can sing tenor."

—

Henry Ford

The limbic style combines the stability of tradition with a caring responsiveness.

Figure 9-11.
Double dominance in the B and C quadrants: a female-preferred management style.

The double dominant B- and C-quadrant style is quite different. This is a style that combines orderliness, tradition, ritual, and productivity with a strong people-orientation, a sensitivity to feelings, a preference for team participation, and involvement. This style is strongly service-oriented and considers employees, customers, and the community to be high-priority stakeholders. Department stores like Nordstrom's typify this management culture style in action. Social work departments, elementary schools, and personnel departments are also prime examples. This style tends to favor the status quo and doing what's right for the company and the individual. It has a strong production orientation, but not at the expense of the people involved. A strong loyalty often accompanies the limbic style. As with the cerebral style, whether the emphasis is on one quadrant or another depends upon the individuals and the prevailing management culture.

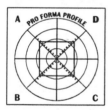

The multidominant style enables a manager to respond to a diverse set of business issues.

Figure 9-12.
The Whole Brain Management style: Equally dominant in all quadrants.

A multidominant management style is one that can readily access all four quadrants and apply the features of the different styles in situationally appropriate ways. To be able to make use of this style, an individual must be able to access the differing styles on a relatively level playing field. To put that in other words, think of a four-quadrant, four-mode pool of style options that the multidominant person could draw from as situationally required: eight discrete styles as just described. While the multidominant style could be available to any manager in any function, those managers who have work requirements that involve all four quadrants are the ones most likely to apply it. The CEO would probably be fully advantaged by this style. But this doesn't mean that other types of managers, in engineering, finance, business development, or manufacturing, would not have occasion to apply the flexible style.

Being situational is the key requirement to the full application of the multidominant style. By this I mean the ability to make application of the quadrant-specific style characteristics. For example, a manager who deals with a financial issue not only in an analytical style, but also incorporates organized, interpersonal, long-range strategy, and expressive thinking style will greatly enhance the outcome. Contrast this with a manager that is limited to just an analytical style. Another example would be a human resource development manager who is trying to affect a culture change by implementing an effective cash management program but is limiting his implementation style within the confines of a participatory humanistic approach. In this example, the absence of the structured, organized B-quadrant style, the quantitative, logical A-quadrant style, and the integrating-synthesizing D-quadrant style seriously discounts the likelihood of success.

To be an effective practitioner of the multidominant style requires an opportunity to apply it frequently enough that an appropriate array of competencies can be developed. Managerial and leadership positions that have a high frequency of multidominant opportunity include plant manager, project manager, multifunction team leader, executive secretary, and, of course, chief executive officer. The daily, weekly, and monthly in-basket of these positions can be so wide-ranging that flexibility of style options is a real advantage, if not necessity. Since only 2.5 percent of the population have preferences for all quadrants, being *situationally-whole brained* is the viable solution. This means that those styles that are not our most preferred need to be available for timely application in situations that could benefit from such a style.

There is something to be said about consistency, but managing in only one style can be limiting if the situation requires shifting to a style that is more effective. Consider an individual whose work requires effective management behavior in a budgetary situation with finance, a design review session with engineering, deciding on appropriation requests from manufacturing, reaching a decision on the architectural plan for the new headquarters building, responding to the

"The man who always knows how, will always have a job. The man who also knows why will always be his boss."

—

Ralph Waldo Emerson

MANAGEMENT STYLES MATRIX		
A-Quadrant Style	**A/D-Quadrant Style**	**D-Quadrant Style**
The single A-quadrant style is typically "authoritative," "directive," and "all-business."	The A/D cerebral style combines preferences for technical and experimental thinking.	The D-quadrant style is holistic, risk-oriented, adventurous, and entrepreneurial.
A/B-Left-Mode Style	**MULTIDOMINANT Style**	**C/D-Right-Mode Style**
The A/B-quadrant, left-mode management style is well-defined, practical, and realistic.	The multidominant style enables a manager to respond to a diverse set of business issues.	The C/D-quadrant, right-mode style is open-minded, intuitive, and flexible.
B-Quadrant Style	**B/C-Quadrant Style**	**C-Quadrant Style**
The single B-quadrant style is typically consistent, conservative, and risk avoiding.	The B/C Limbic style combines the stability of tradition with a caring responsiveness.	The single C-quadrant style is personable, interactive, and intuitive.

B C

Figure 9-13. Management style matrix. Scan the styles to find the most appropriate one for your situation.

recommendations of the art selection committee for the main lobby, and conducting the annual manpower review with the human resources representatives from each of the major functions. These multiple events are scheduled to take place over a three-day period. Consider for a moment the range of management styles that could be applied to maximize the success of each separate event. The advantage of style flexibility is clear whether the position is that of a plant manager, head of a multifunctional division, or chief executive officer. Add to that impressive list of circumstances the need to represent the company in a legal suit and to be interviewed by the press in conjunction with the plant expansion. Being situational in each separate event is similar to "rising to the occasion" as the situation demands, even though the experience base is not equally distributed, and even though the preference for managing your way through each unique event is not equally high. Being able to switch back and forth between styles eventually allows for the acquisition of the competencies to meet each different need.

Throughout this book, there are quadrant walk-around models that are designed to achieve whole brain results. By forcing a walk-around of the four quadrants, these models help diagnose whether the attributes of each quadrant have been factored into whatever domain the model is addressing. This walk-around concept applied to management styles can help us determine which style is most appropriate, whether it be in a staff meeting, in dealing with a customer complaint, in running an annual meeting, or in dealing with the media. Figure 9-13 offers an eight-element universe of managerial styles that emerge from Whole Brain Technology.

In general, the most flexible situational style is the one that will produce the best results from any organization, with the caveat that, whatever the style, the needed competencies required by the business must be available to meet daily business needs. Style alone cannot produce bottom-line results.

So What?

- Since the world of management is made up of all combinations of preferences and avoidances, all possible management styles are present in the business world.

- Male styles are primarily left mode and cerebral, while female styles are primarily right mode and limbic.

- Style flexibility contributes to managerial effectiveness.

- The multidominant management style matrix (four quadrants, four modes) is a whole brain tool enabling a manager to diagnose style usage and to select appropriate style applications.

Communication

Chapter Headlines

♦ Effective communication is fundamental to the success of business processes.

♦ Differing mental preferences contribute to the level of success or failure of communication processes.

♦ Alignment between communication pairs can range from effective to very ineffective.

♦ Due to basic male/female brain dominance differences, male/female communication pairs are candidates for miscommunication.

♦ We experience the world around us as enhanced or filtered through our profile of mental preferences.

"After all, when you come right down to it, how many people speak the same language even when they speak the same language?"

—

Russell Hoban

There is hardly a single topic more fundamental to the business process than communication. I believe it is also true that there is hardly any process more susceptible to failure than the everyday activity of businesspeople talking, writing, and somehow signaling to each other. A major contributor to the success or failure of the communication processes we use is the way our different mental preferences influence the way we send and receive information.

It's quite likely that most of us think that we see the world exactly as it is, and that our view is complete and accurate. My studies indicate that for the vast majority of us this is simply not the case. In essence we are experiencing the world around us as filtered through our profile of mental preferences. Where we have strong preferences we are seeing and hearing things close to the way they actually are. However,

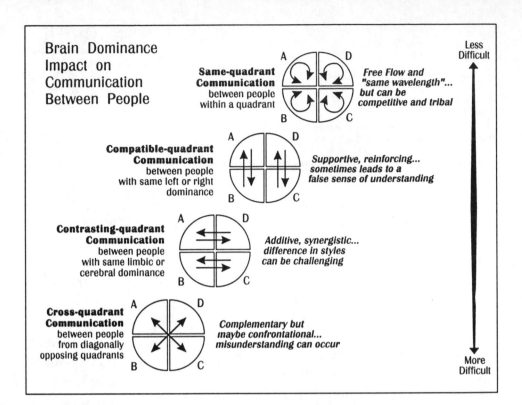

Figure 10-1.
Communication continuum: Communication between those with different thinking styles.

in our areas of lesser preference we are likely to be partially blind and deaf. And in our areas of avoidance there is little doubt that we don't see or hear accurately at all.

If we built a continuum of communication success, the high point would occur between two individuals with nearly identical profiles and equal experience in the same profession. At the opposite end would be a pair with opposing profiles, where one person's preference is the other's avoidance and where they hold entirely different levels of experience, such as an A-quadrant insurance company actuary and a C-quadrant kindergarten teacher.

Figure 10-1 indicates that the most effective and least difficult communication takes place between people who have the *same quadrant* preference and are in the same occupation. These two people are on the same wavelength, so to speak, and words are likely to mean the same thing to each due to their similar preferences and occupations. Somewhat more difficult and less effective communication takes place between two people whose profiles are in *compatible quadrants,* such as the left mode A and B and the right mode D

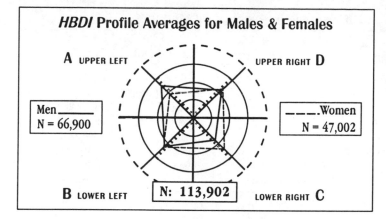

Figure 10-2.
Average profiles of men and women from current computer database.

and C. The next lower level of communication success occurs between individuals representing *complementary quadrants,* such as A and D and B and C. These complementary quadrants represent interconnected structures in the brain that are able to relate to each other in ways that often lead to creative thinking outcomes.

The most difficult end of the communication continuum is where opposing quadrants are involved in the transaction, such as the B and D quadrants and the A and C quadrants. B-quadrant administrators and D-quadrant art directors in an advertising agency, and A-quadrant financial managers and C-quadrant employee counselors are such pairs. When the differences in thinking preferences and work requirements are both severely out of alignment, effective communication is least likely to occur. And when it does succeed, it is the result of intense focus and motivation on the part of the people involved. They really want to make it work.

From our database we can conclude that men and women are, on the average, equally strong candidates to experience the difficulties of the A/C communication situation just described. Why? More men statistically prefer the A quadrant and least prefer the C, whereas women prefer the exact opposite (see "Adam and Eve in the Workplace," Chapter 4). I believe it to be the root of what has been described as the "Men are from Mars and Women are from Venus" syndrome. The fact that these differences contribute to the attraction between men and women increases the likelihood that a lot of relationships will be stressed or actually ruptured because of the inherent communication difficulty brought about by the combining of opposing quadrants.

"You cannot speak of ocean to a well-frog, the creature of a narrower sphere.

You cannot speak of ice to a summer insect, the creature of a season."

—

Chuang Tzu,
"Autumn Floods"
(4th-3rd c. B.C.)
tr. Herbert A.
Giles

Differences in Processing Modes			
	A Upper Left	**B** Lower Left	**C** Lower Right	**D** Upper Right

	A Upper Left	**B** Lower Left	**C** Lower Right	**D** Upper Right
Descriptors	analytical authoritarian critical factual logical mathematical quantitative rational	articulate conservative controlled data collector detailed dominant sequential technical reader	emotional intuitive (of people) musical reader (personal) spiritual symbolic talkative	artistic holistic imaginative intuitive (of solutions) simultaneous spatial synthesizer
Skills	analytical financial problem solving scientific statistical technical	administrative implementation organizational planning regulatory supervisory	expressing ideas interpersonal teaching training writing (cor- respondence)	causing change conceptualizing generating ideas integrative trusting intuition visualizing
Typical Phrases Used	"Break it down" "Critical analysis" "Hardware" "Key point" "Knowing the bottom line" "Take it apart" "Tools"	"By the book" "Establishing habits" "Law and order" "Play it safe" "Self-discipline" "Sequence" "We have always done it this way"	"Human resources" "Human values" "Interactive" "Participatory" "Personal growth" "Team work" "Team development" "The family"	"Blockbusting" "Broad-based" "Conceptual "Cutting edge" "Innovative" "Play with an idea" "Synergistic" "The big picture"
Typical Derogatory Phrases (Zingers) Used By Others	"Calculating" "Cold fish" "Nerd" "Number cruncher" "Power Hungry" "Uncaring" "Unemotional"	"Can't think for him/herself" "Grinds out the task" "One-track mind" "Picky" "Stick-in-the-mud" "Unimaginative"	"A push over" "Bleeding heart" "Corny" "Talk, talk, talk" "Touchy-feely" "Gullible" "Sappy"	"Can't focus" "Dreams a lot" "Head in clouds" "Off-the-wall" "Reckless" "Unrealistic" "Undisciplined"

Figure 10-3.
Typical processing modes for each quadrant.

Figure 10-3 was developed to help explain the differences in processing modes on the basis of the four-quadrant model. In this case the four quadrants are shown as vertical columns, with the horizontal rows indicating key descriptors, occupational choices, and typical phrases used. The words chosen are only characteristic examples; there is a wide variety of possibilities. It is easy to see how specialized jargon can develop around occupational choices and mental preferences. I believe this tends to increase the likelihood of misunderstandings taking place between people with different preferences, working in different occupations.

A	D
◆ Does it use facts? ◆ Is it quantified? ◆ Does it show clear analysis? ◆ Is it to the point? Is it logical?	◆ Does it look at the big picture or overview? ◆ Is it visual and colorful? ◆ Does It use metaphors? ◆ Does it look at the future? ◆ Is it conceptually sound or clear?

Communication Walk-Around

B	C
◆ Does it provide details? ◆ Is it in sequential order? ◆ Is it neat? ◆ Is it in a recognizable, "appropriate" format?	◆ Does it use experiences that relate to the audience? ◆ Are there examples to illustrate the point? ◆ Is it helpful and user-friendly? ◆ Does it acknowledge emotional issues?

Figure 10-4. Communication Walk-Around Exercise. Walk around each quadrant to diagnose your communication style.

The challenge for business managers is to find ways of communicating with diverse employee populations so that the *intended communication* actually takes place, regardless of differences in the way people perceive. When the intended communication is significant, it is necessary to design and deliver it in ways that allow for understanding to take place in all four quadrants. My experience clearly demonstrates that the use of illustrations, graphics, examples, stories, and metaphors greatly enhances the likelihood that the intended meaning is conveyed to a wide range of people.

The fail-safe assumption is that the receiving population is mentally diverse. I would recommend that each significant point be delivered in all quadrants and modes. When information *must* be understood as intended, there is no other option other than to employ all quadrants and modes of the Whole Brain Model in delivering that communication.

A useful tool to insure a whole brain communication is to apply the four-quadrant Communication Walk-Around Model to the significant points of the intended message. This is a problem-solving/avoiding process that forces a review of the intended communication in each of the four quadrants.

Suppose, for example, that a company president has just drafted a statement for the corporate newsletter. His first key point is: "It is our strategic intent to double this business in the next five years." He wants to be sure people understand his intended meaning, so he tests his draft statements by eliciting new reactions from each of the four quadrants of the Communication Walk-Around Model (figure 10-4).

"Precision of communication is important, more important than ever, in our era of hair-trigger balances, when a false, or misunderstood word may create as much disaster as a sudden thoughtless act."

—

James Thurber

1. Quadrant A: "Double the business in the next five years"? Just what did he intend to convey: Double the sales? ...profits? ...number of employees? ...total assets of the business? By asking himself questions about the factual content of his proposed statement, he realizes that he has to be more precise in his language. What he really means is that the strategic intent is to double the *revenues* of the business, specifically, to grow from $2 billion to $4 billion in annual revenues.

2. Quadrant B: His draft statement does not address the organizational implications of doubling the revenue. Does he mean that this is to occur without any increase in staff on the basis of the same organizational arrangement? He discovers that he has failed to build into the statement his intention to create three new strategic business units to accomplish this doubling of revenues.

3. Quadrant C: If he now includes a reference to three new business units, what might that do to employment? How would it affect the morale of existing employees? His statement must stipulate or strongly imply that the strategic intent is not to double employment to achieve a doubling of revenue, nor to double the work of each employee. The significant increase in market focus should allow the doubling of revenue to take place with minimum increases in numbers of employees and extra workload for current employees.

4. Quadrant D: The initial draft statement limits the strategic intent to five years. In reality, the strategic intent is to grow the business indefinitely, and the doubling in five years is just the first of a series of milestones stipulated in the long-range plan. The statement needs to add how this strategy is part of a 25-year vision.

The benefit of the walk-around process is that it forces a quadrant-by-quadrant review of the intended communication. It is clear from the walk-around in figure 10-4 that the draft statement will have to be modified in order to convey what the president intends. For example, he may want to revise the statement as follows: "The strategic intent of the first five years of our long-range plan is to double the revenues of our business by reorganizing into three strategic business units, which will provide the level of market focus that will allow us to achieve this goal with a minimum of staff increases." To make sure his message is understood by all, he could have slides or overheads graphically depicting the growth plan, and a handout that documents his statement and stipulates when and what kinds of organizational changes are needed. Addressing the C quadrant, he may offer to an-

" 'Out of sight, out of mind,' when translated into Russian (by computer), then back again into English, became 'invisible maniac.' "

—

Arthur Calder-Marshall

A UPPER LEFT	UPPER RIGHT D
◇ Uses facts to illustrate points ◇ Very matter-of-fact ◇ Expresses emotions abstractly ◇ Appears to display little or no emotion regardless of the situation	◇ Asks questions that lead to other questions: *Why? How?* ◇ Speaks in phrases ◇ Stops in mid-sentence thinking others obviously know

How the Brain Communicates

◇ Asks questions that have answers: *Who? What? When? Where?* ◇ Speaks in sentences and paragraphs ◇ Completes sentences and paragraphs	◇ Face is animated - eyes flash, etc. ◇ Uses expansive nonverbal gestures ◇ Uses stories to illustrate points ◇ Talks out loud or to self to learn
B LOWER LEFT	LOWER RIGHT C

Figure 10-5.
Differing expectations of listeners according to mental preferences representing the four quadrants.

swer any questions or concerns or to meet on an individual basis if the changes directly affect an individual.

An additional tool to help improve the communication process is this four-quadrant model of how communication takes place. There are communications options for each quadrant that are characteristic of the type of thinking that is employed by individuals holding those preferences. Increased awareness of these differences aids the communication process by enabling people to say more precisely what they mean and to listen more purposefully to what they hear. Improving communications does more than just relieve personal frustration. When the whole organization improves, bottom-line results must also improve.

I doubt that anyone would argue about the importance of effective communication. In all aspects of business and personal life, near or at the top of everybody's list of contributors to success is communication among members of a team. We can also include here the family, since in many ways the most successful families function like a team.

Whole brain teams, which are comprised of individuals representing all four quadrants and all four modes, present a particularly difficult communication challenge. Taking into account the models in this chapter, contemplate the communication struggles of an eight-member team whose members are all unique in their preferences, and whose preferences,

"No one would talk much in society, if he knew how often he misunderstands others."

—

Johann Wolfgang von Goethe

taken together, represent a balanced distribution of all the quadrant characteristics. There is a strong possibility that each team member is communicating more effectively in his or her area of preference, less effectively in his or her area of less preference, and perhaps not at all in his or her area of avoidance. This means that in the ideal whole brain team situation there are communication patterns of highly variable effectiveness on any given discussion point. Team members who understand this reality will ask questions if they don't understand or will offer paraphrasing or embellishment of their principle points as they are offered. Phrases such as, "By that I mean . . ." or "For instance . . ." or "This illustration will explain what I mean . . ." or "This page of the handout explains what I mean . . ." or "I offer this metaphor in explanation . . ."

"When the eyes say one thing, and the tongue another, a practised man relies on the language of the first."

—

Ralph Waldo Emerson

Of course, it takes a savvy team to engage in this kind of interaction, but the reality of team communication needs due to differences in perception requires that this understanding take place. When whole brain team members learn how to express themselves in ways that are true to their thinking style but sensitive to other members' styles, the chances are good that the team will be highly effective.

So What?

■ Effective communication is fundamental to successful human interaction and very susceptible to failure in family, social, and business situations.

■ Communication processes are typically filtered through an individual's screen of mental preference, and therefore causes occasional "blindness and deafness."

■ The challenge for business managers is to maximize the *intended* communication to a corporate whole brain organization.

■ Whole brain teams are greatly advantaged by whole brain communications.

■ Useful take-away tools will help managers and whole brain teams diagnose and, through better understanding, be able to greatly improve their communication processes.

Teams: Maximizing Results Through Mental Diversity

"No one can whistle a symphony. It takes an orchestra to play it."

—

H. E. Luccock

Chapter Headlines

♦ Organizations of more than 100 members are likely to be a balanced composite of all four quadrants and therefore are an ideal pool from which to select homogeneous and heterogeneous teams.

♦ Homogeneous teams can quickly achieve a consensus of opinion and will typically respond in ways predictably consistent with their quadrant preference.

♦ Heterogeneous teams behave in entirely different ways. They experience difficulty in reaching consensus, but because of their diversity can be synergistic and therefore ideal for creative/innovative assignments.

♦ High-performing teams share common characteristics of key functions, such as: visualization, intensity, focus, and imagination.

E ach individual in an organization has a distribution of mental preferences that can be displayed in the form of an *HBDI* profile. As reported earlier, an organization with more than 100 members is likely to have a well-balanced distribution of individual profiles in all four quadrants and all four modes. The composite average of all individuals approximates a balanced whole brain. Because of the relatively equal distribution of this employee pool in the four quadrants and four modes of the Whole Brain Model, it is easy to form teams

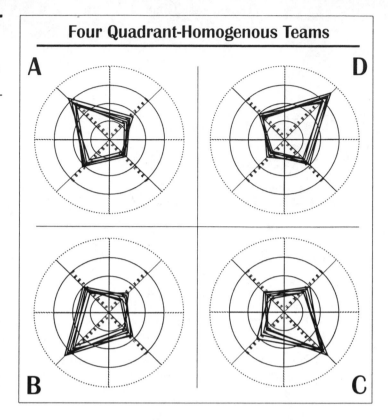

Four Quadrant-Homogenous Teams

of five or six individuals who have approximately the same profile—that is, their coalition of mental preferences will be quite homogeneous (figure 11-1).

The consequences of forming teams this way have been demonstrated many times in public sessions attended by about 100 business managers. For example, let's create four teams, each with a strong lead characteristic in each of the four quadrants—that is, a five-member A-quadrant team, in which each member has a strong primary in the A quadrant. Using the same model, imagine a five-person B-quadrant team, a five-person C-quadrant team, and a five-person D-quadrant team. In each case, the strongest preference in each of the teams will be in a particular quadrant.

If I then simultaneously ask the members of all four teams to describe the work that turns them on, there will be highly consistent responses from each five-member team. But these responses will be extremely different from one team to the next.

For example:
- The A-quadrant-oriented team will quickly reach a consensus around work activities that are logical, analytical, quantitative, and rational.

- The B-quadrant team, on the other hand, will quickly coalesce around organized, structured, detailed, and administrative-type work.

- For the C-quadrant team, working with people will be an absolute must. They will cite a need for their work to give them an opportunity to develop interpersonal relationships, to express their feelings, and to work in tandem with other people.

- In contrast, the D-quadrant group will describe themselves as creative, conceptual, and experimental risk takers.

If this same task were given to the same four teams, but instead of having them respond in one large room you sent them to four separate conference rooms and gave them 15 minutes to reach a consensus and return, the results would be quite different. The first groups back would predictably be the A and B teams. The C team would typically return a few minutes late. But the D team would, in 90 percent of the cases, have to be sent for, because D-quadrant-oriented people would have the most difficulty complying with the time rules of the exercise.

A general characteristic of homogeneous teams is the ability to reach a consensus quickly. People who think alike tend to come to agreement quite rapidly. Since they are on the same wavelength, they have similar interests. Words mean about the same thing to them, and their approach to a given situation is likely to be quite similar.

What would happen if you reconfigured the four teams into four new teams, with each representing a fairly equal distribution of preferences across the four quadrants? Each team would be a little composite whole brain. Now, if you gave them the same assignment, "What Work Turns You On?" it would be extremely difficult for each team to reach a consensus. And if they were assigned to four different rooms and given 15 minutes to reach agreement, none of the teams would be back on time. A characteristic of heterogeneous teams is the difficulty of reaching consensus. The opposite is true of homogeneous teams.

"Where all think alike, no one thinks very much."

—

Walter Lippmann

Figure 11-2.
Examples of
reorganizing
population of
homogenous teams
into whole brain
heterogeneous
teams.

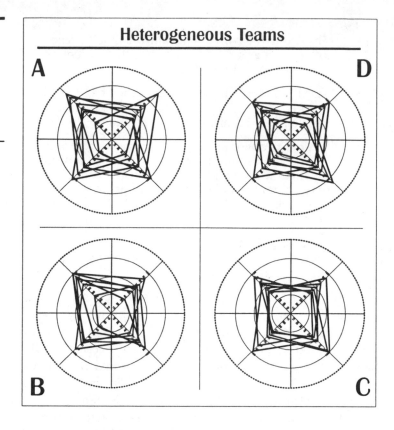

Heterogeneous Teams

A   D

B   C

Another example of the differences in team behavior and
outcomes occurs in problem-solving situations. In our first
example, we form four homogeneous teams, give them the
same identical problem situation, assign them to separate team
rooms, and give them four hours to come up with a solution.
Typically, all four teams of this type will report back in approximately half the time allocated with a range of reasonably adequate solutions. The A and D teams will come back
first and have the best solutions. The B team will be in third
place, and the C team will return last. If the exercise is repeated with the heterogeneous teams, all the teams will likely
take the full amount of time and several will ask for more
time. Instead of a single solution, all the teams will have
several alternative solutions. In most cases, these alternative
solutions will be superior to the consensus solutions reached
by the homogeneous team. Words like "creative" and "innovative" would describe the heterogeneous solutions. Words
like "obvious" or "adequate" would characterize the homogenous team solutions.

These conclusions are not based on one or two samples, but on literally hundreds of workshop and consulting experiences. The outcomes are quite predictable.

There are some key issues that need to be understood and resolved before the benefits of these different teams' concepts can be realized. The *power* of the homogeneous approach to team formation lies in rapid consensus building. This can be an advantage when time is of the essence. This approach can also produce less than optimum results, since the rapidly formed consensus excludes alternative approaches. Another likely outcome of homogeneous groups is that they tend to rapidly establish group norms and an overall group culture. In the nonbusiness world, gangs and tribes exhibit some of these same characteristics.

The heterogeneous teams face an entirely different group issue-dealing with differences among the members. In the ideal heterogeneous group the differences are significant. One person may have extremely strong preferences for logical, analytic, quantitative processes and a distaste for anything dealing with feelings and emotions, while another team member may have the exact opposite set of preferences. Another pair might be made up of a highly experimental, risk-oriented, adventurous spirit who abhors the status quo, and another member who is highly traditional and security-minded. These differences can be synergistic and positive or they can be hostile and disruptive. For these reasons, to optimize team performance, it is essential that the heterogenous team build a climate not only tolerant of differences but actually celebrating differences.

Diversity in thinking can be the basis of creative thinking. As described in other chapters, this can actually occur within a single individual whose mental preferences allow for the interplay of different mental processes. In the team situation there often has to be an investment in team building in advance of real on-line application. In all cases, the human assets are too precious to waste by putting people together on a haphazard basis without understanding the consequences. Let me emphasize that, by and large, the consequences of team formation in both the homogeneous and heterogeneous approaches are, to a large extent, predictable.

In the case of heterogeneous team formation, some theorists might say, "Oh, all this is is applying constructive dissonance." My answer is "Absolutely not!" In constructive dis-

> *"I use not only all the brains I have, but all I can borrow."*
>
> —
>
> *Woodrow Wilson*

sonance the objective would be to sustain the dissonance with the hope that something positive would, from time to time, result. The dissonances are constant. The heterogeneous diversity I'm talking about is based on synergy, which resolves the diversity with a creative outcome. When this occurs, it doesn't take long for diverse individuals to begin to respect and honor the differences that brought about the synergy. In my experience, this is a much more positive way to take advantage of the reality of differences in the workplace.

Experience has shown that once individuals experience the stimulation, excitement, and creative outcomes of heterogeneous team membership they can participate in a heterogeneous team made up of different members without going through an elaborate learning curve. In other words, heterogeneous team skills once acquired are transferable to other heterogeneous group situations. Given the 100-member organization described earlier, they could, through a series of team engagements, become a highly flexible candidate pool for almost limitless combinations of heterogeneous teams. Such an organization would be well on its way toward being a critical mass with great creative potential and ready to unleash that potential at any given time.

> *"None of us is as smart as all of us."*
>
> —
>
> *Ken Blanchard*

High-Performance Teams

The ability to profile employees' mental preferences provides an opportunity to assemble teams that can perform at quantum levels higher than the norm. Not only can the profile data provide the basis for building a heterogeneous team that has a greater potential for creativity and innovation, but profile data can also reveal the presence of a critical, mental skill—that is, a particular mental preference of the team members that allows the team to have a common capability and still be heterogeneous. For example, Frank Peschanel, an associate in Germany, reports that in the case of software engineers, one of the specialized mental capabilities that all high-performing teams have in common is the ability to mentally visualize the objective of their software design. Being able to have a unified view of the design objective enormously facilitates the team's creative interaction around the proposed design. Imagine for a moment the difference between a diverse team having a common design objective and one that doesn't

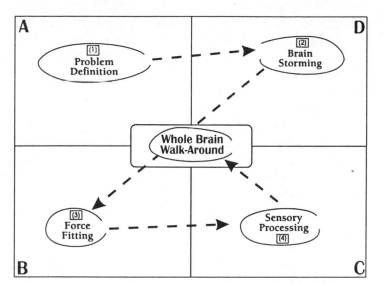

Figure 11-3.
The different stages of process storming.

have this common point of view. In the first case, you have the analogy of a jigsaw puzzle with five or six people pooling their resources and finding and inserting the right pieces. In the second case, you have the five or six people working on separate puzzles that have nothing in common other than that they are jigsaw puzzles.

This common characteristic of visual capability can be identified by applying the *HBDI* and a supplemental questionnaire relevant to the team task. This combined input will greatly facilitate the building of a team whose high-performing potential has a greater chance of being achieved.

Another characteristic of high-performance teams is the ability to bring more than one creative process to bear on a particular problem situation. The process is similar to brainstorming except that in this case we are not using a single process to develop ideas, but are applying multiple processes in a manner that could be called "process storming." The number and quality of ideas generated by this creative strategy is significantly greater than that which would occur when employing a single process. Good teams that apply process-storming techniques can become high-performing teams.

Another characteristic of high-performance teams is intensity and focus. The level of interest of the team members and the task at hand is usually very high, so there is also a high level of inner motivation to apply to the team task. This strong motivation contributes to *focus* on the team task and

"Problems can become opportunities when the right people come together."

—

Robert Redford

commitment to achieve its goal. It is frequently the case that the strength of an individual's preference is predictive of the intensity of his or her team interaction. *HBDI* profiles that are particularly "spiky" provide advanced evidence of the likelihood of this intense team interaction occurring. This level of intensity requires experienced team leadership to deal with the potential interpersonal dynamics.

High-performance teams made up of diverse members who have the common characteristic of *imagination* are also likely to be very creatively productive. Teams with diverse preferences but with the common quality of imagination are usually capable of higher forms of synergy than teams without these characteristics. Imagination helps them make effective use of diverse capabilities such as logic, analysis, and intuition, as well as organizational and interpersonal skills.

A key ingredient in team performance is the climate in which the team functions. The extent to which this climate is supportive, nonbureaucratic, flexible in meeting team needs, and rewarding of team performance, is the degree to which the team can take advantage of its own inner resources to achieve its goals without counterproductive interference from outside the team. Taken together, these ingredients contribute to high team performance. When there is a creative champion in the team or a management champion supportive of its work, the likelihood of team success is further optimized.

> *"Progress is 95 percent routine teamwork. The other 5 percent relies on restless, inner-directed people who are willing to upset our applecart with new and better ideas."*
>
> —
>
> *Michael LeBoeuf*

So What?

■ Organizations can become a dynamic pool of diverse, synergistic team members.

■ Such critical mental skills as visualization and imagination, when they are common characteristics of all team members, can elevate team performance.

■ "Spiky" profiles give advance evidence of team intensity.

■ A supportive, noninterfering team climate is essential to sustained high performance.

■ The presence of creative champions on the team helps guarantee high performance, and the presence of management champions supportive of the team's work can raise performance to optimum levels.

Productivity and Job Design

Chapter Headlines

♦ High productivity is based on the combination of individuals being turned on by particular work and then being aligned with that work in their jobs.

♦ Understanding the mental preferences of individuals and the mental requirements of the work they do represents a new management skill and priority.

♦ Individuals and their work can be brought into better alignment by modifying the work or reassigning the individual.

♦ Application of Whole Brain Technology to improve the alignment of individuals with their work results in significant increases in productivity.

"In business, respect for the individual means acknowledging that every individual wants to do good work and to contribute to the success of the organization."

—

Keshavan Nair

If we can identify motivational work for an employee, and either assign that person to an existing job where that work is the basis of that job, *or* design a job that is in alignment with that worker's passion, we have made the individual/organizational coupling that is needed for high productivity.

My concept of individual and organizational productivity is based on the combination of people being turned on to a particular kind of work and then being aligned with that work in their job. One measure of alignment is the degree to which employees are turned on by their work. By *turned-on*, I mean work that is so interesting to them that if they had the opportunity to choose they would select it for its stimulation and pleasure, because the performance of it is rewarding in itself. Desire for this type of work is at the top of Maslow's hierarchy of needs. It's called self-actualization. The opportunity to perform turn-on work is a major ingredient of motivation, since motivation always comes from within a person. Allowing people access to their turn-on work pulls them into performing at their highest level of work performance. Can you imagine the kind of productivity that would result? Can you imagine the level of satisfaction and fulfillment that both the individuals and their managers would enjoy? This, to me, is the answer to the age-old quest for increased productivity. Contrast this approach with the following typical example.

"I think it is an immutable law in business that words are words, explanations are explanations, promises are promises—but only performance is reality."

—

Harold Geneen

The traditional business approach to raising productivity is to have people work harder, to have supervisors oversee employees at work. The factory supervisor occupies an office on a mezzanine level overlooking the factory floor from which he or she can observe the work effort without even getting up from the desk. The supervisor of clerical employees can scan the "bull-pen" office layout for anybody who is not fully attentive to work. Added to this method of management by monitoring, there is the mistaken notion that managers motivate employees (rather than people motivating themselves) and "push them" into work that is not turn-on work and often is actually turn-off work. These and all the other similar supervisory tactics are nothing more than substitutes for paying attention to the established preferences and competencies of employees and matching those to the mental requirements of the work.

Business has traditionally sought productivity improvements of 3, 4, or 5 percent, and leaders proudly proclaim in annual reports that they achieved that dramatic 3 percent increase in productivity. Productivity increases I am talking about are of the order of 20, 30, 40, and 50 percent. The work that has to be done to achieve these is managerial work, not production work. If management does its job in advance of the assignment of work, then the management skill required is how to keep out of the way of productive employees rather than how best to oversee at work employees whom they assume are nonproductive.

These concepts are so simple and straightforward it is amazing to me that managers don't recognize their application as a major solution to productivity and job satisfaction issues. Instead of working in these positive terms, all too

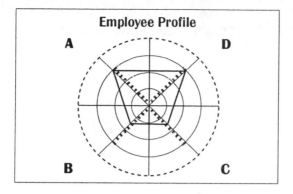

Figure 12-1.
Profile of an
employee.

often we tackle productivity issues by downsizing. It is only then that affected employees have an opportunity to try anew to align themselves with work that turns them on—but now outside the company they could have done it for.

Whole Brain Technology provides new tools for management to increase productivity. Achieving alignment between individuals and their work requires a methodology of diagnosing the mentality of each. Here, the *HBDI* is used to identify and measure the mental preferences of individuals, which is the first step in identifying the work that turns them on. The Turn-On Work Exercise, although not as detailed as the *HBDI*, can provide the direction of a person's turn-on work. Let's back up a minute and look at a typical employee's profile representing thinking-style preferences. Remember that this is a coalition of preferences across a spectrum of thinking options that represent the whole brain. These preferences, which are the result of that employee's Brain Dominance characteristics, lead inevitably to an array of interests in alignment with those preferences. It is quite likely that as that person pursued educational options he or she chose courses that would lead toward competencies in good alignment with their preferences and interests.

Now take a look at a range of job pro formas that the employee might be assigned to perform in figure 12-2. One of the advantages of Whole Brain Technology is the capability of diagnosing the mental requirements for work. Using the Whole Brain Model as a diagnostic tool provides management with a way of diagnosing the mentality of the work elements that constitute a job assignment. Jobs can be thought of as an aggregate of tasks composed of work elements. Each work element can be diagnosed in terms of the mentality required to perform it. This means that it is possible to pro-

"If you keep doing what you've always done, you'll keep getting what you've always got."

—

Peter Francisco

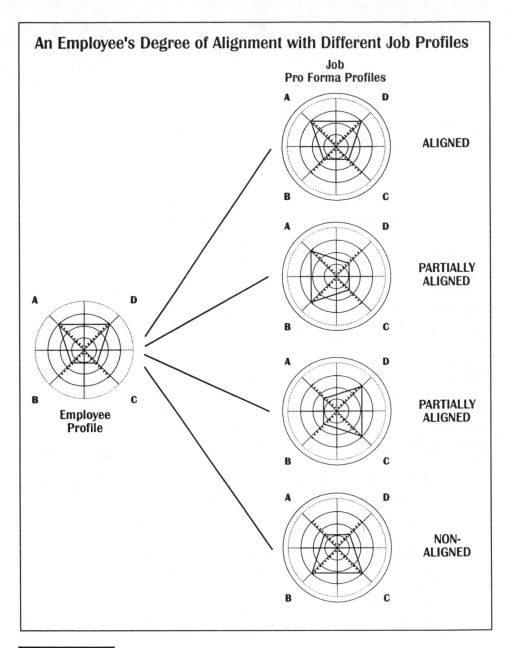

An Employee's Degree of Alignment with Different Job Profiles

Job
Pro Forma Profiles

ALIGNED

PARTIALLY
ALIGNED

PARTIALLY
ALIGNED

NON-
ALIGNED

Employee
Profile

Figure 12-2.
An employee's *HBDI* compared with pro formas of jobs ranging from aligned to nonaligned with employee's preferences.

file and even design the total job on the basis of the distribution of mental requirements needed to perform it at an optimum level. For example, analytic work elements, such as analyzing the information in a financial report, are A quadrant in their mentality. Detailed, administrative work elements, such as filling out and sending off applications and forms, are B quadrant in their mentality. Interpersonal-type work elements, such as contacting a customer, are C quadrant in their mentality. And work elements that require strategic thinking, such as brainstorming on a more effective way to beat the competition or innovating products, are D quadrant in their mentality. Once a pro forma profile of the job is complete, as demonstrated in Chapter 4, it can be compared to the mental preferences of the individual, and the degree of alignment can easily be determined. Here, then, are pro forma profiles of a range of jobs from fully aligned to totally non-aligned.

Assume for the moment that the *HBDI* profile is an accurate representation of the employee's preferred modes of thinking and that the pro forma profile of the jobs is an accurate representation of the mental requirements of those jobs. It is easy to come to the conclusion that when the employee's mental preferences are in alignment with the job's mental requirements, everybody wins. The better the alignment, the higher the productivity potential. When the managerial climate is supportive of the alignment initiative, higher productivity is more likely. Why isn't this high-probability solution to job design and employee placement immediately adopted by managers everywhere? There are some possible answers. It's too different from traditional solutions to be worth a try. Without a guaranteed outcome, it's too risky to try. Managers may not have the proper tools to assess the mentality of the work and those performing it to achieve proper alignment.

"Choose a job you love, and you will never have to work a day in your life."

—

Confucius

All too frequently, no effort is made to understand the job requirements on the basis of the needed mental preferences and thus the associated competencies required to perform it. From my perspective I find that jobs are typically not designed at all but rather represent pieces of needed work that are assembled into an approximate whole. The reason I use the word *approximate* is that the total job is typically never quantified in terms of what's required to perform it. Not only do we assemble jobs this way, often on the basis of administrative convenience, but we also fill jobs this way. It is rare, indeed, that we know the mental preferences of job candidates and even rarer that the related competencies coming from those preferences are taken into account. Therefore, it's lucky if we end up with any reasonable alignment between an individual's capability and the requirements to perform the job. In my experience of working with hundreds of companies I have seen a massive nonalignment between employees at all levels and the work they are assigned to do. By "massive," I mean that more than half of all employees are in an active state of nonalignment.

The Consequences of Misalignment and Occupational Mismatches

What are the consequences of this lack of alignment? In severe cases, the litany starts with poor productivity, poor quality, absenteeism, and work-related accidents. From the employee's point of view the consequences are low motivation, low satisfaction, low fulfillment, deteriorating health, and all too frequently, substance abuse to get through the day.

In between the best case and the worst case are hundreds of thousands of workers at all levels, from maintenance up to senior staff, who are nonaligned to a degree that affects not only their performance but also their job satisfaction and fulfillment.

Suppose you were in a job that required you to do work that was diametrically opposed to your mental preferences and acquired competencies. It's likely that you would feel strange, maybe like a "fish out of water." Now also suppose that this is your only job opportunity and that you have financial obligations that require you to stay employed. What do you do? Chances are that you will hang in there and try to survive.

Consider the likelihood that over half of the world's workforce is to a certain degree out of alignment with the work it is assigned to do. That is, the mental preferences of these workers and the competencies they have acquired are, to a degree, mismatched with the mental requirements of the work to which they have been assigned. This mismatch can be minor or it can be so severe that the work is either not done or is done in such an indifferent way that it's not the job that was intended by the employer. This is not to say that there are not instances when a person with a profile strikingly different from the norm can't perform the job. But when this happens, it is certain that the way it is done will be very different from the employer's intentions.

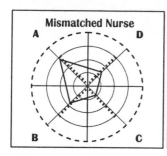
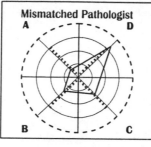
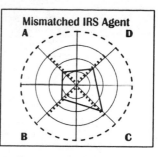

Take for example, a nurse with a strong A-quadrant-oriented profile of 1-2-3-2. This person actually has an avoidance in the C quadrant, which is the strongest quadrant for the nursing norm. The nurse's approach to her job would be more like a doctor. She would be technically smart and highly clinical in her approach to her patients. She would have little genuine "bedside manner" but her nursing technique would be close to perfection in a clinical sense. She might make an excellent operating room nurse under extreme medical circumstances. However, under normal conditions on the nursing floor, she would stand out as totally different from the rest of the staff. She would likely be considered very competent but unfeeling.

Consider next a pathologist with a profile 3-2-2-1+. In this example you have a person performing a highly specialized, extremely technical medical job who has an avoidance in the quadrant that is the preferred norm for pathologists around the world. On the other hand, this person has a strong primary in a quadrant that is known for experimentation and risk taking. This is not the behavior expected of a pathologist. Would you want your tissue diagnosed by such an individual? I would anticipate that most would ask for a second opinion.

Now consider an IRS agent with a profile that is strongly C-quadrant-oriented—a 2-2-1-2. In this case, you might have a person who would be able to deal with the financial details of an agent's job, but might do so with a very strong interpersonal approach to the assignment. Some people might even want to arrange a multiyear contract should they be audited by an agent with such a strong humanistic approach.

You get the point that there should be a strong alignment between the mental requirements of the intended work and the mental preferences of the person performing that work.

Figure 12-3.
Nurse mismatched with occupational norm; Pathologist mismatched with job profile; IRS agent mismatched with job profile norm.

"Job enrichment has been around for 60 years. It's been successful every time it has been tried, but industry is not interested."

—

Peter Drucker

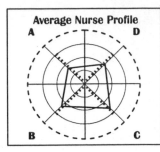

Average Nurse Profile

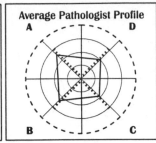

Average Pathologist Profile

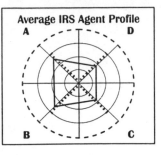

Average IRS Agent Profile

Figure 12-4.
Profile norms for nurse, pathologist, and IRS agent.

While there is bellcurve of acceptable deviation from the norm, as soon as you get into the extremes it is not likely that the assigned work is being performed as intended. It is hard to believe that otherwise smart managers are sometimes blind to the extent of the job assignment mismatch taking place in their business. As Henry Mintzberg has said, "Isn't it strange that smart people can be so dull?"

How to Turn Misalignment Around

My advice is to try assessing the work and those doing it in a small work group where job design issues and job assignment practices are sufficiently flexible to accommodate such a demonstration. In our office, we often pull in employees from different departments to get a good mix of mental preferences for a project. Sometimes a finite project will reveal preferences for work and competencies much more visibly, especially if the team leader is there to witness this in action. Use the job design worksheet to get started, and plan for transition periods for realignment. If you aren't in a managerial position, talk to your supervisor and team up with the human resource department to problem solve your misalignment issues.

"Every calling is great when greatly pursued."

—

Oliver Wendall Holmes, Jr.

One of the advantages of Whole Brain Technology is that it is teachable and, therefore, transferable. Many hundreds of individuals with an inclination toward human resource development or personnel management have demonstrated a uniformly high ability to grasp these concepts and apply them. This says that a relatively small number of people could be trained in this process and could bring about the needed changes in job redesign and employee assignment to those jobs so that there is an optimum alignment between the employee and the job, and between the job and the needs of the business. Perhaps you have been misaligned yourself and know the lack of motivation and pain that results, or you've been the manager and been frustrated by the inability of your organization to perform at its optimal level. If so, I hope this chapter has given you some options to pursue. As a manager, you have a great opportunity to enhance the productivity in your area of responsibility by aligning your staff's preferences with the required work whenever possible.

So What?

■ All too frequently, jobs are assembled without regard for the mental requirements to perform them, and incumbents are placed in those jobs without regard for their mental preferences and the need for alignment.

■ Nonalignment of employees with their work leads to poor performance, low productivity, and low job satisfaction.

■ Whole Brain Technology can provide answers and solutions to misalignment situations.

■ Specialists can be trained to implement this available technology in their areas of responsibility.

"Whether
you are a
depart-
ment head
or a super-
visor, the
principle
remains
the same:
Meet your
responsi-
bilities
before you
ask others
to meet
theirs."

—

Keshavan
Nair

Supervision, Delegation, and Followership

Chapter Headlines

♦ How the *HBDI* is used to check the mental compatibility of workers and the work and solve poor performance problems.

♦ The quality of the manager/subordinant relationship impacts on the effectiveness of their communication and therefore, the delegation process as well.

♦ Degree of alignment between manager and subordinant is a determining factor in the level of delegation success.

♦ What are the characteristics of a good follower and what are management's expectations of a good follower?

A Supervisory Case: Solving A Performance Problem

Mary Frankel is an Employee Benefits Supervisor in the HRD department of a Fortune 500 company. She has a dozen benefit clerks reporting directly to her and feels that eight of them are responding very well to her supervision. They appear to understand the work and she can trust them to perform their duties as assigned. Their performance reviews all range from satisfactory to excellent.

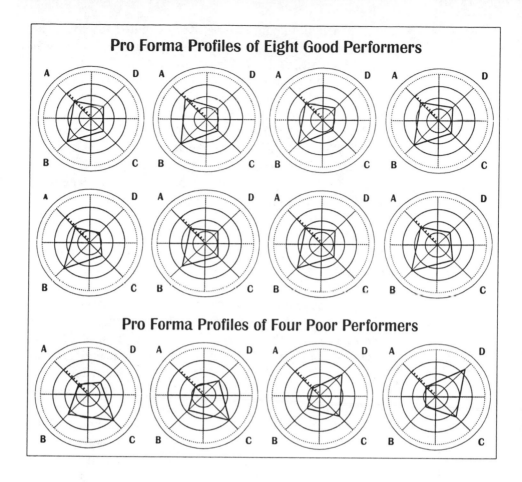

Pro Forma Profiles of Eight Good Performers

Pro Forma Profiles of Four Poor Performers

But, Mary has severe problems with her four other benefit clerks, and is frustrated because she cannot seem to get them to perform to the standards she has set. After a number of attempts to solve these performance problems, (which primarily concern accuracy, timeliness, and completeness of reports), she decides to administer the *HBDI* to the total group to see if the resulting profiles will give her a clue as to what the performance problems are. (Eight of the 12 profiles are very homogeneous and are strongly tilted toward the B quadrant, which is also her preference. This is the group that is performing well. Of the remaining four, two are strongly C quadrant, one is double-dominant C/D, and the fourth is strongly D quadrant.)

The job description of a Benefits Clerk is as follows: Administer the company's benefit program in strict accordance

Figure 13-1.
Profiles of 12 members of a benefits department; how profiles can help identify the cause of poor or good performance.

with Benefits Bulletin 101-A. Keep detailed records of all transactions with employees, including correspondence, verbal discussions, and benefits claims. All activity is to be entered into the computer database on a daily basis and must be available for verification at all times. Summary reports are due quarterly and annually. Performance will be evaluated on the basis of the company's Zero Defects Program.

Mary looks at the four profiles that are radically different from the homogeneous group of eight and says to herself, "Oh. Now I get it. I've got four people whose preferences are significantly different from those who are performing well and therefore they seem to be badly out of alignment with the job specs." This confirms her hunch that if these profiles are so different from the ones who are doing the job the way it should be performed, there must be a good commonsense explanation.

Mary does a quick review of the key descriptors and work elements data of the group of eight and the group of four and comes to the conclusion that none of the four employees exhibit the common preferences of the eight who are performing well. These include strong preferences for highly detailed, organized, procedural, administrative work activities. As a matter of fact, the profiles show that two of the four actually seem to avoid these kinds of work activities. Further review shows that three of the four have strong preferences for the interpersonal aspects of the job, and their personal files indicate complimentary feedback from employees on their personal visits to the Benefit Office. It is clear that these three clerks take a personal interest in the employees' transactions.

The fourth benefit clerk has a profile that is diametrically opposed to the eight who are doing their jobs well. This clerk seems more interested in bending the rules than in complying with them. She likes to invent solutions to employee problems. She often overlooks missing pieces of needed information and writes little notes indicating that through verbal discussion she is satisfied with the employee's submission on the various benefit forms. It becomes clearer and clearer to Mary that this person is really marching to a different drum and is not properly assigned in the component.

She decides to give each person with performance problems a chance to write a description of their job as they understand it and then to write a description of the job as they would like to perform it. She feels that this process will reveal the nature and extent of any job alignment problems.

A Benefits Clerk's Description of Her Existing Job Responsibilities

As a Benefits Clerk, I see my job as administering the company's Benefits Programs and explaining them to each employee with whom I come in contact. My job requires me to keep detailed records of all transactions with the people I work with, and to enter into the computer, on a daily basis, all transactions. I am supposed to send in summary reports each quarter and at the end of each year.

—Benefits Clerk, A. J. Anderson

The Same Benefits Clerk Describes How She Would Like to Perform Her Job

As a Benefits Clerk, I would like to perform my job quite differently from what is written in my job description. I understand the need for detail, but the reporting requirements limit my ability to deal with the actual problems that employees have. They always want to talk about their personal issues. They want to be heard. I don't feel that is my job responsibility, but I would like it to be since I notice that in those cases where I do listen, the problems seem to lessen or disappear. I don't like the detailed, "mechanical" aspects of my work as laid down in the job description. I really dislike paperwork. I would much rather listen and be helpful. I am good at that. That's what my employee cases seem to need and that's what I'd like to provide.

—Benefits Clerk, A. J. Anderson

The Source of Motivation

Motivation of employees is a key issue at all levels of supervision, management, and leadership. As I travel around and work with and talk to people in charge of other people, I continue to find them making a fundamental mistake. They continue to believe and behave as if they are responsible for an employee's motivation. Countless books, articles, and seminars have attempted to convince generations of leaders that the motivation of workers does not come from the manager. In all cases, it comes from within the employee. Why is this so hard to grasp? A possible answer is that we have established a cadre of leaders who think that visible action on their part is the primary way to lead; that you must *do* something or you will not be viewed as a leader by those who are led.

"If he works for you, you work for him."

—

Japanese Proverb

The facts of the matter are that we all motivate ourselves. This inner self-motivation can be encouraged in a number of ways by supervisors, managers, and executives:

1. Provide employees with *"work that turns them on."*

2. Provide a work *climate* that allows this turn-on work to be performed in ways that satisfy and fulfill the worker.

3. Provide incentives and rewards that supplement the self-actualization that the worker is already experiencing.

4. Provide the necessary tools, materials, and support that allow the worker to optimize quality performance.

5. Stay the hell out of the way!

This surprisingly direct and simple process is founded on two human resource basics:

1. Know the employees. Understand their preferences, their expectations, and their job needs.

2. Understand the mental requirements of the work. This requires an investment in time, energy, and skill to diagnose the work elements of the tasks to be performed, and then constructing a pro forma profile of the job.

The next step in this process is exceedingly elementary in concept, but impossible to carry out if the preceding steps have not been rigorously performed. This next step is bringing the worker into alignment with the work.

Happy workers perform at higher levels and often higher than the quality and production standards. It would be a serious mistake to write this off as "touchy, feely" stuff. For me, this is plain common sense. Supervising, managing, and leading in the ways that I have suggested will, I believe, unleash the latent productivity of workers to the organization and to its objectives and goals.

Delegation

I do not believe that the effectiveness of the delegation process is dependent on the manager having the authority to fire a nonresponsive subordinate. I believe that any manager worthy of the name, should be able to delegate successfully on the basis of the shared understanding of the task and its priorities and of the shared goals of the organization. Consider for a moment a team leader who has no organizational power other than his team leader role, but has the need for members of the team to accept his delegation of work tasks. Here we are not dealing with the tools of authoritarian management, but rather with the sophistication of getting work done when you are not the manager. Geoff Bellman's book, *Getting Things Done When You Are Not in Charge* (Berrett-Koehler 1992), is an outstanding source of wisdom in this domain. I have tried to provide in this book as many examples as I can to illustrate the consequences of aligned, misaligned, and nonaligned business relationships. Even under the best of circumstances in which two individuals are clearly on the same mental wavelength, there is a need for testing understanding and clarifying any discovered misunderstanding because there is always the possibility of a competitive outcome from two people who are strongly aligned in the same quadrant. The conclusion must be, therefore, that even under the best of circumstances the person in charge—whether a manager or a team leader—is at risk if he or she assumes that the person to whom they are delegating really understands the nature of that delegation in terms of:

1. The specifics of the task to be performed.
2. The priority determined by the person in charge.
3. The precise due date when action is required.

The many references in this book to the consequences of mental preference all lead to the high probability that alignment between a manager and an employee will result in effective communication around the delegated task to be performed, and that various degrees of misalignment or nonalignment represent a low probability that effective communication will take place. It stands to reason that if the employee does not completely understand the delegated task, does not accurately assess the priority, does not capture the delivery date, and does not comprehend the consequences of failure, there is a high probability of disaster.

A
- Are the facts understood?
- Have money matters been resolved?
- Have technical needs been met?
- Is the proposed delegation logical? Rational?

D
- Are future consequences known?
- Is the big picture understood?
- What subtleties are involved?
- What does your intuition tell you?
- Are there creative opportunities?

WHOLE BRAIN DELEGATION WALK-AROUND

- Are there sequential steps that are critical?
- Have dates and timing issues been considered?
- What are the risks?
- Will the organization be affected?

B

- Have all those affected been involved?
- Have all relationship issues been taken into account?
- Are there team impiications?
- Are values in alignment?
- Are there training needs?

C

Complicating the delegating process are the typical dynamics of a boss-subordinant relationship. The manager feels that the work to be done is simple and straightforward and the employee doesn't want to appear stupid, so the delegation communication from the manager is often inadequate and the feedback from the employee is frequently misleading. The inadequacy of the communication is compounded by the likelihood that both verbal and nonverbal aspects of the manager's communication are, to some extent, misunderstood or misinterpreted by reason of their mental differences.

Here is another quiz: On a scale of 1 to 10, with 10 being the most successful, diagnose each of the following manager/subordinant delegation outcomes.

Here is a tool that can substantially increase the probability of successful delegation by offering a method of testing for understanding and clarifying misunderstanding. This tool is called a Whole Brain Delegation Walk-Around. It can be easily adapted to application by either the manager *or* the subordinant since the objective is mutual understanding.

Delegation is often taught "by the numbers" and is often encouraged as a characteristic of good management. That is, you do it in a certain series of known steps and you get it off your personal agenda because, after all, managers are supposed to get work done through others and not do it themselves. I believe that Whole Brain Technology brings a different level of sophistication and comprehension to the delegating process:

1. Through its diagnostic tools it offers an early warning system.

2. Through its communication tools it offers techniques to improve the written and verbal aspects of the process.

3. Through the Whole Brain Delegation Walk-Around tool it provides an effective method of testing for understanding and a road map for achieving the needed understanding for effective delegation to take place.

Followership

What is a good follower and how do you become one? Do you blindly follow leadership from above? I think that military followership demands obedience to commands: "Take hill 207. The enemy forces are in the woods directly ahead. I want your squad to annihilate them." Is blind adherence to command what we mean by "followership"? In a business example, suppose a business is doing $100,000 annually with customer A. The CEO says, "I want that increased to $200,000 by the end of the year." Contrast that with "Your compensation will be based upon the level of performance with regard to customer A. The bonus on top of your annual salary will be adjusted on the basis of any increase above current levels, including a doubling of our billings to customer A," or "Your continuity of service is dependent on increasing the billings from customer A. If you can't do it we will find someone else to fill your position."

What do we expect our followers to do? Take the initiative, toe the line, follow orders, interpret our leadership situationally? Almost every one of us is a follower to a certain degree. As a follower yourself, how would you define your role? When, as a follower, I was asked that question

"Hold yourself responsible for a higher standard than anybody else expects of you."

—

Henry Ward Beecher

many years ago, I surprised myself somewhat by answering this way: "One of my key objectives in this position is to generate enough cashflow to earn my salary as early in the year as I can. If I can pay for myself by June, that means that everything after June represents added value to the organization. If I can pay for myself by April, that's even better, and if I can pay for myself as early as March, I will beat my stretch goal for the yearly performance of my entire component." Over the years I have found this personal goal to be much more motivational to me than achieving the budgeted performance negotiated with my boss. I was going to do *that* anyway, but by paying for myself or my whole operation as soon in the year as possible, I rewarded myself for my performance. It was actually a higher standard than that expected by my leader, so as a follower I set my own standards of performance at a higher level than my boss' expectations. I think many, many employees set higher standards for themselves than their leaders set for them. I feel such an approach is one way to achieve outstanding followership.

Another approach in achieving followership excellence is to work with your manager to make as much as possible of your job to be turn-on work for you. Once you know the work that really turns you on, you need to take the initiative to identify those work elements that are available in your occupation that can be made a part of your job assignment. The greater the percentage of turn-on work in your job, the more interest and passion you will have for doing the work, and therefore the better your performance will be.

If *you* are the manager, establish a climate in your component that will encourage the followers in your organization to take the initiative to identify *their* turn-on work. Like the first approach, I believe this turn-on work approach is also a win, win, win solution to achieving high-level followership. It is a win for you, it is a win for your manager, and it is a win for your organization.

In summary, followers need good leaders and good leaders need good followers. The organization in which they work needs a climate that encourages both leaders and followers to flourish. There is not much in the domain of management that can be better than this combination.

"There is no traffic jam on the extra mile."

—

Anonymous

So What?

- The *HBDI* is a valuable tool for diagnosing employee performance situations.

- Motivation comes from within and it is essential to match employees with work that turns them on.

- Alignment of the employee within their work is a key to effective supervision, good performance, and employee satisfaction.

- Whole Brain Technology offers useful diagnostic tools to managers and team leaders to help them improve their delegation effectiveness such as the Communication Walk-Around on page 119 and the Delegation Walk-Around on page 146.

- Outstanding followership is a key requirement for effective management and high individual performance.

- An effective approach is to provide a climate that encourages followers and their managers to maximize the percentage of turn-on work in their job assignment.

14

Whole Brain Training and Development

"The only safe assumption is that every learning group represents a corporate whole brain."

—

Ned Herrmann

Chapter Headlines

♦ Groups of almost any size represent balanced learning styles.

♦ Learning preferences and learning avoidances are both of key importance.

♦ Whole brain design and delivery of key learning points is a major solution to training effectiveness.

♦ A breakthrough concept is understanding how to be "situationally whole."

As frequently referenced in this book, a major finding emerging from my work is that the world is a composite whole brain, and more precisely, that the business world is a composite whole brain. Organizations of 100, 500, 1,000, and 10,000 employees represent an extraordinarily well-balanced distribution of individual preferences that, taken together, constitutes a balanced whole brain.

The same can be said for a university, a public school system, a high school, or a group of gifted and talented children. This also includes business conventions and seminars. When a large enough group of learners is considered as a whole, it inevitably comprises a composite whole brain. This means that administrators, curriculum development specialists, and teachers must change their assumptions about who is in the classroom or the auditorium. Chances are that every classroom represents a complete spectrum of learning-style preferences. Principals, superintendents, deans, or college presidents armed with this information need to radically change the curriculum development and teaching processes in their institutions if they don't currently deliver the learning product with equal effectiveness across the full learning spectrum.

Absolutely the same is true in business and industry. The people who run the training and development operations in a business are faced with the same identical effectiveness situation, with the significant exception that this is now a *business cost*. Training budgets range from thousands to millions, to as much as billions, of dollars annually. Much of this may be wasted because people are sent to courses that are out of alignment with their learning style, out of alignment with their job needs, and out of alignment with their career path. They typically have been sent to a training course to acquire a specific competence, but often without regard for the degree of match between the learner and the training course. The greater the misalignment, the less the competency will be acquired. My experience tells me that at least half of all people attending in-house training programs are seriously out of alignment in one or more of these specific measures. A rough guess would be that one-third to one-half of the money spent in this way is largely wasted and, depending on the size of the organization, that could amount to thousands, millions, or even billions of dollars.

The first application of my evolving theory of brain dominance was in the domain of management education. This was back in the late 1970s. The more I learned about the role of the brain in the learning process the more curious and skeptical I became about the effectiveness of the programs I was involved with. To satisfy my curiosity I began to evaluate the programs that I was responsible for on the basis of what was actually learned and whether what was learned was what was intended to be learned. The study revealed that what was actually learned covered a wide spectrum within a course-participant group of only 20 people. The study further revealed that less than half of that learning was the intended learning of the training program. This information was so shocking I decided I could not report it to upper management without offering specific ways to correct the situation.

Further inquiry into the learning styles of participants revealed a wide range of preferences, with several significant subgroups showing similar learning-style preferences. Next, I diagnosed the faculty and discovered that they, too, had strong personal learning-style preferences. My curiosity then led me to examine the design of the various courses that were being taught. I discovered that these were rather narrow in the design methods used, and also seemed to match the learning preferences of the course leaders. No wonder we were having problems. The course design and the course leaders seemed to be in good alignment, but this was in turn in good alignment with only a part of the class, perhaps as few as half. This meant that as many as half of the participants were so out of alignment with the course material and the course leadership that they were missing much of what was intended to be taken back to their jobs.

> "Education, learning, and changing are so closely related to problem solving that they may all be names for the same thing."
>
> —
>
> George Prince

As I have said: The business world, taken as a whole, represents a composite array of learning styles equally distributed across the Whole Brain Model. In other words, there is a balanced distribution of learning preferences, with each quadrant and each mode equally represented. But that's not all. There is also an equal distribution of learning avoidances distributed across the four quadrants. And learning avoidances are even more significant than learning preferences because they turn people off. A turned-off learner is a waste of educational time and effort as well as corporate time and money.

What to do? Most training programs have a discrete number of key learning points. These represent the essence of the program. These are learning points that the course leader would die for. These key learning points represent the essence of the intended take-away learning—that is, what the sponsor hopes is actually taken away and independently applied to their work by the participants. In a one-day session, there might be six to eight key learning points. In a two-day workshop, there might be 12 to 16, and so forth, with a max, perhaps, of 24. And that's a stretch for even the brightest participant to understand and take away. What if these key learning points, the six or eight you would die for, are designed and delivered in ways that reach each participant's

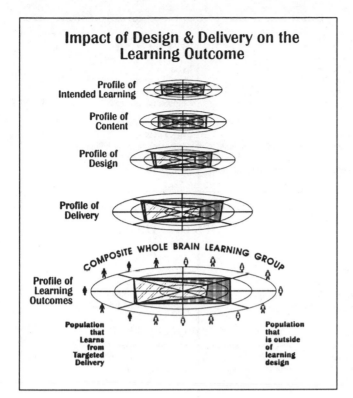

Impact of Design & Delivery on the Learning Outcome

Profile of Intended Learning

Profile of Content

Profile of Design

Profile of Delivery

COMPOSITE WHOLE BRAIN LEARNING GROUP

Profile of Learning Outcomes

Population that Learns from Targeted Delivery

Population that is outside of learning design

Figure 14-1.
A whole brain group receiving intended learning due to a whole brain design compared with a delivery that addresses only left-mode styles.

learning preference and evade each learning avoidance? This strategy would yield entirely different results. The key intended learnings, the design and delivery focus of the training program, the peripheral "nice to know" topics, would have a lesser priority or be eliminated entirely. Each key learning point would be delivered in three or four different ways, representing the different learning styles. These might include an item of prework, a handout, an experiential exercise, a short video, a team activity, a metaphoric approach, a lecturette, and a case study. These are all standard techniques, but instead of applying them purely for diversity of method purposes, they would now be applied with strategic precision to each key learning point. This would mean that an engineer who strongly prefers rational theories, databased cases, and written reference material covering each learning point, would get those inputs but would also be exposed to a metaphoric film and a stimulating team exercise—all focused on the same intended learning point. Each of these different methods would be optimized in terms of its design and delivery so that even those approaches that are potential turn-

Figure 14-2.
The Learning-Style
Model summarizes
learning styles by
quadrant and
suggests forms of
delivery for
successful learning
communication.

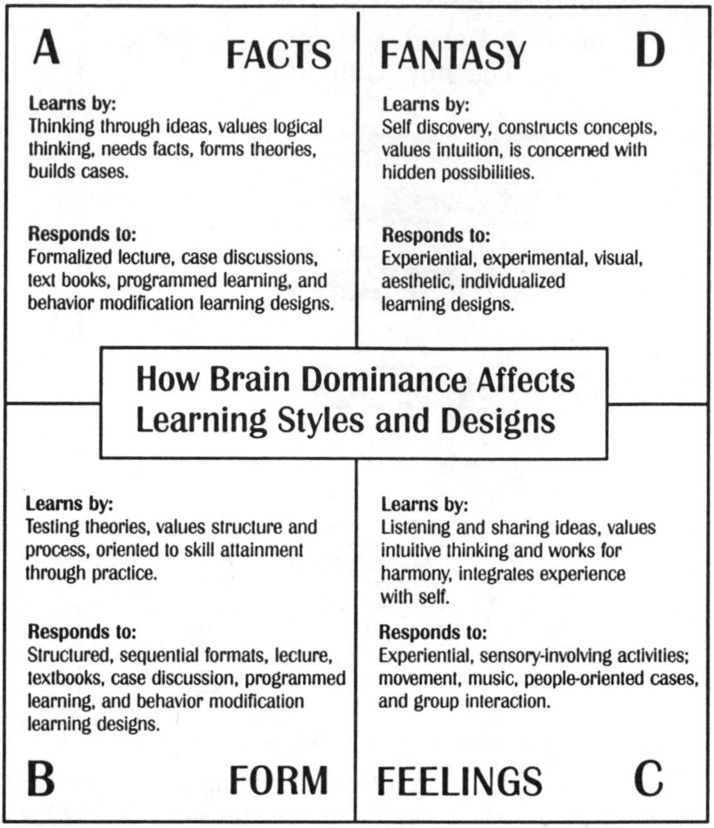

A FACTS	FANTASY D
Learns by: Thinking through ideas, values logical thinking, needs facts, forms theories, builds cases.	**Learns by:** Self discovery, constructs concepts, values intuition, is concerned with hidden possibilities.
Responds to: Formalized lecture, case discussions, text books, programmed learning, and behavior modification learning designs.	**Responds to:** Experiential, experimental, visual, aesthetic, individualized learning designs.

How Brain Dominance Affects Learning Styles and Designs

Learns by: Testing theories, values structure and process, oriented to skill attainment through practice.	**Learns by:** Listening and sharing ideas, values intuitive thinking and works for harmony, integrates experience with self.
Responds to: Structured, sequential formats, lecture, textbooks, case discussion, programmed learning, and behavior modification learning designs.	**Responds to:** Experiential, sensory-involving activities; movement, music, people-oriented cases, and group interaction.
B FORM	FEELINGS C

offs are so well done that this likelihood is minimized.

The process I've just described is called Whole Brain Teaching and Learning and has been demonstrated over the years since 1979 to be an extremely viable approach to dramatically increasing the effectiveness of training and development programs. Sounds like common sense, doesn't it? So why isn't that the way that all training and development departments operate? Well, overcoming resistance to change is hard enough, but in the domain of education, resistance represents the proverbial brick wall. This is painfully true in the public sector, and as private citizens we shake our heads and poke fun at it. But it is also true in the business sector, but our feelings are less intense because we feel that we are in charge. But it's not the bottom-line operating people that are in charge. In training and development we are dealing with a domain that is extremely difficult to measure. We can add up the dollars, but we are less able to add up the effectiveness of that investment.

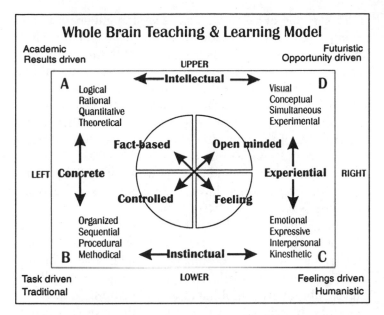

Figure 14-3.
The Whole Brain
Teaching and
Learning Model
points out styles for
each quadrant and
left, right, upper, and
lower modes as well.

What I am describing in terms of different learning styles and different levels of comprehension and different levels of bottom-line learning is not merely theoretical. The viability of this technology has been demonstrated in over 300 workshops attended by more than 5,000 business people. The more typical business situation that I have described is a reality because most of us have experienced it ourselves. What most organizations need is a command level *champion* who has the interest, understanding, passion, and authority to install a Whole Brain Teaching and Learning process in that company.

CEO and Top Management Training

A high percentage of managers who attend advanced management development programs say, upon graduation, "My boss should have taken this course. This stuff is good, but I really can't implement all I've learned until the boss buys in by having attended himself." The consequence of this reality is that there is an immediate and substantial discount on the take-away learnings of most managers who have a boss who excludes himself or herself from advanced management training.

This is kind of a Catch 22 and I've thought about it, and experienced it, over the course of 40 or 50 years. I don't know how you spring CEOs from their 60-hour-a-week jobs, even for two or three days. And I think it takes at least that long to bring about any enlightenment, much less change. I still don't know how to equip managers with the confidence and courage to apply what they have learned to their work, independent of their bosses. That's really not teachable; it's motivation and courage that comes from inside.

For senior managers and CEOs, I would start off by breaking down the walls that have accumulated over the years, that have to a degree insulated them from their direct reports and the layers below. They need to rediscover who they really are and to be comfortable with that knowledge. As they process their own *HBDI* profile, they will be largely affirmed in their own self-knowledge, but in most cases they will also gain significant insights about their leadership style and management approach and why their relationships with key people vary in effectiveness.

Once they have a better understanding of themselves and a working grasp of Whole Brain Technology, they can begin to see opportunities to optimize their approach to decision making, staff development, and dealing with key leadership issues. A breakthrough concept for many will be the idea that we can achieve the value of whole brain thinking by being *situational* in our daily activities. The idea is not to attempt to change the unchangeable but to take advantage of the flexibility we all have to become situationally more effective across a broad range of key leadership issues.

Since CEOs, as a general occupational group, are perhaps four times as likely as others to be multidominant, there is a strong likelihood that they have even more mental options than they are currently using. An example would be strategic thinking—not the rigors of strategic planning but the kind of thinking that should precede strategic planning. Experience has demonstrated that it's quite possible to open up senior managers to their strategic thinking potential in as short a time as three days. Once experienced, this mode of thinking becomes almost instantly more available on a daily basis.

I don't think that the CEO training priorities should deal with any of the standard functional issues, such as advanced finance or quality control. These are functions that others can carry out under their leadership. What is needed are ways to unleash their thinking capability across the mental aspects of the key leadership issues they are faced with. Their career path has already demonstrated an enormous capacity to deliver the system requirements. To optimize the business they must now go beyond their day-to-day mental boundaries. For this reason, they must be able to access and develop those mental processes that are still at the lower levels of their learning curve. In addition to strategic thinking are such modes as problem solving, intuitive thinking, conceptualizing, visualizing, and creative processing. All of these are like ripples in a pond. They generate additional ripples.

Affirmation is a key in the training of higher-level managers. Since they have built their careers on delivering to the bottom line, they must, in most cases, have positive feedback early on that they can perform in these new ways of thinking.

Years ago I asked a class in advanced management whether they could draw. About eight hands out of 100 slowly raised. When I asked them if they would like to be able to draw, 80 hands shot up without hesitation. AHA! What would happen if I taught the 80 how to draw? What if I affirmed them in their desire? What would that lead to? What would be the consequences? Well, I wasn't able to teach that particular group of 80, but over the years many hundreds of managers have learned to draw. The objective is not to have them become artists, although some have. The objective is to help them to do something they had always aspired to but could not do because they had no good way to access their latent capability. Once accessed, the affirmation was enormous. Suddenly they could "see." Not for the purpose of drawing, which of course they now could do, but for the purpose of *understanding* more of the world around them. They are probably very good at thinking analytically.

This is the kind of stuff that CEOs and top managers need to be able to do. They can hire experts in finance and strategic planning and computer technology. What they can't hire is their own ability to think strategically, visually, intuitively, globally—to project their leadership out into the future.

The human brain is still quite malleable at 55 or 60, much more so than we used to think. Significant learning can still take place at this age and well beyond. The benefits to the business of having a business leader able to think more effectively are beyond calculation.

Figure 14-4.
A comparison of a
CEO's profile to that
of the corporate
culture and the
misalignment in the
B and D quadrants.

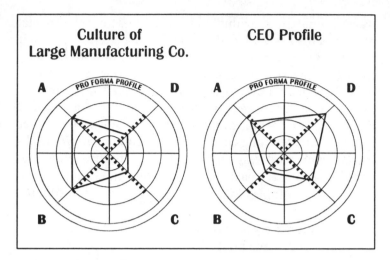

Culture of Large Manufacturing Co. | CEO Profile

The Metamorphosis of Whole Brain CEOs

Given the reality that most management cultures of large companies are left mode (A/B) dominant, how is it possible for a CEO who has a four-quadrant profile including strong right mode (C/D) preferences and competencies to survive the career path to the top?

I have diagnosed a number of cases in the context of Whole Brain Technology and here are my observations.

In all cases, the future CEOs apparently met or exceeded the left mode A/B quadrant system requirements by applying situational competencies to achieve outstanding bottom-line performance (figures 14-4 and 14-5). Their right mode C/D quadrant preferences were not very visible outside the privacy of their office. I don't think that they consciously managed their behavior so that it was visibly aligned with the management culture. I think they intuitively sensed that "when in Rome, you behave as a Roman."

As promotions were earned and their responsibilities and authority widened, they began to naturally behave in ways that encouraged their right mode C- and D-quadrant behaviors to be more openly applied. Again, I don't think this was particularly deliberate but rather an expression of their growing confidence that they had the right stuff and that therefore they should use it. As they attained senior management positions and felt more confident in their future, they also felt more secure in managing in accordance with their own per-

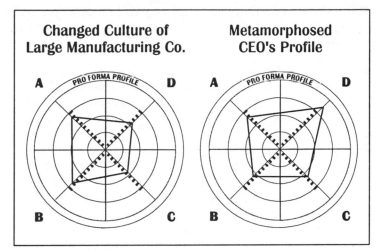

Figure 14-5.
The adjustments of a CEO's thinking styles to accommodate an evolving and changing corporate culture.

sonal style. As one well-known CEO said to me when he was still VP, "Ned, I like what I do and I like the way I do it. I have been successful so far and in the long run I will be more successful. I don't want to learn other ways; I am confident of my ways."

Future CEOs, when still at the VP level, could take more calculated risks, share their vision of the future, talk in more global terms, make more humane decisions, and in general, champion the human asset of the business. In these ways they were able to be "nice guys" in addition to "tough guys."

These future CEOs were able to talk in terms of long-range goals rather than focusing exclusively on short-term results. And they could usually do these things without fear of being ridiculed by their competitors for the senior positions. At this point, they had consolidated their authority and power and were able to lead on the basis of their personal style. No longer was there a need for them to situationally role-play the style approved by the culture. They had migrated from the middle management cultural norms to setting up senior management cultural norms. As CEOs, they would be able to consolidate their influence and establish a leadership culture of their own design.

So What?

- Traditional approaches to the design and delivery of intended business learning are often ineffective and extremely costly; much of the investment is wasted.

- Whole brain design and delivery technologies provide participants with intended learning take-aways for independent application to their work.

- Organizations with leaders who can champion this technology can acquire it for their own benefit, both in significantly improved learning outcomes and significantly improved return on their training investment.

- It is really up to the high-level managers to have the courage and confidence to apply their new learning independent of their bosses' specific approval. This is a continuing dilemma.

- High-level managers are usually good at analytic thinking and can hire experts on finance and planning. What they need to acquire for themselves is the capacity to think visually, intuitively, creatively, and strategically. This key learning is available, and senior managers, including CEOs, owe it to themselves and their companies to acquire these mental skills.

- Potential CEOs can migrate through the organization by applying their left mode competencies and skills situationally to excel in meeting organizational requirements. To succeed, much of their right mode preferences are temporarily suppressed.

- As success results in promotions, and increased authority and organizational power is acquired, the future CEO is able to personalize his or her leadership style and shape the leadership culture in the direction of his or her preferences.

PART III

Whole Brain Leadership

The CEO's Key
Leadership Issues

Chapter Headlines

♦   CEOs need to be involved in the creation of key company documents, such as vision, mission, and value statements and annual reports.

♦   These statements are often developed separately and are out of alignment.

♦   Whole Brain Technology provides a method of diagnosing the mentality of these statements, which can lead to their alignment.

"The only limits are, as always, those of vision."

—

James Broughton

The CEO's incoming mail, whether it be electronic or paper, covers the entire gamut of the business. By fax, E-mail, Fed Ex, or postal service, the office of the CEO is kept continuously informed about what's going on. The challenge is to read it all. However, there is one category of written material dealing with key leadership issues that is primarily *outgoing* rather than incoming: the vision statement, statement of mission, core values, and annual report. These documents establish the purpose and direction of the business and must, in fact, represent the thinking of the leadership of the business, and specifically of the CEO. There is no escaping the personalization of these critical documents through the CEO's active involvement and sign-off.

Figure 15-1.
Key leadership pro
formas for a U.S.
corporation.

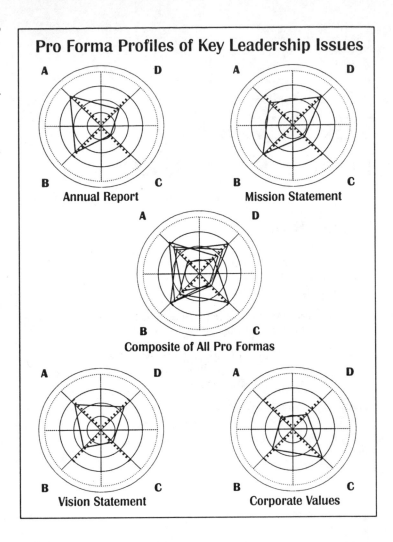

Pro Forma Profiles of Key Leadership Issues

Annual Report

Mission Statement

Composite of All Pro Formas

Vision Statement

Corporate Values

In most cases, these documents are developed separately and at different times in the CEO's tenure. Therefore they reflect thinking that may be appropriate to those different situations and time frames. In spite of this, I believe it is a requirement of business leadership that these written statements be consistent, one with the other, and that taken together they document the purpose and direction of the business on an everyday basis. We can't have last year's values and this year's vision. We can't have an annual report that conveys a different message than the current mission on which daily decisions are being based.

Whole Brain Technology provides a method for diagnosing the mentality of each of these documents or statements on a consistent basis that therefore permits comparative analysis. For example, here is an array of what I refer to as the "key leadership" issues of a large U. S. corporation.

These pro forma profiles were created by diagnosing the mentality of each descriptive word, sentence, paragraph, or page of a particular document on the basis of the Whole Brain Model. Also included were any charts, graphs, financial data, or illustrations. For example, a page of financial data would be diagnosed as an exclusively A-quadrant element of the complete document. An illustration of a family enjoying a picnic, in which the company's products were displayed, would be considered primarily a C-quadrant element, with perhaps a D-quadrant contribution if the products were being newly introduced. In contrast, a page devoted to the manufacturing assembly line operation and its production results would contribute a strong B-quadrant element to the overall diagnosis. In this way, the brain dominance characteristics of the statements and documents are diagnosed and aggregated into an overall profile of that key leadership issue.

Even to the untutored eye, it is clear that the key leadership issues shown in the illustration are reasonably consistent in the rational and analytic A quadrant, less consistent in the organized, structured B quadrant, and even less consistent in the conceptual, visionary D quadrant. They are flagrantly inconsistent in the humanistic, interpersonal C quadrant. This lack of alignment lessens the credibility of the leadership. The profiles strongly suggest that management proclaims values that are not actually carried out, that management describes things to the investing public that are not experienced by the customers and employees, that the good intentions embedded in the vision statement are more of a pipe dream than a reality.

I find it extremely revealing that, in the vast majority of cases, it is the C quadrant that is consistently out of alignment. This is where the rubber tire of leadership credibility meets the hard pavement of employee reality. The documents invite people to compare intentions with performance.

Let me give you an example. I was invited to present my Whole Brain Technology story to the board of a billion-dollar communications company. I was ushered into the green room, adjoining the boardroom to await my appointment. As I looked around the well-appointed room, I noted a portrait of

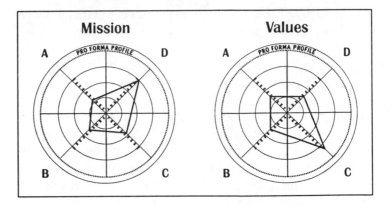

Figure 15-2.
Pro forma profile of a communications company's mission statement corporate values.

a distinguished-looking gentleman who was apparently the founder, and on either side were framed, parchment documents describing the mission of the organization and its core values. The Mission Statement was a very impressive, well-crafted document, impeccably handlettered on fine grain parchment, handsomely framed, and mounted next to the founder. Its profile is shown in figure 15-2.

I had just finished preparing this profile when a staff member indicated it would be another 10 to 15 minutes before I could come into the boardroom, so I decided to do a pro forma profile of the company's corporate value statement, similarly framed, on the other side of the founder. In like manner, I diagnosed each word in terms of its brain dominance characteristics and aggregated the individual elements into an overall profile (figure 15-2, profile on right).

I was then invited into the boardroom and offered a seat next to the president. After a brief introduction, I was given 45 minutes to present my material, during which time there were numerous questions and nonverbal reactions to what I was saying. This segment was followed by an open discussion of application possibilities of my work to this organization. At the end of the allotted time, the president said, "Ned, I would like to give you a departing gift. Here is a card containing the mission and corporate value statements upon which our business is based. This card is carried by thousands of our employees who are proud to work for this great company." As I accepted the card, I glanced at it and it contained the two statements that I had just diagnosed before entering the meeting. When I got back to the hotel, I took half an hour to document my experience in the boardroom, including capturing a generous sampling of statements that I

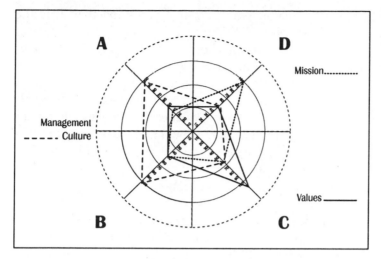

Figure 15-3. Composite pro forma of mission, values, and management culture.

could quote verbatim. Seeing the possibility of a small case history, I then developed a pro forma profile of my experience with the board. Shown in figure 15-3 are all three profiles plotted together.

My wife Margy, who always accompanies me on these trips, expressed an interest in a Japanese dinner that night. So we found a nearby restaurant that features open seating around individual grills. We were seated next to a young couple, and the four of us were the only patrons at that particular grill, so we had a chance to converse. When I asked what they did and where they worked, they both indicated that they were professional employees working for the same company that I had just visited. It didn't take much probing for them to reveal their lack of satisfaction with their work for that company. In their own words they described a pious, crass, self-serving management that did not live up to its stated objectives. When I took the president's plastic card out of my pocket they burst into laughter. After a minute they said that not only didn't they carry those cards in their wallets, but they trashed them as soon as they discovered the company was not living up to the values as they were stated. They both indicated that they were actively looking for a better place to work and would leave in a heartbeat if the opportunity presented itself.

It's seldom that I have the opportunity to so quickly verify the consequences of such a gross misalignment as these pro forma profiles reveal. To have credibility, the words describing key leadership issues must be matched by leadership be-

"The reality is that we lose respect for our leaders if we do not approve of their conduct— public or private. Leaders who do not command our respect reduce the legitimacy of their leadership and lose our trust."

—

Keshavan Nair

> "When CEOs are asked how much of the knowledge in their companies is used, they typically answer, 'About twenty percent.'"
>
> —
>
> Charles Handy

havior. No matter who puts the words together, it is the responsibility of the CEO to make certain that the intent of those words is translated into leadership action. Prior to Whole Brain Technology there was no easy way to diagnose these kinds of leadership statements, and therefore they have been promulgated without regard for the leadership mentality they reveal and the consequences of their misalignment with management behavior. Now that there is a way to diagnose the mentality of these statements, it should be a New Year's resolution of management to make certain that they are strongly aligned—unless of course, they don't give a damn about their credibility.

The concept of brain dominance leads into a whole array of alignment issues—the alignment of our mental preferences and our educational choices, the alignment of our mental preferences and our occupational choices, the alignment of those things that turn us on and our actual work assignment. As it turns out, I believe that most of the business world is out of alignment rather than in alignment—that it is a relatively rare event for people to be truly aligned with the activity that they are involved with, whether it is going to school, pursuing a career, or performing a job.

I would anticipate that Maslow's notion of self-actualization would occur more frequently when there was a strong alignment between how we think and what we are doing, and that the level of effort required to engage in that activity would be more relaxed, freeflowing, and therefore more efficient in the use of our mental faculties. When we are out of alignment we have to struggle to perform, because what we are doing is not really what we are interested in doing.

> "Imagine the implications for a company if it could get that number up to thirty percent."
>
> —
>
> Betty Zucker

My imagination takes me to an organization where an effort has been made to understand the mental preferences of the people in the organization and to understand the mental requirements of the work of that organization, and then to sort out and divide up the work into packages of activities that can be matched to the mental preferences of the people in the organization. This would allow there to be individual alignments between people and their work not only at the micro level, but also at the macro level, where the whole organization is in alignment. Can you imagine the performance of such an organization?

Another application of the alignment concept is to an organization that develops a vision, a specific mission, a set of goals and objectives, and a definition of its values and then compares the alignment between the mentality of each of those issues and the alignment of the total array considered from the standpoint of the organization as a whole. Experience tells us that it would be rare indeed for all these significant business issues to be in alignment without conscious preparation.

Consider next the annual report of such an organization in which the objective of the annual report is to tell the story of that business to the investing public and to its employees. The story being told by the annual report is often not the story intended to be told. Imagine what the business results might be if full alignment were achieved. What a positive influence that would have on all concerned.

Looking more closely at the alignment issue, it is likely to be the case that different functions of the business are at different levels or degrees of alignment. For example, the engineering function may be in stronger alignment than the manufacturing function, and the marketing and sales organization at a different level of alignment than engineering and manufacturing. Under these conditions, it is less likely that potential success of the integrated business can be achieved.

I believe one of the roles of the CEO is to diagnose these alignment issues and do something about them. There are, of course, two sides of the equation: the vision, mission, and goals of the organization on one hand, and the orientation of the human asset on the other. The CEO needs to be in a position to affect both. He or she can change the vision, change the mission, change the objectives of the organization to better meet the reality of its human asset. The CEO can also change the nature, the mix, the capability of the human asset to better meet the vision, objectives, and goals of the organization. One of the significant ingredients of the decision process is the ability to diagnose, to measure, and to compare.

Whole Brain Technology provides an important way to quantify aggregate brain power in terms of the composite averages of each function of the organization. Through the ability to develop pro forma profiles of the key leadership issues, such as the vision or the mission or the goals and objectives, the CEO is able to better understand the relationship between those issues and the organization as a whole and by its functions. For many businesses, the availability of

"The standard of leadership depends not only on the qualities and beliefs of our leaders, but also on the expectations we have of them."

—

Keshavan Nair

this tool represents the first time the CEO and staff possess a way of assessing the degree of alignment between these major aspects of the business.

I see an opportunity for each individual to seek alignment of the various segments of personal and business life by making adjustments, not only in the mental approach we take to those elements, but also in those elements themselves. I think it is safe to forecast that success, fulfillment, and the simple pleasure of our daily existence can improve to the extent that such personal alignment is achieved.

So What?

- For the first time the mentality of key leadership documents can now be diagnosed and brought into alignment.

- When an organization's key leadership issues, statements, and documents are in alignment, its message becomes clearer, and its credibility improves.

Managing Financial Crisis

"I believe that crisis really tends to help develop the character of an organization."

—

John Sculley

Chapter Headlines

◆ Management's traditional ways of taking visible crisis action, such as turning out the lights, or cancelling trade shows, are often counterproductive.

◆ Economic crises often stimulate inappropriate counterproductive management behavior.

◆ Windows of opportunity are usually overlooked because legitimate, safekeeping management thinking runs amuck.

◆ Positive programs like effective cash management yield better results faster.

During an economic downturn, when many companies feel the beginnings of a financial crisis due to falling revenues, management mentality often experiences a lower left B-quadrant downshift. It is very tempting for managers who lean in that direction anyway to have an excuse to do it on purpose. That is, they immediately begin to turn out the lights, set the thermostat at 68, save string and wrapping paper, and in general behave extremely conservatively about any activity involving money, materials, and people. For those who have a high need for visible action, putting on the brakes is an obvious first option that observers of the managerial process can note and applaud.

When the question is asked, "What's management doing?" it's comfortable and easy to answer, "They are taking the lead in saving money." Travel is curtailed. Expense account rules are tightened. Trade shows are cancelled. Time clocks are installed. Purchasing ground rules are severely tightened. Building for inventory stops. Advertising is pulled. Hiring ceases and layoffs begin. This is crisis mentality, which responds in the only way it knows how—a mindless retreat to safekeeping supervision of all identifiable processes in the business. And it feels good because people are *doing* something.

The thought that this might be a window of opportunity for a particular product line never survives its initial introduction as a creative idea. The thought that this is the time to advertise, and do so more creatively than before, is not given serious consideration. The idea that investing in the retention of the trained workforce is rejected out of hand. The even more outrageous thought that this is an ideal time to further develop key employees is shot down as it is being verbalized into a recommendation. The senior vice president raises questions about the company's standard paper pads that have two thin red lines down the left side of the paper. He says "You know, this costs extra money. Is it absolutely necessary?" Expensive computers that work better when they are operated continuously are turned off in order to save on the electric bill. As this juggernaut of cost-saving ideas gains momentum, the ruling is made that all employees will now turn in their frequent-flyer miles to the company account.

This kind of thinking typifies legitimate, needed B-quadrant mentality that has run amok. For some managers who were brought up under traditional, status quo, safekeeping, security-minded management, it represents a return to sanity. They welcome it and collaborate enthusiastically to make it the management culture of survival. In many situations, however, it is just the opposite. It is a return to past practices that have taken a whole generation to overcome. Management is asked to turn in its sharpshooter expense-control rifles for broad gauge shotguns and to fire at will at anything with a dollar sign that moves.

It takes a certain leadership strength to stick to the vision that brought the company this far, to reexamine current events with a view toward midcourse corrections rather than a 180° turnabout. Appropriate leadership actions include: a four-quadrant Walk-Around of the decision process in each of the company's key functions as well as at the CEO level, applications of creativity rather than a crowbar to problems, and diagnosis of the economic facts of life with a simultaneous assessment of appropriate risks and respect for the leadership intuition that brought us this far.

The period of business crisis is a time to be situationally whole brained. It is the time to develop multiple options rather than considering only those that are security-minded and safekeeping, to employ savvy leadership rather than micromanagement. This is a time for wide-angle binoculars and celestial telescopes rather than microscopes.

Business crisis conditions call for creative solutions. This is a time to organize creative teams and assign them to areas of opportunity. A prime area for creative action is cash management. In the typical case, cash management is the responsibility of the finance function only. In point of fact, everybody in the organization is involved in cash management. I would recommend that instead of the many negative actions that have just been described, a very positive organizationwide effort would focus on effective cash management. Every member of the organization should be part of a team, and each of these teams should be heterogeneous (that is, comprised of people who together represent a full range of mental preferences). Each person broadens the scope of the team's constructive actions and recommendations.

Organizations that launch effective cash management campaigns are universally surprised by the results. There is cash *everywhere*. The exact amount depends on the functions and size of the organization, but the total is always a pleasant surprise.

The effective cash management program that I designed for General Electric in the late 1970s generated over $500 million in its first year of implementation. A major benefit of launching an effective cash management campaign is that the organization becomes trained in those techniques and attitudes that sustain the positive effect for several years after the launching of the initial effort. In fact, effective cash management changes the culture of the organization. Instead of employees feeling isolated from the organization's everyday problems, individuals become part of the solution. It has been my experience that teams that find $50, or $5,000, or $100,000 are so fulfilled by team results that they are motivated to continue their efforts.

The key outcomes from programs like effective cash management are positive, quantifiable, visible results. Compare

"You must deodorise profits and make people understand that profit is not something offensive, but as important to a company as breathing."

—

Sir Peter Parker

these outcomes to the typical, negative, demotivational activities that result from crisis management. As a matter of fact, programs like effective cash management can be so successful that the crisis is avoided altogether.

Listed below are some criteria to keep in mind in developing crisis-avoiding programs.

1. The results should be quantifiable, easy to measure, and reportable.

2. Official score keeping should be the responsibility of the business function involved (usually finance).

3. The program should be organizationwide, involving a maximum number of individuals.

4. Heterogeneous teams of up to seven people should be formed, including all functions and locations. Their assignment should be to find all the cash in a specific segment of the business.

5. Results of the program should be reported as soon as possible, widely and regularly, on a specific schedule.

6. The reporting process should focus on team results.

7. Teams should be given recognition in the company newspaper and specific rewards.

8. The rewards should be real and meaningful, and proportional to the amount of cash formed. They should reflect the culture of the organization.

9. Senior management should be involved in the recognition and reward process.

So What?

■ Opportunities created by the crisis are usually not taken advantage of.

■ Positive programs such as effective cash management can generate needed cash quickly, and therefore reduce the economic threat. Negative programs usually don't produce much cash, but do demotivate employees.

■ Specific criteria are needed to help ensure effective program design.

Ways to Make Reengineering Work

Chapter Headlines

♦ Reengineering is actually a whole brain process being implemented all too frequently by left mode management in counterproductive left mode ways.

♦ Too often, reengineering focuses on cost reduction instead of process reinvention.

♦ Most organizations are sufficiently diverse to provide whole brain reengineering project leadership and whole brain implementation teams.

♦ Reengineering is an opportunity for the whole organization to "go creative."

> *"Everyone's role perception tells you their assumptions about how things are supposed to operate around here.*
> *To re-engineer a company, those perceptions have to be aligned with today's realities, not wistful memories of yesterday."*
>
> —
>
> *Charles Geschke*

Who hasn't heard about reengineering? It's the buzz word of the early 1990s. It's a great concept, but a terrible word. In the context of Brain Dominance as described in this book, reengineering is strictly an A-quadrant word. However, to *work*, it must be a whole brain process. And to be completely honest about it, a lot of so-called reengineering interventions have not worked. (This is freely admitted by the gurus who invented reengineering.) My belief is that if the interventions had been properly conceptualized, managed, and carried out, the vast majority of reengineering efforts would have been wonderfully successful.

Figure 17-1.
National Inventors
Hall of Fame: a pro
forma composite of
the 84 members
showing the strong
A/D cerebral mental
preference of
inventors (also
displayed in figure
9-10).

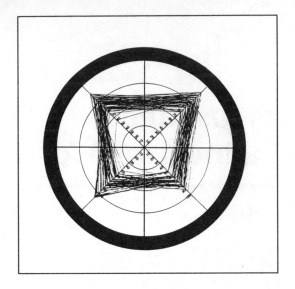

In Brain Dominance jargon, the word *reinvention* is actually a cerebral description of what should take place. The process of invention is very clearly a double-dominant cerebral A/D-quadrant activity. Data from the National Invention Hall of Fame and the Lawrence Livermore National Laboratory demonstrate that the 1-2-2-1 profile is clearly the norm for the inventive mind. The A quadrant contributes logical, analytical, rational, quantitative, financial, and technical mental processes. The fact that the imaginative, conceptual, holistic, experimental D quadrant represents half this synergistic cerebral combination makes all the difference in the thinking process. When we add the necessary qualities of the B quadrant, with its specialization in form, sequence, chronology, and implementation, to the required qualities of the C quadrant, with its specialized preferences for interpersonal relationships, work, spirit, and communication expressiveness, we have a much more mentally complete process.

In reengineering, *process* is the operative word. Reinvention of a business is targeted to the key processes involved in that business. This could mean the entire sales process or just the billing process. It could be as comprehensive a process as new product development or manufacturing automation, or so limited a process as the training of production line workers. A key characteristic in identifying a process for reinvention is that it must involve a change of state, and it must also be a process critical to the success of the business.

Paul Gustavson, President of OPD, one of the country's most successful consultancies in organizational design, uses this simple example to explain what kind of processes are candidates for reinvention. He diagnoses the bakery business as having three critical-state change processes.

1. The first bakery process involves taking raw materials and mixing them together to create batter.

2. The second process involves shaping the batter into the form of a cake and baking it.

3. The third process involves icing and decorating the basic cake to create an attractive birthday or wedding cake.

Each of these processes is discrete, and each causes a change of state from raw materials to batter, from batter to cake, from cake to a wedding cake. The reinvention or reengineering challenge is to creatively change one, two, or all three of these bakery processes in order to reduce the cost, decrease the time, improve the taste, enhance the appearance, or achieve all four simultaneously. Add to those results already described a reduction in the number of people required, and you now have a miniexample of reengineering at its simplest.

An operative word above is *creatively.* Without creativity, reengineering efforts are often "awkward examples of management muscle," which may get good marks for intent, but very bad marks for results.

If you trace the motivating force behind the typical reengineering project, you will often find a management decision based on left mode A- and B-quadrant thinking. The objective of the reengineering intervention becomes so narrowly focused on cost reduction, for example, that creative possibilities are not even considered. The strong left mode thinking style becomes the basis for the decision-making style, which in turn becomes the basis for the operational style of dealing with the problem situation. These styles reinforce each other to such an extent that a fragile, creative idea doesn't have a chance. In addition to smothering creativity, the strong left mode management decision process also influences the make up of the teams or project groups that have been assigned to carry out the reengineering intervention. It is all too easy for left mode managers to select left mode teams to carry out their mandate. After all, they are selecting people in their own image to implement their perception of needed action.

One of OPD President Paul Gustavson's favorite statements is that "Organizations are perfectly designed for the results they achieve." This is a devastatingly accurate prediction of the bottom-line results of the business organization. If success is to be the final result, then we must design the organization to be capable of producing that result. I would add to Paul's quote that it is the leadership of the organization that determines the outcome. Organizations, taken as a whole, represent a composite whole brain. This means that the mental diversity is already in place as a candidate pool from which to select the teams to implement a reengineering project. The missing element is whole brain management.

> *"Organiza-*
> *tions are*
> *perfectly*
> *designed for*
> *the results*
> *they achieve."*
>
> —
>
> *Paul*
> *Gustavson*

Step 1. Install a whole brain management team in the leadership roles of a reengineering project.

Step 2. Create whole brain implementation teams.

Step 3. Apply appropriate creative processes in all the activities of the leadership and implementation teams.

To optimize reengineering interventions and help guarantee their success, organizations need to "go creative," and by so doing will reenergize the entire business.

So What?

- Reengineering interventions are too often failing to produce the intended results.

- Too often reengineering projects are led by left mode management incapable of conceptualizing the intervention in whole brain terms.

- Organizations are perfectly designed for the results they achieve.

- Economic crises require tough, savvy, future-oriented management decisions.

CEOs
Around the World

Chapter Headlines

♦ Leadership behaviors and styles differ for CEOs working in European, Asian-Pacific, and North American countries.

♦ Preferred work elements of CEOs are consistent across cultures, national boundaries, and genders.

♦ The best CEOs adapt their behavior to the region or country where they operate, but all of them share a set of universal competencies that transcend national boundaries.

♦ The international *HBDI* database clearly shows that the CEO occupation is multidominant.

♦ A recent study by the author of 697 male CEOs and 76 female CEOs from many countries reveals a surprising consensus of thinking styles, work preferences, and likely competencies.

> *"The world is round and the place which may seem like the end may also be the beginning."*
>
> —
>
> *Ivy Baker Priest,*
>
> *1905-1975*

Our international database clearly shows that the typical CEO is multidominant and has at least two, usually three, and often four, strong primaries and therefore has a wide array of thinking options. As an occupational category, CEOs have four times the number of four-quadrant-balanced profiles than any other occupational group because that is the mental nature of the work they do. An in-basket study of CEOs over a two-week period, including their daily calendars, clearly indicated a wide functional diversity and therefore multidominant nature of their work. In all cases all four quadrants were almost equally involved.

According to the Hay Group's *International CEO Leadership Study* of March 1995, cultural factors play a significant part in differentiating the behavioral characteristics of successful CEOs in different parts of the world.

The Hay study raised these questions:

1. What does it really take to lead an international business successfully?

2. What are superior CEOs doing differently from their average counterparts?

3. How can we ensure that future CEOs will have what it takes to excel in international organizations?

The study was based on 51 CEOs of top performing corporations in 14 countries. The countries include: Belgium, Canada, France, Germany, Hong Kong, Italy, Japan, Mexico, the Netherlands, New Zealand, the Philippines, Spain, the United Kingdom, and the United States.

The Hay study found that while the best CEOs adapt their behavior to the region or country where they operate, all of them share *universal competencies* that transcend national boundaries but which must be modified based on the culture in which they are being used.

Figure 18-1.
Distributing traits in the Whole Brain Model.

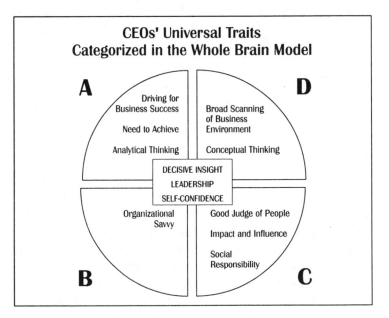

CEOs' Universal Traits
Categorized in the Whole Brain Model

A

Driving for
Business Success

Need to Achieve

Analytical Thinking

D

Broad Scanning
of Business
Environment

Conceptual Thinking

DECISIVE INSIGHT
LEADERSHIP
SELF-CONFIDENCE

Organizational
Savvy

Good Judge of People

Impact and Influence

Social
Responsibility

B

C

The competencies fall into three distinct clusters:

1. *Sharpening the focus*—broad scanning ability, analytical and conceptual thinking, decisive insight.

2. *Building commitment*—organizational savvy, good judgment of people, leadership, impact, and influence.

3. *Driving for success*—a need to achieve, self-confidence, and social responsibility.

I have translated key Hay study findings into the Whole Brain Model so that the results can be approximated in the form of the four-quadrant model by locating the mentality of the key characteristics in the appropriate quadrants. For example, the universal traits, just described, fall into all four quadrants and therefore confirm the multidominant nature of the CEO role.

Murray Dalziel, Managing Director of Hay Europe, says: "Executives who operate in their local culture require little conscious adaptation beyond their corporate culture. Some global executives think they can impose their wills and personal styles no matter what culture they are operating in, but they do this at their own peril. . . . they must be flexible enough to change the ways they use their universal competencies. . . .The ability to adapt leadership styles across cultures determines whether the executive will win the game."

The Hay study found cultural differentiation in four broad areas. These include *relationships*, *objectivity*, *planning*, and *implementation*. In the area of relationships, CEOs in different parts of the world took distinct approaches to building personal relationships—and these approaches were very much aligned with the prevailing culture. In Asian-Pacific countries, successful CEOs displayed a mastery of personal interaction—conducting business through the gradual development of trust and mutual respect among their counterparts in the business community and the public sector. They feel that short-term financial gain is less important than creating and maintaining these relationships. In this Far Eastern culture, successful CEOs excel in competencies known as *developing mutual respect* and *relationship building*.

In contrast, the study found that successful North American CEOs represent the opposite end of the personal rela-

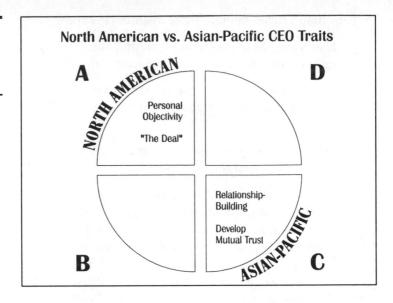

Figure 18-2.
Results of Hays Study of North American and Asian-Pacific CEOs.

tionship continuum. While they may possess the capacity to form relationships, in the practice of their business, they stress the *contractual outcome*. "The deal's the thing" is their credo. Decisions are made on the basis of price, performance, quality, and other such objective criteria. For example, the study cited one North American CEO who observed about a deal that he made: "These people weren't particularly pleasant, but that was irrelevant. They offered the best price." In the U. S. culture, successful CEOs demonstrate high levels of competency known as *personal objectivity*.

In the Whole Brain Model, personal objectivity, and "the deal" translate into A-quadrant thinking. By contrast, gradual relationship building and developing mutual respect translates into C-quadrant thinking (see figure 18-2).

In the planning area, the study indicates that many European CEOs tended to heavily emphasize the development of detailed plans that are clearly communicated to subordinates. They demonstrate superior development of a competency known as *rational planning*. In the Whole Brain Model this would be a combination of the A and B quadrants and would place rational planning in the left mode.

On the other hand, North American CEOs who are more concerned with implementation focus their efforts on setting the general direction of the plan and then finding the best person or people to carry it out. This style is characterized

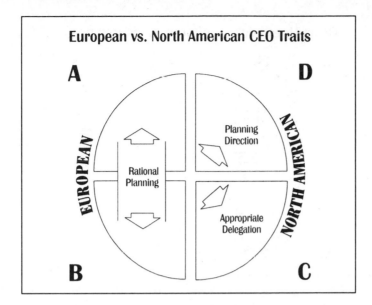

Figure 18-3.
European versus
North American CEO
mentality.

by a sense of urgency and is often seen in fast-paced, changing environments. In the Whole Brain Model this form of implementation is more right mode than left mode because it deals with the general direction of planning rather than with specific details or the delegation of responsibility to the individuals best suited to carry it out. This is a combination of the D and C quadrants and therefore is right mode thinking.

In terms of authority, the study indicates a basic dichotomy between those CEOs who tend toward centralized authority—that is, toward taking a clear stance as the leader and decision maker during interactions with subordinates—and those who are more participatory in the leadership role and allow their staff to make collective decisions. On this basis the study indicates three *leadership patterns* (figure 18-4).

The lesson to be learned is that while CEOs tend to have more options in their thinking processes than most occupations, the way they carry out their role is influenced by the culture in which they operate. They must be able to be flexible in their leadership style and be able to culturally adapt their business competencies to better align with local cultural norms.

According to Geert Hoestede, a European cultural expert, the business culture of Germany is like a "well-oiled machine"; that of France is like a "pyramid"; and that of England is similar to a "village market." When interpreted in terms of

Figure 18-4.
Hoestede model of
cultural patterns in
Europe.

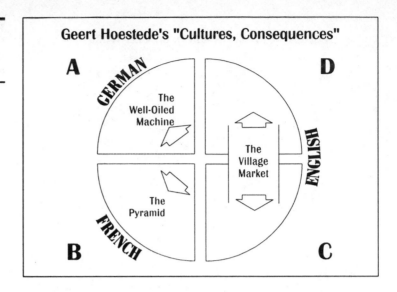

Geert Hoestede's "Cultures, Consequences"

the Whole Brain Model, the three cultural metaphors are distributed as shown in figure 18-4.

Motivated by the Hay study, I conducted an independent study in 1995 of 697 male CEOs employing *HBDI* profiles administered by our international affiliates in six countries—the United States, Germany (Roland Spinola), France (Lionel Vuillemin), England (Dennis Martin), Australia (Mike Morgan), and Turkey (Savas Tumis). Parallel with the study of male CEOs, I also conducted a study of 76 female CEOs from the United States, Germany, and England.

The composite averages of male CEOs in each of the six countries are shown in figure 18-5, along with the overall average profile for all 697 male CEOs. These profiles, representing CEOs from six countries, show a similarity in thinking styles, indicating a relatively uniform distribution of mental preferences for the CEO occupation worldwide.

Country-by-country differences appear when the *HBDI* data is diagnosed in greater depth. One of the most powerful sections of the *Herrmann Brain Dominance Instrument* focuses on a forced ranking of 16 so-called work elements. These are shown in table 18-1 and as part of the *HBDI* in Appendix B.

All individuals completing the *HBDI* survey form are asked to assign values—from 5 (very best) to 1 (worst)—to all 16 work elements. I have diagnosed the work elements data in order to establish an overall consensus rank order for the CEOs in each of the six countries. A general consensus

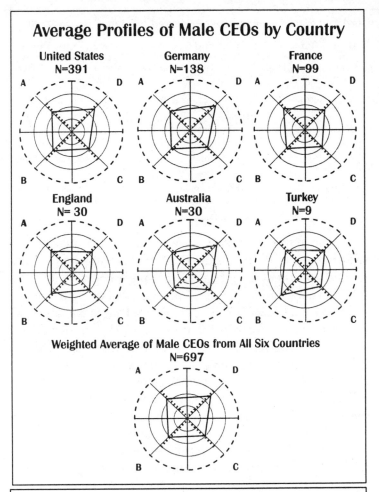

Average Profiles of Male CEOs by Country

United States
N=391

Germany
N=138

France
N=99

England
N= 30

Australia
N=30

Turkey
N=9

Weighted Average of Male CEOs from All Six Countries
N=697

Figure 18-5.
Average profiles of 697 CEOs collected from Ned Herrmann Group's international affiliates administering the *HBDI* on a regular basis.

Table 18-1. Work Elements Reprinted from the *HBDI*

Analytical	Planning
Administrative	Interpersonal Aspects
Conceptualizing	Problem Solving
Expressing Ideas	Innovating
Integration	Teaching/Training
Writing	Organization
Technical Aspects	Creative Aspects
Implementation	Financial Aspects

emerges on the ranking of preferred work elements among the 697 male CEOs in the *HBDI* database for the United States, Germany, France, England, Australia, and Turkey.

In diagnosing the six-country average ranking of male CEO work elements in the four-quadrant model, the distribution

Table 18-2. Rank-ordered Work Elements Most Preferred by Male CEOs in Study

The *top four* out of 16 work elements in the consensus rank order for male CEOs are:	There is further consensus in the work elements ranked fifth through eighth:	This third set of work elements is ranked ninth through twelfth by male CEOs:	There is a particularly strong consensus on the four least preferred work elements:
1. Problem Solving	5. Analyzing	9. Creative Aspects	13. Administrative
2. Organizational Aspects	6. Planning	10. Innovating	14. Writing
3. Interpersonal Aspects	7. Expressing ideas	11. Implementation	15. Teaching/Training
4. Conceptualizing	8. Integrating	12. Financial Aspects	16. Technical Aspects

of the 16 ranked elements by most preferred quadrant is shown in table 18-2. This distribution, favoring the D quadrant, is consistent with the quadrant preferences established by the average profile of all 697 male CEOs (see figure 18-5).

In five out of six countries, *Problem Solving* is the universal choice of the top work element priority. Also, in five out of six countries, *Technical Aspects* is the universal choice of the bottom ranking work element. Australia is the country out of alignment with these two work elements, ranking *Technical Aspects* high and *Problem Solving* low. While there is relative consistency at the top and bottom of the list of 16 CEO work elements, there are significant differences in the ranking of the middle of the list (5 through 12), country by country. Table 18-3 lists the work elements rank-ordered by country compared to the six-country composite average.

Work Elements Analysis of Male CEOs

The surprisingly low ranking in the six-country average of *Financial Aspects* (12), *Writing* (14), and *Technical Aspects* (16) strongly suggests that these three important work elements are of generally low interest and priority and are therefore likely to be delegated to key staff members.

The key low ranking of *Teaching/Training* (15) is alarming because it implies that male CEOs in general have a low interest and priority in this important function, which in my experience needs strong CEO support to be effective enough to meet the needs of the business.

CEOs in the United States, France, and England rank *Innovation* (6.6) higher than *Creativity* (10.3). This confirms, at least for this sample, greater business acceptance of *Innovation* than for *Creativity*. As pointed out in Chapter 21, this greater acceptance of innovation is unfortunate because creativity clearly represents the body of knowledge outside of business. Business needs *both* creativity and innovation.

Table 18-3. Rank-ordered Work Elements of 697 Male CEOs Listed by Country

U. S. A. (N=391)	Germany (N=138)	France (N=99)
1. Conceptualizing	1. Problem Solving	1. Analytical
2. Problem Solving	2. Conceptualizing	2. Interpersonal Aspects
3. Interpersonal Aspects	3. Organization	3. Problem Solving
4. Innovating	4. Planning	4. Implementation
5. Expressing Ideas	5. Analytical	5. Organization
6. Analytical	6. Integration	6. Integration
7. Creative Aspects	7. Creative Aspects	7. Expressing Ideas
8. Organization	8. Expressing Ideas	8. Conceptualizing
9. Integration	9. Interpersonal Aspects	9. Planning
10. Writing	10. Implementation	10. Innovating
11. Administrative	11. Innovating	11. Writing
12. Planning	12. Financial Aspects	12. Creative Aspects
13. Financial Aspects	13. Writing	13. Teaching/Training
14. Implementation	14. Teaching/Training	14. Technical Aspects
15. Teaching/Training	15. Technical Aspects	15. Financial Aspects
16. Technical Aspects	16. Administrative	16. Administrative

WEIGHTED AVERAGE (N=697)

1. Problem Solving
2. Organization
3. Interpersonal Aspects
4. Conceptualizing
5. Analytical
6. Planning
7. Expressing Ideas
8. Integration
9. Creative Aspects
10. Innovating
11. Implementation
12. Financial Aspects
13. Administrative
14. Writing
15. Teaching/Training
16. Technical Aspects

England (N=30)	Australia (N=30)	Turkey (N=9)
1. Problem Solving	1. Conceptualizing	1. Interpersonal Aspects
2. Analytical	2. Organization	2. Problem Solving
3. Planning	3. Planning	3. Organization
4. Organization	4. Creative Aspects	4. Integration
5. Expressing Ideas	5. Technical Aspects	5. Expressing Ideas
6. Innovating	6. Interpersonal Aspects	6. Financial Aspects
7. Implementation	7. Integration	7. Administrative
8. Interpersonal Aspects	8. Administrative	8. Planning
9. Conceptualizing	9. Expressing Ideas	9. Creative Aspects
10. Integration	10. Innovating	10. Analytical
11. Financial Aspects	11. Teaching/Training	11. Writing
12. Administrative	12. Financial Aspects	12. Innovating
13. Creative Aspects	13. Problem Solving	13. Implementation
14. Teaching/Training	14. Analytical	14. Teaching/Training
15. Writing	15. Writing	15. Conceptualizing
16. Technical Aspects	16. Implementation	16. Technical Aspects

Figure 18-6.
Weighted average
profiles of male and
female CEOs and
rate of differentia-
tion.

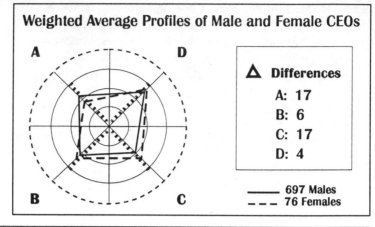

Weighted Average Profiles of Male and Female CEOs

△ **Differences**

A: 17

B: 6

C: 17

D: 4

——— 697 Males
— — — 76 Females

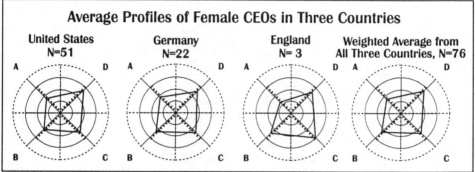

Average Profiles of Female CEOs in Three Countries

| United States N=51 | Germany N=22 | England N= 3 | Weighted Average from All Three Countries, N=76 |

Figure 18-7.
Average profile of
female CEOs in
three countries and
the overall weighted
average.

New Female CEO Study Provides Comparative HBDI Data

This may be the first time that female CEO data has been reported and diagnosed alongside male CEO data. While the female CEO data is only one-tenth of the male CEO data (76 women compared to 697 men), and represents only three countries instead of six, I feel it is interesting, important, and valid. Of the three countries involved, the United States, Germany, and England, 96% of the female CEO data comes from the United States and Germany.

The weighted average profiles of 697 male CEOs and the 76 female CEOs are shown separately (figure 18-6) as well as displayed on the same grid (figure 18-7) for comparison purposes.

As with the male CEOs, there is a general consensus of work element ranking among the 76 female CEOs in the *HBDI* database from the United States, Germany, and England.

Table 18-4. Rank-ordered Work Elements Most Preferred by Female CEOs in Study

Weightd Average (N=76)	USA (N=51)	Germany (N=22)	England (N=3)
1. Organization	1. Problem Solving	1. Organization	1. Administration
2. Interpersonal	2. Expressing Ideas	2. Conceptualizing	2. Planning
3. Problem Solving	3. Conceptualizing	3. Integration	3. Creativity
4. Conceptualizing	4. Interpersonal	4. Interpersonal	4. Implementation
5. Planning	5. Organization	5. Analytical	5. Interpersonal
6. Expressing Ideas	6. Analytical	6. Expressing Ideas	6. Organization
7. Analytical	7. Planning	7. Planning	7. Integration
8. Integration	8. Innovation	8. Implementation	8. Writing
9. Administration	9. Administration	9. Writing	9. Analytical
10. Creativity	10. Creativity	10. Problem Solving	10. Teaching/Training
11. Implementation	11. Writing	11. Creativity	11. Conceptualizing
12. Innovation	12. Integration	12. Administration	12. Expressing Ideas
13. Writing	13. Teaching/Training	13. Financial	13. Problem Solving
14. Teaching/Training	14. Implementation	14. Teaching/Training	14. Innovation
15. Financial	15. Financial	15. Innovation	15. Financial
16. Technical	16. Technical	16. Technical	16. Technical

Table 18-5. Women's Rank Ordering of Work Elements in Relation to Men

The top four work elements for females are the same as for males except in a different rank order:	Again, the next four work elements are identical to the male CEO listing except for the order:	This third tier has three out of four in common with those chosen by the male CEOs:	In this set ranked last, three out of the four work elements match those chosen by the male CEOs:
1. Organization	5. Planning	9. Administrative	13. Writing
2. Interpersonal Aspects	6. Expressing Ideas	10. Creative Aspects	14. Teaching/Training
3. Problem Solving	7. Analytical	11. Implementation	15. Financial Aspects
4. Conceptualizing	8. Integration	12. Innovation	16. Technical Aspects

Table 18-4 represents the rank order of *HBDI* work elements for the female CEO population in the study.

In view of these differing global male/female mental preferences, I feel it is remarkable that the male/female CEO data is so consistent. For example, consider the following lists of rank-ordered *HBDI* work elements in tables 18-6 and 18-7.

The four work elements for both male and female CEOs are identical, but in a slightly different order. *These represent personal mental work activities carried out largely by the CEOs themselves and not delegated to staff members.*

Figure 18-8.
HBDI profile norms
for entire *HBDI*
computer database.

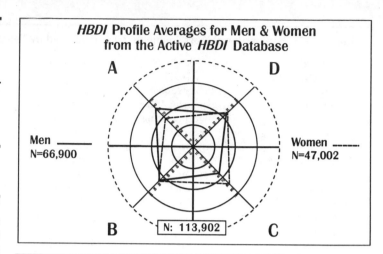

HBDI Profile Averages for Men & Women from the Active HBDI Database

Men ——
N=66,900

Women - - - - -
N=47,002

N: 113,902

**Conclusions
from CEO study
using the *HBDI***

The thinking style
preferences of both
male & female CEO's
are strikingly similar.
Both genders are well
distributed in the four
quadrants; however,
the weighted average
profiles shown in Fig.
18-6 display an over-
all "tilt" toward the
conceptual, future-ori-
ented, entrepreneur-
ial D quadrant.

CEO specific prefer-
ences displayed in
Fig. 18-6, while seem-
ingly similar to the
population at large as
shown in Fig. 18-8,
actually exhibit less
than half the signifi-
cant differences in
the A & C quadrant
preferences that oc-
cur in the general
population. This A/C
shift is characteristic
of males & females in
all occupations, in all
countries, and in all
cultures. This study
reveals that CEO's of
both genders are
more balanced and
less differientiated in
the A and C quad-
rants than any other
occupational group in
our database.

Table 18.6 Rank Ordering of the Top Four *HBDI* Work Elements

697 Male CEOs, Six Countries	76 Female CEOs, Three Countries
1. Problem Solving	1. Organizational Aspects
2. Organizational Aspects	2. Interpersonal Aspects
3. Interpersonal Aspects	3. Problem Solving
4. Conceptualizing	4. Conceptualizing

Table 18.7 Rank Ordering of the Bottom Four *HBDI* Work Elements

697 Male CEOs, Six Countries	76 Female CEOs, Three Countries
13. Administrative	13. Writing
14. Writing	14. Teaching/Training
15. Teaching/Training	15. Financial Aspects
16. Technical Aspects	16. Technical Aspects

Three out of four work elements are identical for the male
and female CEOs, but again in a slightly different order, except for Technical Aspects, which is in last place on both
male and female lists. *I believe these work elements represent
mental work activities that are largely delegated to other staff
members rather than being carried out by the CEOs themselves.*
It is apparent that the occupation of CEO requires a discrete set of interests, preferences, and competencies that are
generally consistent across country, cultural, and gender
boundaries. The Hay study reveals at least two universal CEO
competencies, and the study I conducted identifies four work

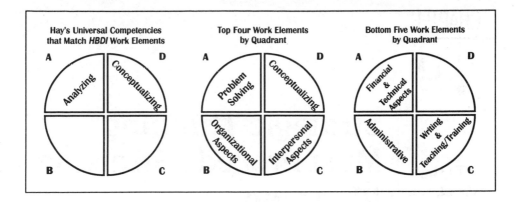

| Hay's Universal Competencies that Match *HBDI* Work Elements | Top Four Work Elements by Quadrant | Bottom Five Work Elements by Quadrant |

preferences and likely universal competencies for both male and female CEOs. The study of CEO *HBDI* data also identified six *least-preferred* work elements and likely *least-developed competencies* for both male and female CEOs. The lack of least-preferred work elements in the D quadrant is in alignment with the strong D-quadrant preferred composite profile of the 773 male and female CEOs in this study.

HBDI profile data confirms this by revealing significant differences in CEO work interests and priorities in different countries and cultures, even though the profile data is generally similar.

Figure 18-9.
The top four CEO work elements by quadrant compared to the bottom five.

So What?

■ The Hay study concludes that cultural factors play a significant part in differentiating CEO behavior in different parts of the world.

■ Successful CEOs must be flexible in their leadership style and be able to culturally adapt their business competencies to better align with local cultural norms.

■ The Herrmann study identifies a set of thinking style preferences and likely competencies that are consistent for both male and female CEOs in different countries. These appear to be personal mental activities carried out by the CEOs themselves.

■ While CEOs clearly adapt to local conditions and situations, there is an impressive consistency in thinking style preferences in the CEO occupation in many countries and cultures.

Strategic Thinking Must Precede Strategic Planning

"To stay ahead, you must have your next idea waiting in the wings."

—

Rosabeth Moss Kantor

Chapter Headlines

◆ Effective strategic planning requires an ability to think strategically.

◆ Strategic thinking is primarily a D-quadrant mental process.

◆ Strategic planning expertise and consultation is much more available than strategic thinking expertise and consultation.

◆ There are proven ways of tapping into and unleashing an individual's creative potential.

Strategic planning is not a walk in the park. It's actually a pretty difficult process and it requires a great deal of home-work, scanning of the environment and competitors, and research into customers' needs—and not only those that are served and already articulated, but those that are unarticulated and unserved. In the typical case, senior executives plunge into strategic planning because they think it's the thing to do, without ever really knowing what it is or how to do it. Many senior executives don't know what a strategic plan is nor how it differs from an operating plan. Strategic plans deal with products, markets, customers, and with the business envi-

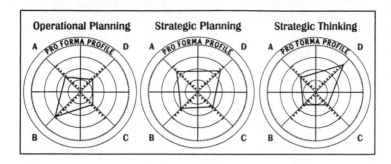

Figure 19-1.
Strategic thinking/
strategic planning
pro forma.

ronment in which those markets and customers are served. There are a number of experts on strategic planning but very few on strategic thinking. It is my view that strategic thinking must, in most cases, precede a strategic plan.

In the Whole Brain Model, strategic thinking is largely a D-quadrant process. Strategic thinking deals in futures, in patterns, in trends, in nuances that require an ability to sense emerging strategies in the middle of daily business chaos. It deals more in fuzzy logic than in the kind of logic that we use to analyze and diagnose. Where much of strategic planning can be described in facts and quantified in numbers, strategic thinking is best revealed in metaphor, through creative models, through doodles, sketches, and in intuitive flashes. Strategic thinking is largely conceptual, whereas most strategic plans have a visible structure and sequence. How, then, do executives and managers who are trained in the reality of the here and now, who quantify with facts and numbers, make sense out of a cloud of smoke or a handful of air? Well, it takes a totally different mind-set and you don't acquire it just by reading about it. In my experience, most managers need to go through a transition stage. They need to metamorphose into a mental state in which they place the same value on the insights emerging from a metaphoric model as they would on a spreadsheet of production numbers or on the diagnosis of a customer's annual report.

In working with a large number of managers and senior executives in the process of making this metamorphosis, I see the following capabilities as essential steps along the way of transition:

1. Strategic thinkers must understand their own mentality. That is, they need to know the reality of their own thinking preferences, which result in their everyday business behaviors. Managers are often capable of do-

"Imagination is the beginning of creation. We imagine what we desire; we will what we imagine; and at last we create what we will."

—

George Bernard Shaw

ing certain things very successfully and at the same time totally incapable of doing other things. A case in point is the ability to develop a strategy, or even to understand what a strategy is. There are some very successful business managers who cannot fathom an annual report, or for that matter, a financial statement.

2. Whatever their profile of mental preferences, strategic thinkers must be able to make use of their D-quadrant mental capabilities, at least situationally. They must have a sense of the future, be able to take a risk and to perceive patterns. They must be able to deal with ambiguities, to think in metaphor and to visualize. They must be able to think holistically—that is, to see the big picture. And lastly, they must be able to access, respect, be aware of, and trust the validity of their own intuition.

Now all these capabilities are available to each of us in our existing array of mental options, in different degrees. It's likely that we used these mental processes as children, but we began to be talked out of their validity by all the influential people in our lives. These forms of mental processing are not typically advocated in the business environment, but many successful CEOs use them frequently, whether they are aware of it or not.

For example, on a major transaction such as an acquisition, when the time for decision arrives and all the facts are in, the CEO leaves the cluttered boardroom and takes a short break out on the balcony. After a few minutes he or she comes back and says, "We're gonna go!" There are no new facts. That decision is based on an instant holistic review of all the factors involved, and an intuitive conclusion to take action.

3. Strategic thinkers need to get smart in areas where we are currently somewhat dumb. There are proven ways of tapping into and unleashing an individual's creative potential, previously self-censored intuition, or clarity of vision in seeing patterns.

4. Strategic thinkers need to be open to new ways of thinking and learning. An example of a critically important technique is to think metaphorically. One of my valued colleagues, Ayn Fox, developed a process in which participants in a learning session select an adult toy as an object that has attributes that describe themselves. For

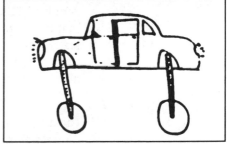

example, "I am like this kaleidoscope because I have many facets of interest that constantly change." Or, "I am like this electronic plasma sculpture because I, too, radiate energy in all directions."

I adapted an idea that came out of the Wharton School to use car metaphors to reveal a person's attitude about a company or a customer or an employee, by drawing little sketches of cars that reveal the kind of car he or she prefers, the model of that car, and how it is accessorized. You can use these sketches to draw forth a person's point of view with respect to his or her own company and a competitor, or to the company today and ten years into the future. These metaphors have the power of revealing unarticulated thoughts and therefore are extremely useful when thinking strategically.

5. Strategic thinking can be accessed through a technique called "metaphoric modeling." This is the use of creative materials to build a model of an organization or company that portrays the most significant attributes of that organization. This is not a literal model of the headquarters building, but rather a metaphoric construction that reveals attributes not previously articulated.

Imagine, for a moment, building a metaphoric model of your company, and next to it a model of your key customer. In between the two models are the connections (or absence of connections) that represent the relationships you have with your key customer. In the many hundreds of times that I have used this technique, I cannot recall a single instance in which the modelmaker did not discover something new and important about the company or the key customer. The process is very engaging.

6. Another process to add to the above is the pro forma

Figure 19-2.
Two examples of car metaphor drawings revealing different views from differing perspectives.

"Imagination is more important than knowledge."

—

Albert Einstein

profile technique (see Chapter 15). You start by guesstimating the profile of a company's annual report, vision statement, mission statement, and statement of core values. The profiles are then analyzed in terms of their alignment with each other and the corporate culture.

7. Try a guided fantasy that takes you five to ten years into the future to respond to key questions about the company's mission, products, markets, and customer expectations. Discuss the consequences of going out into the future with your colleagues.

As you can see, these are not the usual types of management activities such as gathering and analyzing data. The techniques are so indirect that they seem like a back road, but in reality they represent a shortcut to attaining the perceptions needed to build a strategic plan. What look like clouds of smoke that you can't grab are actually elements of solid understanding that defy rational processing.

A whole universe of techniques can be mixed and matched to apply to different business situations and make the transition of traditional thinkers to strategic thinkers a more likely outcome. The fresh perspectives that are gained through this transformation greatly benefit the more formal strategic planning processes that follow. The individuals involved are now much more sensitive to patterns, trends, nuances, and unarticulated needs and opportunities. They are able to better conceptualize and visualize existing relationships and future projections. They are, in a word, smarter about the process of strategic thinking and its follow-on action step, strategic planning.

"A moment's insight is sometimes worth a life's experience."

—

Oliver Wendall Holmes, Sr.

So What?

■ Strategic planning is a difficult process that often doesn't work because the mentality to conduct it is not understood and therefore not practiced.

■ The level of success with typical left mode executives is very high.

■ Awareness, familiarity, and particularly skill in D-quadrant strategic thinking are important ingredients in effective strategic planning.

Organizational Change

Chapter Headlines

- Creativity is a key to positive organizational change.

- The best solution to creative change involves the whole organization going creative.

- Positive, creative change can become continuous and keep an organization in a constant state of renewal.

> *"You must be the change you wish to see in the world."*
>
> —
>
> *Mahatma Gandhi*

As a new CEO, Jack Welch of General Electric once complained that trying to bring about change "was like running into a brick wall. I give all these speeches, but nothing ever happens."

In my experience, organizational change is best accomplished by "going creative." Change is frequently viewed as negative. It's uncomfortable to change the status quo. "We're doing great. Who needs it?" Even though change is inexorable and must happen if the organization is to survive, it is still fiercely resisted, particularly by the bureaucracy. However, if we change the context of change and think of it in terms of creativity, a lot of the negativity simply evaporates. In contrast to change, creativity is thought of as positive. It's reaching out to solve problems, to make improvements, to resolve leadership issues, not to cause them.

This is not to say that "going creative" eliminates all the barriers to change. Some people need to move past the stage of denying that change is necessary. Others need to move past the resentment, discomfort, and even anger, that their

Figure 20-1.
Going creative
change model.

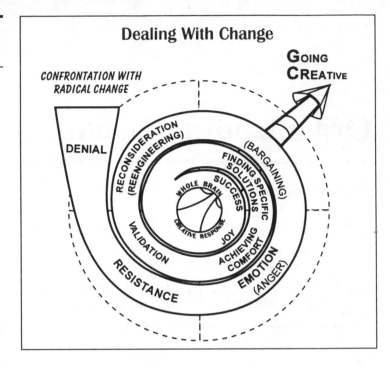

Dealing With Change

CONFRONTATION WITH
RADICAL CHANGE

DENIAL

RECONSIDERATION
(REENGINEERING)

(BARGAINING)
FINDING SPECIFIC
SOLUTIONS

SUCCESS

WHOLE BRAIN
CREATIVE RESPONSE

VALIDATION

JOY

ACHIEVING
COMFORT

EMOTION
(ANGER)

RESISTANCE

GOING
CREATIVE

*"Every day
the world
turns
upsidedown
on someone
who thought
they were
sitting on top
of it."*

—

Glenn Tullman

lives are being affected by the change process. But these emotions are relatively temporary, even though they are distinct parts of a process. The onset of change in an organization is like the death of an individual. Elizabeth Kubler-Ross, a renowned expert on death and dying, describes death as a process that starts with denial. Once past that stage there is anger—why me? Once past anger, we enter a stage of acceptance. "O.K. It's going to happen, so how can I allow it to happen with grace, humor, and dignity?" It's at this stage in the change process that creativity offers the best alternative.

Now that we've accepted the fact that it's *going* to happen and *must* happen, let's have it happen creatively. Let's make the best of it, which means not just tolerating change, but through creativity, making it a positive, constructive process that reaches a conclusion that is better for everybody than the prior condition.

We are really dealing here with two processes. One is the change process and the other is the creative process that provides solutions to change. Because they are processes, they are describable and teachable. These characteristics greatly reduce the personalization of change and therefore its emotional content.

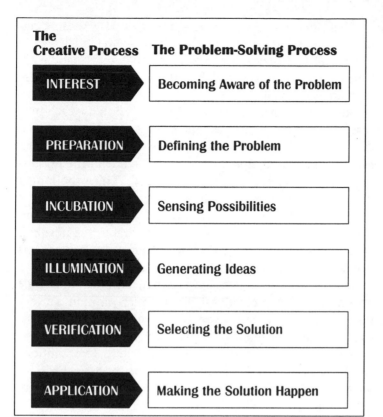

The Creative Process   **The Problem-Solving Process**

The Creative Process	The Problem-Solving Process
INTEREST	Becoming Aware of the Problem
PREPARATION	Defining the Problem
INCUBATION	Sensing Possibilities
ILLUMINATION	Generating Ideas
VERIFICATION	Selecting the Solution
APPLICATION	Making the Solution Happen

Figure 20-2.
Creative process chart.

Creativity itself is a process. It starts with interest and understanding—*interest* in the situation that requires change and *understanding* that change is inevitable and is, in the final analysis, the only constant. The next stage is preparation. This is the information gathering stage where the reasons for change become fact based. Moving the need for change from personal opinion to quantifiable fact removes much of the emotion from the process.

Next comes the stage of incubation. This is the period when the facts requiring change are contemplated in a relatively emotion-free climate so that idea generation can take place in a positive frame of mind. Sooner or later, this incubation stage leads to an AHA!, which can blossom into a possible solution. Illumination can be more than just a single idea. It represents a stage of the process where alternative solutions are identified and developed into real possibilities. These possibilities then need to be verified as realistic solutions to the change issue. When verification occurs then application of the potential solutions can begin.

These two processes, change and creativity, when diagnosed from the perspective of the Whole Brain Model, clearly involve all four quadrants (see figure 20-2 and Chapter 23, "Managing Creativity Through Multiple Processes"). Because both are describable, rational processes, a foundation is provided for the needed actions to take place. Because each process has a distinct orderliness and sequence of steps required, there is a structure to build the rational foundation on. Because of this foundation and structure, many of the reasons requiring change become depersonalized. This is no longer the whim of an individual in management, but rather the reality of the business situation that demands action. And while both processes engage all four quadrants, the imaginative idea-generation stage leading to alternative solutions is primarily a D-quadrant function.

Once viable alternatives have been determined, the whole organization can go creative. That is, it can move into a very positive, energetic, and even playful community exercise. Every member of the organization can be purposefully involved in the creative change process. Alternative solutions can be selected that represent a win for most of those involved. When thought of in this way, creative change can become an annual event. You don't have to wait around for change to be required for survival. You assume that change is always needed and that we need to find out now what particular aspect of change is the current priority, and then get on with it. We have annual budgets; we have annual performance reviews; we also need to annualize the change process. It is not a major conceptual leap from continuous improvement to continuous change management.

So What?

- Change carried out creatively transforms a negative need into a positive outcome.

- An entire organization can be inspired by its leaders to "go creative."

- By changing, an organization can avoid dying.

- Change is best thought of as a process involving the entire organization.

PART IV

Whole Brain Creativity and Innovation

Applying Creativity and Innovation in Organizations

Chapter Headlines

♦ Creativity is part of the human condition and takes many forms.

♦ Creativity and innovation are different in ways important to business success.

♦ Unleashing creativity can make the winning difference, but there are consequences for the organization's culture.

♦ A lack of understanding of creativity results in waste of money and missed opportunities.

> *"The things we fear most in organizations—fluctuations, disturbances, imbalances—are the primary source of creativity."*
>
> *Margaret J. Wheatley*

Creativity is part of the human condition. It is an important aspect of life from early childhood to old age. It takes many forms; from child rearing to learning languages, to arts and crafts, to cooking, to gardening, to composing, dancing, writing, problem solving, and inventing. These are just a few of the many aspects of life that help define the domain of creativity. Out of this list, the words *problem solving* and *inventing* strongly suggest a business application of the creative process. It is the business application of creativity that is the focus of this chapter.

In describing what creativity is and how it works, I will often use the word *innovation* in partnership with *creativity*. The reason is that many businesspeople use the term *innovation* in place of *creativity* because they feel more comfortable with the former term. Actually, I believe there are significant differences between creativity and innovation. I will present an argument that strongly suggests that business needs both, but they are, in terms of process, a bit different and I will describe what those differences are. If your competitors have the same products, the same markets, the same customers, and the same delivery systems as you do, unleashing the creativity of your organization can make the winning difference.

Unleashing Creativity

It is a foregone conclusion that business executives would like to unleash the creativity they are sure is locked up in their organizations. They talk about it in staff meetings, write headlines about it in the plant news, and proclaim it as a company goal at the annual meeting. How many of you have heard the CEO say: "What this company needs to do is to unleash the creativity of its employees"?

"If you want to succeed, double your failure rate."

—

Thomas Watson

Just for openers, unleashing creativity means that risks will have to be taken. Mistakes will be made, rules will have to be changed, and the status quo will be challenged. In fact, business assumptions will have to be reconsidered and leadership concepts will have to be altered. You can count on the fact that none of these consequences are what leadership had in mind. All they wanted was the fruits of creativity, not the challenges to the status quo that are integral to the creative process.

There are consequences to unleashing creativity that are often not considered. The creative process is not "business as usual." It's like having 100 or 1,000 or 10,000 tightly wound springs suddenly releasing their energy into the organization at random. The business leader underestimates the power of creativity and tries to manage and control it. This approach is effective only if you want to inhibit the natural flow of creativity. In order to cultivate creativity, you have to understand the process.

A good metaphor for the creative process in the brain is zigzag lightning. This implies freedom within the cranial cavity for the creative spark to occur. People must be free to think in whatever ways allow the process to unfold. A person who is mentally handcuffed by the constraints of his or her work will be less able to think and function creatively. For successful results to be achieved, full permission for independent action must be granted. You may have to jump through some hoops to convince the resisters that this is worth the effort, but once you do, you can expect the kind of results that the following anecdote reveals.

Creativity Surfacing in Day-to-Day Business Situation

The story is told by Alison Strickland, a leading expert on creativity and one of our creativit y training leaders. There was a business that, like many, was short of ideal office space and also short of computers. The available office space was in a converted factory loft where there were support columns that got in the way of an attractive office layout. Most offices ended up with columns in the wrong place and therefore were considered undesirable by people who had a choice, and so they went begging. At this time the company also had a critical shortage of personal computers. It seemed that everybody wanted an attractive, pillar-free office *and* a computer. The people in charge tried several solutions, but nothing seemed to work until this *creative solution* was offered: Anybody who selected an office with a pillar in it was given a personal computer installed in that office. Both problems were solved simultaneously. With the incentive of having a computer to use, the unattractive space suddenly became premium office space. This is an excellent example of win/win creative problem solving.

The Creative Climate Developed at the DuPont Spruance, VA, Plant: A Case Study

Over a three-year period, DuPont implemented a plan to increase the creativity and innovation in several of its plants. In their effort to "go creative," several of the technical managers there got interested in our whole brain approach to problem solving and sent a number of their researchers to our Applied Creative Thinking (ACT) workshop. After the

"My definition, then, of the creative process is that it is the emergence in action of a novel relational product, growing out of the uniqueness of the individual on the one hand, and the materials, events, people, or circumstances of his life on the other."

—

Carl Rogers

program had been implemented, I was invited to present the fundamentals of the Whole Brain Model and Whole Brain Creativity to upper management at an annual meeting. At our suggestion, they created a videotape with comments from several staff members and managers who had benefited from all aspects of the program. In addition to our ACT workshops and customized programs, DuPont made use of several creativity experts to provide a well-rounded approach. The following excerpt from the tape is a mixture of explanatory comments and candid remarks from those involved in the program. It is a good illustration of many of the suggestions I make in this chapter for implementing a successful program.

"Creativity is not a special gift of the few, but rather a common event of the many."

—

D. and J. Sanders

Creativity...Innovation—these words have been said before, but they've taken on a whole new meaning to the professionals of Kevlar Technical at the DuPont Spruance plant.

"People are excited about coming to work and doing their jobs, and seeing how they can do it a lot better."

"I'm hooked on creativity and innovation."

"I view creativity as looking at the same thing that everybody else looks at and seeing it differently."

With emphasis placed on the value of increased education, environment, and reinforcement in the workplace, people at Kevlar Technical and other site functions were given the space they needed to improve their performance and were exposed to an education in creativity and innovation.

"If you want to make your organization more innovative, it has to start with the leadership of your organization. It has to start with your management."

"People were static in the DuPont way of doing things but when they realized management did have value for innovation and creativity, slowly they have opened up....It helps to give people the skills and the techniques to learn their creative problem-solving process."

One day, the plant was faced with a major problem. It needed creative and innovative problem solving right then. Here's an account of the situation and how a solution was found as told by the problem solver himself:

"We were having a crisis problem in our plant...some vacuum hoses were becoming delaminated...they were collapsing, the vacuum was lost, and the continuity was terrible. We spent roughly 18 hours fighting hard on that problem. It was tough. I'll never forget that. I got home, the problem still bothering me. I went to bed...stayed up all night with the problem still throbbing like a toothache...Finally I fell asleep."

Floyd, the Spruance plant employee telling the story, goes on to explain how he saw the solution to the problem in a dream.

"It hit me. One of the ways to prevent hoses from collapsing is to put a spring inside."

Floyd envisioned an industrial-strength Slinky, and as he learned at ACT, he got up around 5:00 a.m. to capture his idea on a piece of paper so he wouldn't forget it. That morning Floyd told his group leader, Jean, about the Slinky idea.

So Floyd comes to me and says, "All we've got to do is to get this Slinky—you know, those Slinkys that look like this, and I'm going to stick it inside that pipe. That's going to solve your problems." It absolutely did. We must have had ten engineers trying to reformulate those hoses, reformulate the glue...trying everything and having no success at all. Floyd solved the problem just like that with his Slinky.

Because Floyd Ragsdale believed in his dream and came up with an innovative solution to an impossible task, Dave Tanner, his technical director, presented Floyd with a Creative Thinking Award in the presence of plant management. The segment ends with this statement:

In managing a truly great global organization, leadership is the guiding light toward its success. Jean Prideaux (Floyd's manager) is one such leader.

The videotape goes on to give other examples of how DuPont's program has had a direct and positive affect upon dealing with impossible tasks. Because of the necessary bottom-line mentality of business, it is often difficult to sell an organization on the benefits of creativity and innovation until they've seen positive results. This is a classic Catch-22. Here are some other classic obstacles to prepare for as you contemplate going creative.

Breaking Down the Barriers to Creativity

When it comes to solving multifunctional problems, borders between corporate functions should disappear. For example, solving a product design problem that occurs during the manufacturing process involves both the engineering function and the manufacturing function. Often an administrator from one function will be charged with relaying communication from one functional department to the other. This type of project coordination constantly interrupts and distracts the problem solvers. Because the information is traveling through a third party, misunderstandings and inefficiency are the result. It allows bureaucracy to block a process which, by its very nature, must be free-flowing in order to take place—free from functional barriers.

Subjecting creative functioning to standard procedures is like throwing a monkey wrench into the gears. This scenario can be easily avoided with a bit of planning and cooperation. Instead of the problem solvers working independently of each other and communicating through cumbersome corporate channels, a crossfunctional creative team can be formed to work specifically on the problem. Given the popularity of specialized task teams, knowing how to effectively construct crossfunctional teams will be a requirement for any manager.

I recall a large tire company that converted an obsolete factory building into its new product development center. The architectural design featured offices and laboratory areas that were highly structured, stark, shiny spaces that were conceived more as showplaces than as creative work spaces conducive to messy experimenting. Neatness was the order of the day. There could be no papers on desks, no books out of their library shelves, no materials to obstruct the mirror-shiny desk surfaces. The company's primary product—tires—was considered too dirty to be allowed in these pristine spaces.

Creativity is fundamentally a messy process. The more you structure it, order it, and routinize it, the more you will shut it down. You will recognize these management actions as primarily left mode behaviors. They result from A- and B-quadrant-preferred thinking that leaves out the needed contribution of the right mode. These are just some of the reasons why an understanding of the nature and source of creativity is so vital to its application in business and industry. The $100,000,000 invested in the conversion of the old factory is only a fraction of the losses that the business incurred. The big loss was in the missed opportunities that resulted from shutting down creativity instead of unleashing it.

So how can you be supportive of the creative process? Given the typical corporate culture, you may have to move slowly and carefully. Time and time again, our experience has shown that if you can just convince the organization to take a risk by running a workshop, bringing in creativity experts, or engaging in the creative process, success will emerge.

However, you may encounter some problems along the way. The listed consequences in figure 21-1 are only a sampling of the possible results of unleashing the creative potential of an organization. In a very real sense, giving an organization permission to be creative changes the rules of the road that may have existed for years, if not decades. The culture of the organization must be carefully reoriented to

• Risks will have to be taken.	...You bet, that's how creativity is defined!
• Mistakes will be made.	...Grant permission to make them.
• Rules may have to be changed.	...Eliminate or change unnecessary rules.
• Status quo will be challenged.	...Encourage and reward challenging the status quo.
• Assumptions will be reconsidered.	...Have management take the initiative.
• Concepts will be altered.	...Work toward aligning them with a renewed vision.
• Permission for independent action will be required.	...Management buy-in and reward for this is essential.
• Functional boundaries will be breached.	...Boundaries that are retained will be porous.
• Organizational relationships will change.	...Flexibility will need to be modeled and encouraged.
• Work content and procedures will be rethought.	...Work redesign and even reinvention will be initiated.
• Bureaucratic walls will be lowered.	...Bureaucracies will not be tolerated.
• Counterproductive traditions will be reexamined.	...Not just reexamined, but abandoned.
• Accelerated change will take place.	...Management will have to take the lead in pushing for and supporting needed change.

accommodate such significant changes; if this is not done, then a lot of people may be put in jeopardy because they will be playing a new game under obsolete rules. Some companies, such as Lockheed, set up a *skunk works* (a specialized facility) to contain the new creative behavior within a specified geographic location. Under these conditions, a creative champion can unleash to his or her heart's content without confronting the not-yet-ready cultures that exist in the more traditional parts of the company.

Figure 21-1.
Listing of the Consequences of Unleashing Creativity.

Creativity in the Corporation: A Case History

Back in 1976 we were, at least in the world of business, in the dark ages of creativity and innovation. Even the word *creativity* was unacceptable business language. It conjured up thoughts of flaky, impractical, unreliable dreamers who had no sense of the bottom line and who were all too eager to waste resources on nutty ideas and crazy schemes. Pragmatism was the watchword. Bottom-line outcomes were the target. *Innovation* was a much more acceptable word.

When I proposed a creative thinking workshop for General Electric, I was advised that it would be inappropriate and politically incorrect to use the word *creativity* in the title of the workshop. It was therefore called, Productive Problem Solving. This was considered a title in alignment with the corporate culture of the time. When the workshop became a success and the company newsletter wrote a cover story describing it, the two key words, *brain* and *creativity*

"There is no reason for any individual to have a computer in his home."

—

Ken Olson

were deliberately avoided by the editorial writer. Even today, only a small percentage of the books written on creativity describe it as a brain-based process.

Creativity and Innovation: Similarities, Differences, and Why You Need Both

I think of creativity and innovation in both similar and in differentiated terms. They are both mental. They both add value. They both involve process. They both have elements of each other embedded in them, but there are significant differences that those who apply these processes need to know in order to optimize the added value each can contribute.

"What is now proved was once only imagined."

—

William Blake

I see creativity as grounded in originality. The process starts with a bare desk, an empty notebook, an unrecognized beginning. Remember such inventions as the light bulb, television, or radio? These are all examples of new creations. In sharp contrast, I think of innovation as having a beginning grounded in already-invented products or processes. Therefore, I see innovation as building on existing, already-created concepts, ideas, processes, and devices. Innovation then is more in the nature of elaboration, extension, building upon existing results of previous creative activity. Both processes can come up with new and novel ideas, but the needed elements of originality are missing from the process of innovation. An example might be an original piece of music that exists in the form of melody and accompaniment. Up to this point in the process, we are dealing with a product of creativity. When a music arranger elaborates on the original melody and accompaniment and develops a full-blown orchestral arrangement, this is a product of innovation. The original creative element of the finished product is there in its entirety, but now there has been given to it additional value in the form of an arrangement which brings in additional instruments, and additional musical patterns woven around the original melody.

Another example is an unusual kaleidoscope called Illusion. This breakthrough design was developed by Cozy Baker, author of *Through the Kaleidoscope and Beyond*. The design consists of two preexisting elements. One is a kaleidoscope body that is based on the original creative concept of a kaleidoscope. The second element is a clear plexiglass magic wand with colorful sparkles floating in a thick clear gel. Both the wand and the kaleidoscope are preexisting products that have different applications. Both of them are free-standing creative products. Innovation comes into play when we adapt the kaleidoscope with a receptacle into which the magic wand is placed and the result is a quantum leap in kaleidoscopic effectiveness. Two separate creative elements are combined to create a new innovative purpose for the magic wand and the kaleidoscope.

Other examples that come to mind vary widely across our culture and environment. One would be a 747 airplane. The first model was an enormously creative and complicated design. It was an instant success in its original form; however, different applications demanded innovative changes such as reconfiguring the inside of the airplane for use as a cargo carrier, adding an upper deck for greater passenger capacity, and customizing the design for the president's Air Force One airplane. Another application equipped the 747 to airlift the space shuttles from Edwards Air Force Base to Cape Canaveral. All of these modifications had creative elements to them, but they were primarily innovations around a preexisting creative accomplishment. They did not start from a bare desk; they started with an existing product and were driven by application opportunities or customer needs.

In the domain of semiconductors, adapting a 1-inch wafer to a 4-, 8-, and 16-inch wafer has elements of creativity in each of the leaps of size, but fundamentally this is innovation around the original notion of a silicon chip. A strictly creative invention would entail a completely different concept— for example, something that did what chips now do, but better, easier, and cheaper. This is the kind of breakthrough creativity can achieve that is beyond the fundamental limits of innovation. In order to achieve a quantum leap in results, you need both creativity *and* innovation.

When you consider that most businesses need to continuously elaborate on and extend their existing product line *as well as* create new ones, using both creativity and innovation is clearly an advantage. This requires a paradigm shift. Innovation occurs largely within the existing paradigm of a product or a process, whereas creativity can be in a totally different paradigm. Since it is not bound by the past, it is entirely original, with a starting point that is based upon a new need or problem to be solved. Creativity can be a fresh concept or a breakthrough idea resulting from experimentation or just playing around.

Original versus Applied Thinking

If you step back from people's thinking behavior, I think there are two categories that stand out in sharp relief. One category is that of original thinker. These are people who are frequently on the edge of something new. It is not only a style of thinking or a way of thinking. I believe it to be the result of a personal need. Some individuals simply have to come up with original thoughts in order to be fulfilled.

On the other hand, there are people whose satisfaction comes from connecting up the original thoughts of others in ongoing applications of their own thinking process. They are less interested in originating ideas and more turned on by interconnecting and applying the ideas of others to meet a given situation.

It is interesting to observe these two styles in action. Person #1, the original thinker, is coming up with a stream of ideas on a given topic and person #2, the connector, is seeing these new ideas as pieces of a jigsaw puzzle that suddenly fit and bridge together two thoughts that have been adrift but now are interconnected and whole.

These are only two of the many styles of thinking we need in everyday business. They fit so neatly together that it's almost symbiotic. Original thinkers are often so prolific that they place little value on their thoughts as they spill out in ordinary conversation. The interconnectors, on the other hand, are constantly circling around the conversations searching for morsels of information that interconnect the loose ends of their own open thought processes. In many cases they serve as instant appliers of what is otherwise lost in the informal process of daily interaction.

In the domain of creativity, there are those who are idea generators and there are those who are problem finders. Idea generators have a special knack for throwing off original ideas that have no particular home in terms of potential solutions. They are free radicals, so to speak. In contrast, problem finders are constantly identifying unsolved problems that need fixing, although they are not personally capable of coming up with potential solutions. Again, a potentially symbiotic relationship.

"Humanity cannot forget its dreamers; it cannot let their ideals fade and die; it knows them as the realities which it shall one day see and know."

—

James Allen

Every once in a while we find a single individual who is capable of thinking in both these different styles in given situations. He or she is not only the original thinker but also the interconnector, not only the idea generator, but also the problem finder. I can't imagine a business in which this type of thinking would not represent added value.

Library research reveals that for every book with innovation in the title, there are 100 with the word creativity in the title. While both innovation and creativity are processes, there are ten times more creative processes than there are innovative processes. It is my judgment that the body of creative literature, processes, tools, and techniques is many times the length, breadth, and depth of the body of work that comprises innovation.

In general, I am underwhelmed by the level of knowledge of creativity in American business today. The body of creative work that exists in the corporate setting is simply an unknown in most American business organizations. It has been avoided by many leaders because the word *creativity* conjures up an image that is in conflict with a down-to-earth corporate culture. In the absence of that knowledge, many well-intentioned but largely untutored leaders take the innovative fork in the road rather than seeking the dual highway of creativity and innovation. The net result is that they are limiting themselves to only one path of success. Creativity and innovation are companions on the dual path of success for American business. Both are there to be understood, to be learned, to be taught and applied. The successful corporations of the future will be those that take competitive advantage of this dual opportunity and train their employees in both creativity and innovation.

> *"The future never just happened. It was created."*
>
> —
>
> *Will and Ariel Durant*

So What?

- There are consequences to unleashing creativity that require a change in business assumptions and leadership concepts.

- Creative climates can be developed to encourage everyday creativity to solve troublesome business problems.

- Such creative climates allow crossfunctional teams to break down traditional functional barriers.

22

The Brain Is the Source of Creativity

Chapter Headlines

♦ Idea generation is a neural event and therefore the brain must be the source of creativity.

♦ The brain is an electrochemical organ that produces electrical brain wave states that are precise, measurable, and characteristic of humans.

♦ The theta state is a natural brain state conducive of creativity.

♦ Neurotransmitters fuel synaptic activity, which is the source of idea generation.

Here is a brief introduction to the creative process as it occurs in the brain so that you'll know specifically what I mean when I say the brain is the source of creativity. Creative thought processes are the result of specialized mental modes that respond situationally to life's experiences. Idea generation is, in fact, a neural event. Neural transmitters streaming across the synaptic gap convey the electrochemical elements of an idea in formation. While we don't know precisely how ideas occur, we do know they arise in specialized parts of the brain which, through massive interconnections, can come in contact with other ideas and together form the basis of synergy.

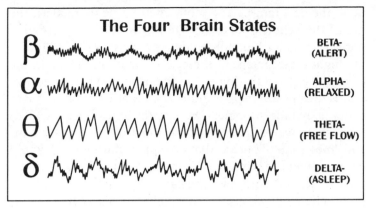

Figure 22-1.
Four key brain waves common to all human beings.

The Four Brain States

β   BETA-
    (ALERT)

α   ALPHA-
    (RELAXED)

θ   THETA-
    (FREE FLOW)

δ   DELTA-
    (ASLEEP)

Plugging into Your Brain

Although every brain is unique, all brains are electrochemical. Electrical brain waves supply a convenient measure of the brain's operating status at any given time. Just as we are a coalition of the four thinking selves, (rational, safekeeping, feeling, and experimental), we are equipped with four brain wave states: beta, alpha, theta, delta—each one specialized for a particular kind of neural activity. The more we understand these brain wave states, the more we are able to consciously engage in them to enhance our thinking, through such methods as biofeedback. Brain wave states are defined by electrical frequencies measured by cycles per second, or by Hertz.

Beta represents the aroused, alert state. The frequency ranges between 13 Hertz and about 30 Hertz. The higher the number, the more aroused or alert the brain state. *Alpha* represents the absence of arousal. This is a calm, meditative state and is defined by brain wave frequencies of 9 to 12 Hertz. The next state, *theta*, represents a very open, free flow creative state. The brain wave frequencies for theta are 5 to 8 Hertz. The final brain wave state is *delta*. Delta represents deep, dreamless sleep. The frequency range for delta is .5 to 4 Hertz.

My early experiments with brain wave states measured by an electroencephalograph demonstrated that all of these brain waves are typically present at any given time but vary greatly in terms of distribution of beta, alpha, theta, and delta brain waves. When a person is fully alert and engaged in performing a task, a high percentage of that person's brain waves will be in the beta range. The more intense, the more alert, the higher the frequency of those beta waves. At the other end of the spectrum an individual who is deeply asleep will have the highest percentage of their brain waves in delta and the deeper the sleep, the lower the frequency. When that individual dreams, every 90 minutes the coalition of brain waves shifts to include an increasing amount of theta waves. It is these theta waves that introduce some of the fantasy trips and "movies in the head" that take place during REM (rapid eye movement) dreaming. When we are in deep contemplation or idea incubation we are likely in an alpha state. Later in this chapter I will discuss in detail how each of these states corresponds to the stages of the creative process. I have just addressed the *electro-* aspect of *electrochemical*; now I will introduce the chemical aspect that fuels our synaptic activity.

The Chemistry of Creativity

Creative and innovative thinking work best when the brain is up to the challenge of increased synaptic activity. Whether you are feeling sharp or dull at any given moment can be due to the chemistry in your head. Some people refer to their bad brain days as, "I'm just not thinking straight today." Other times the ideas and thoughts just keep coming, and you may think to yourself, "I'm really sharp today." And when you are really on top of it, you may not only feel turned on, but also creative and smart.

This is how it works. The brain is an electrochemical organ. Neurotransmitters are the chemical agents that cause synapses to take place, which in turn produce electrical potentials, which together with the chemical reactions, power the brain in its thinking processes. There are about 50 neurotransmitters, such as serotonin, which stimulate synaptic interchange. Each neurotransmitter has a matching receptor that's like a lock and a key. If there are no matching receptors, then the neuron-to-neuron synapse will not take place. When the synapse does not take place, we are less sharp. When synapses do take place, we have the potential for being smart and creative. The greater the synaptic activity, the more likely that ideation will take place.

In order for the chemistry of the brain to work, the brain must be properly fed. What we eat and drink fuel not only our bodies but our brains as well. There are so-called smart

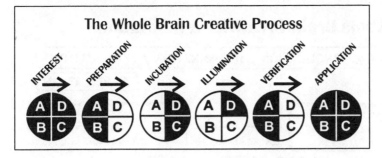

The Whole Brain Creative Process

INTEREST → PREPARATION → INCUBATION → ILLUMINATION → VERIFICATION → APPLICATION

Figure 22-2.
Creative process correlation with four-quadrant model.

foods and drinks that stimulate our mental activity by fueling the neurotransmitters that are the basis of synaptic interaction. Choline is such a neurotransmitter. The greater the flow of neurotransmitters, the greater the synaptic activity.

The detailed inner process of synergy that takes place naturally in the brain is a key characteristic of both creative and innovative thought. Although these two processes have a lot in common, it is important to discuss their individual uses.

Whole Brain Creativity and Innovation

Most descriptions of creativity refer to it as a strictly right brained process. The model of applied creativity and innovation I will describe here is a process from concept to completion and takes advantage of all of the brain's specialized modes. When researching creative processes, I found that the stages defined by Graham Wallas fit my vision of a whole brain creative thinking process. The specialized characteristics of each quadrant and of each mode of the Whole Brain Model are applied in various combinations as the process takes place. A missing quadrant or mode will tend to stall or even shut down the entire process. In order to apply Wallas's original concept to my own, I added two elements which are necessary for the process to be successful and complete. They are interest and application. *Interest* gets the process off the ground. *Application* ensures that the ideas aren't left up in the air but are implemented to solve real problems.

The elements of the expanded process as I apply it are as follows: interest, preparation, incubation, illumination, verification, and application.

The second stage of the process is preparation. This step requires information gathering, analysis of those facts, and

"We may discover that creativity is a common human trait."

—

Isaac Asimov

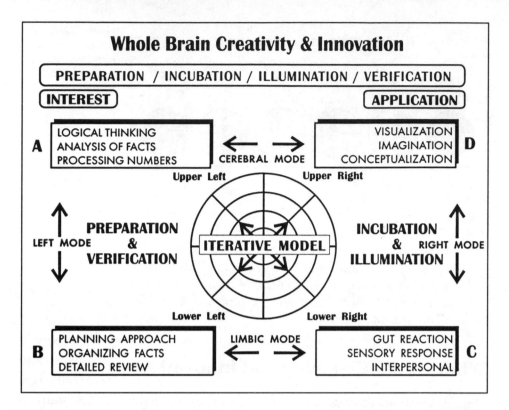

Whole Brain Creativity & Innovation

PREPARATION / INCUBATION / ILLUMINATION / VERIFICATION

INTEREST

APPLICATION

A — LOGICAL THINKING / ANALYSIS OF FACTS / PROCESSING NUMBERS
CEREBRAL MODE
D — VISUALIZATION / IMAGINATION / CONCEPTUALIZATION

Upper Left — Upper Right

LEFT MODE — PREPARATION & VERIFICATION
ITERATIVE MODEL
INCUBATION & ILLUMINATION — RIGHT MODE

Lower Left — Lower Right

B — PLANNING APPROACH / ORGANIZING FACTS / DETAILED REVIEW
LIMBIC MODE
C — GUT REACTION / SENSORY RESPONSE / INTERPERSONAL

Figure 22-3.
Whole Brain
Creativity and
Innovation Model.

the chronological sequencing of them into an accurate statement of the problem.

Consider this situation. You work for a computer hardware manufacturer and you just can't get excited about the design of a monitor for general use. However, your company has recently been open to new applications to give them a competitive advantage. For the last couple of days, you've been thinking about your nephew whose vision is severely impaired and who loves to work on the computer. You have the interest and therefore strong motivation to tackle this problem: creating a computer set up for people with vision problems. In the preparation stage, definition of the exact problem to be solved needs to be stated. Let's say it is "How to improve the readability of type and images on screen for the visually impaired." An analysis of this population's needs would have to be made, along with an assessment of ways a monitor could meet these needs better than what is currently available. The preparation phase requires the application of A- and B-quadrant, left mode thinking characteristics.

The next phase of the process involves incubation. This

is where the brain, now having a problem to work on and motivated by personal interest, processes that problem in both conscious and unconscious ways that allow the brain's natural problem-solving processes to be engaged. This incubation stage of the creative process is clearly a right mode mental activity, making use of intuitive and conceptual understanding to bring potential solutions up to a conscious level. It often works best when we are totally disengaged from the task at hand and are relaxed or dabbling with something else.

Continuing with our problem example, after you've defined the problem and collected the facts, you let all this information simmer, so to speak. This is where your brain makes connections as you shop in the bookstore, looking at large-print books and reading aides. You are not consciously looking for solutions in this stage; you are simply going about your day in a relaxed manner.

Sometimes incubation can take a few hours, or you will continue to incubate as the preparation process continues. This creative problem-solving process does not happen in a neat, chronological manner. An iteration between stages is often necessary before ideas begin to emerge.

The next stage is called illumination, which is frequently referred to as the AHA! or EUREKA! event in the creative process. This is where ideas suddenly pop into our minds as potential solutions, sometimes as an accompaniment to the theta brain waves we experience while daydreaming. The illumination stage integrates all the previous aspects of the creative process that took place in the interest, preparation, and incubation stages. And through integration, synthesis, and synergy, ideas present themselves in response to everything that happened along the way.

Let's go back to the computer monitor project. You have an extra monitor that is torn apart, and you start experimenting at home after dinner. Getting frustrated, you decide to take a break and play with your flight simulator program, equipped with a joy stick. Once you've crashed for the last time, you go to bed and fall into a dreamy state. You dream about your nephew playing on the computer with the flight simulator joystick. Then you notice he's not playing flight simulator but zooming in on certain parts of the screen. He adjusts the colors and the contrast to optimize the image. Then you wake up, with fragmented memories of this dream. All of a sudden it clicks. You grab a piece of paper and jot down "joystick controls image size, buttons control contrast and color intensity...astigmatism correction...high-dot pitch...voice supported..." In a minute your mind is racing, trying to figure out how you can apply the control of a joystick to this computer setup for the visually impaired.

The next needed stage is verification, which requires a hard-nosed, objective review of the potential solution in relationship to the facts of the original problem. Does this new idea have any relationship to the original problem you are attempting to solve? Verification is necessary, since the idea generating activity that results from the illumination process can come up with all manner of potential ideas, some of which have no relationship at all to the problem at hand. They may, in fact, be solutions to problems that occurred some time ago, or could be solutions to problems that have not yet been defined. So a critical assessment of the appropriateness of the potential solution needs to take place before it is applied. This is again a left mode process that takes advantage of the critical, diagnostic, analytic capabilities of the A quadrant.

"Without this playing with fantasy, no creative work has ever yet come to birth. The debt we owe to the play of imagination is incalculable."

—

Carl Jung

Now that you've got some potential solutions to this special computer setup, you critically assess its relationship to the problem. Can this joystick type of control be integrated into a standard computer setup? If an image can be enlarged, the resolution optimized, and color and intensity be easily controlled, will this improve the quality of images and readability by a measurable amount? Or does this concept lend itself to a totally different application? You think this solution will work for your needs, but you have to check it out.

Once a solution is verified, application becomes the next step in the process. This is primarily a B-quadrant activity. As you attempt initial applications, you may need to revisit the verification process. Does the potential solution fit the original problem, and is the application viable? Remember Edison and his hundreds of failed attempts. Does the thing work? What do you need to do to make it work? And when you finally get it to work, does the idea solve the original problem?

As an example of a process that emerged in the illumination stage and didn't pass the verification process, consider a specific adhesive developed by 3M. In trying to create an adhesive that was very thin but extremely strong, they developed a glue that was easily applied but wasn't permanent enough for their purposes. Later on, someone discovered a perfect application for this faulty adhesive: a nonpermanent adhesive to adhere memos to doors instead of tape. Voila! The birth of Post-it notes. Even though this particular adhesive didn't meet the requirements for the original application, another AHA! pointed to a completely different application that could have been easily discarded.

Diagnosing this creative process has only one overarching conclusion: *all quadrants and modes are involved, and the degree to which all of the brain contributes to the process is the extent to which the process is successful.* Leaving out a critical step or an essential mental process will adversely affect the viability of the creative solution or idea.

While these are completely natural processes and often take place without our really being aware of the steps and the sequence, creativity can be greatly enhanced if the process is understood and we engage in it in a conscious way. For this reason, creativity, which *can* be taught, *should* be taught. Our experience is clear: creativity can be unleashed with greater efficiency and success with an individual or a group that has been trained in the creative process. Through that understanding, there is a far greater sensitivity to the climate required for the process to take place and the sensitivity to the fragile nature of idea generation.

Another way of engaging in the creative process is to understand which brain wave states optimize each phase of the process. Experiment, approaching each stage or the process with this information in mind. The creative process most typical of the average businessperson includes: interest, preparation, incubation, illumination, verification, and application. Brain wave research conducted by creativity researchers including myself, suggests that there is a close alignment between brain wave states and the stages of the creative process.

The findings are as follows:

- **Interest** is a general state of alert consideration of a problem situation. The brain state is beta.

- **Preparation** for applying the creative process to a specific problem situation involves beta at the higher frequencies: more intense, more purposeful, more applied.

- **Incubation** of a problem situation following preparation takes place in alpha with the lower-

> *"Creative thinking deals with shades of gray, not with blacks and whites."*
>
> —
>
> *Anonymous*

frequency, high-amplitude brain waves producing the best results of contemplation.

- **Illumination**, which is often described as the AHA! stage of the process, takes place in theta. This is the stage where the potential solution presents itself in the form of an idea.

- **Verification** returns the mental process back to beta, and sometimes occurs at 2:00 a.m., or in the shower, or while commuting to work. This is the stage when an alert evaluation of the potential solution is considered in relationship to the original problem. This is generally high-frequency beta.

- **Application** is the final stage of the process, and continues as an aroused beta level activity.

"Good ideas are not adopted automatically. They must be driven into practice with courageous patience."

—

Admiral Hyman Rickover

The creative process that I have just described takes advantage of the four quadrants of the Whole Brain Model and the three brain wave states that are involved in a conscious processing of the discrete stages of creativity.

Following the Creative Selves Model

As I said earlier, Graham Wallas's model naturally correlates with a whole brain creative process. In the Creative Self Model, the quadrant descriptors reflect the principal aspects of whole brained, applied creativity: the problem-finding self for A, the implementing self for B, the idea-sensing self for C, and the idea-finding self for D.

A legendary example of this creative process is Edwin Land's invention of the Polaroid camera. The process started in the A quadrant, when his 3-year-old daughter Jennifer asked after taking a picture why she couldn't see the snapshot right away. The problem was found. The C quadrant then took over, and in a few hours Land had sensed an idea involving a different kind of camera using a different kind of film. Moving to the D quadrant, he evolved an idea involving two rolls of photo paper and a chemical pod. Shifting to the A quadrant, he figured out the chemistry of his radical idea. Three years of B-quadrant persistence, combined with D-quadrant experimentation and many failures, produced the now ubiq-

Figure 22-4.
The Creative Selves Model.

Our Four Different Selves

A — RATIONAL SELF

Analyzes
Quantifies
Is Logical
Is Critical
Is Realistic
Likes Numbers
Knows about Money
Knows how Things Work

D — EXPERIMENTAL SELF

Infers
Imagines
Speculates
Takes Risks
Is Impetuous
Breaks Rules
Likes Surprises
Is Curious / Plays

B — SAFEKEEPING SELF

Takes Preventive Action
Establishes Procedures
Gets Things Done
Is Reliable
Organizes
Is Neat
Timely
Plans

C — FEELING SELF

Is Sensitive to Others
Likes to Teach
Touches a Lot
Is Supportive
Is Expressive
Is Emotional
Talks a Lot
Feels

uitous Polaroid camera. In total, Land garnered more than 500 patents from applying his creative self.

Mental Diversity and Synergy

I have mentioned before that individuals are not single entities but rather a coalition of four selves—a self-contained team. The diversity within an individual provides the basis for synergy. A rational idea juxtaposed to an intuitive thought can produce a new idea through synergistic interaction. When more than one person is involved, the diversity of mental preferences can significantly enhance both persons' creative potential. Therefore, teams that are assembled to deal with creative problem situations should be formed on the basis of diversity of thinking preferences.

Our experience has shown there is a clear advantage to having all four thinking modes represented on a team (heterogeneous) rather than those with similar preferences (homogeneous). This is not an untested theory, but a popular and successful technique we have employed extensively for the last ten years. It isn't as if a homogeneous team can't come up with a creative solution. The fundamental problem is that homogeneity leads to quick consensus (see Chapter 4, pp. 54-56, and Chapter 11 for more on teams). The members of the team think alike. They are on the same mental wavelength so there is little confrontation of opposing concepts and ideas. No matter how much time is allocated to the homogeneous team they will typically come back early with a workable solution. They say that to take more time to consider the problem is a waste of time and counterproductive. They've already gotten the best answer available and they did it quickly. Early consensus can be an advantage but not in the domain of creativity and innovation. The absence of continued interaction results in missed opportunities. In a direct comparison of homogeneous solutions with heterogeneous ones, the quality of creative team output is clearly in favor of the heterogeneous teams. I would estimate the advantage as over 80%. Considering this clear advantage, why in the world would anybody form a team of other than a heterogeneous diverse group?

Among the reasons are:

1. The people in charge aren't aware of the advantage.

2. They don't have a way of assessing the thinking styles to assemble such mentally diverse teams.

3. They don't know enough about the creative process to understand the significance of diversity.

4. They can't be bothered with these kinds of theories.

So What?

■ The brain is the source of creativity, as it is of all mental processes.

■ As an electrochemical organ, it needs special neurotransmitter fuel to produce synaptic activity, and electrical energy to produce the brain waves that are essential to the creative process.

Managing Creativity Through Multiple Processes

Chapter Headlines

◆ Synergy among the four quadrants contributes strongly to the creative process.

◆ Individuals, if allowed, gravitate naturally to the creative processes that work for them.

◆ Teams can be formed of these creative process champions for multiple applications to major problems.

◆ Creativity, in critical mass, can be extremely powerful and self-sustaining.

Creative problem-solving seminars and creativity courses typically focus on one or two creative processes. Probably the best known is brainstorming. Another is known as "TLC" ("what is Tempting, what is Lacking, and what can be Changed?"). A well-known formalized process is called "Synectics." Another, coming out of Edward DeBono's work, is called "The Six Thinking Hats." Over the years, thousands of individuals have been trained in the Creative Problem-Solving Process originated by the Creative Education Foundation in Buffalo, New York.

Listed in figure 23-1 is a universe of creative processes that totals 77 discrete approaches to creative problem solving. While many people have been involved in the development of these processes, there are only a few original thinkers responsible for the core processes in this extensive universe. The individuals in this list are known throughout the world for their work in the domain of creativity. They, along with their colleagues and coworkers, have played a key conceptual role in the development and teaching of the 77 discrete processes.

Since these processes have been developed by a variety of people for a variety of purposes, they each reflect a particular brain dominance characteristic. That is, when viewed in terms of the four-quadrant model, each process reflects a particular mental orientation. Some are quite logical, analytic, and quantitative, and therefore fall in the A quadrant. Others are consistent with the B-quadrant qualities: more structured, procedural, and step-by-step. The humanistic, team-oriented, and relationship-based methods naturally fall in line with the C quadrant. When sensing solutions is done intuitively, experimenting, conceptualizing and putting problems and solutions in metaphoric terms, the process is very D quadrant. Of course, not all processes fit neatly in one quadrant or another; many represent combinations of quadrants, including left mode (A and B), right mode (C and D), limbic (B and C), and cerebral (A and D) processes. All four modes involve pairs of quadrant preferences and are therefore dynamic. Since adjacent quadrants are interconnected, these four modes take advantage of the potential synergy between the pairs of quadrants. Synergy contributes strongly to the creative process, so interaction among the four modes presents prime opportunities for creative output. This is particularly true of the cerebral mode consisting of the problem-finding A quadrant and the idea-finding D quadrant. These two cerebral quadrants are the most extensively interconnected of all the modes.

And finally, a handful of processes are so multidominant that they might be considered whole brained. Figure 23-1 shows how the 77 processes are distributed among the quadrants and modes of the Whole Brain Model.

In other sections of this book, particularly in those dealing with work, competency, and job satisfaction, I have discussed alignment of a person's mental preferences with the mental requirements of the job. In Chapter 2 you were encouraged to complete a Turn-On Work Exercise in which you selected from a universe of work activities eight that turned

Categorizing the 77 Creative Processes in terms of the Whole Brain Model

A Quadrant

Attribute Listing
Electronic Brainstorming
Bionics
Factual Analysis
Forced Field Analysis
Idea Fisher Software
Kepner-Tregor Process
Mathematica
Method 6-3-5
Operation Research
Pert Program
Problem Definitions
Pure "Logic"
Rational Thinking
Reengineering
Value Analysis

D Quadrant

Brain Writing
Creative Dramatics
Creative Materials (ACT I)
De-Doodling (Juan Carlos Folino)
Dreaming
Free Association
Guided Imagery
Incubation
Intuition (Solutions)
Journeys into Creative Problem Solving, audiocassette, ACL
Lateral Thinking
Meditation
Mess Worksheet
Metaphoric Thinking
Modeling
Play
Sketching
Solution After Next
Synectics
Theta State/Free Flow
Visual Brainstorming
Visualization
Visual Thinking

Multi-Dominant

Applied Creative Thinking Process
CPSI Process
A.C.T. Creative Process Audiocassette
Mind Mapping
Pugh Method
Six Thinking Hats
Story Board
TLC (Tempting, Lacking, Change)
Whole Brain Creativity
Whole Brain Problem Solving Walk-Around

Delphi Method
Detailed
Force Fitting
Idea Evaluation
Implementation Aspects
Instinctual
Morphological
Operation Analysis
Orderly
Scamper
Step-by-step
Strictly Procedural
Time Line Principle
Trigger Concept
Work Simplification
Zero Defects

Expressive
Human Factors
Interactive Brainstorming
Intuition (Feeling)
Kinesthetic Modeling
Passion Point Process
People Design Principle
Sensory Processing
Symbolic
Task Team
Team Process

B Quadrant

C Quadrant

Figure 23-1. 77 Creative processes clustered in terms of the Whole Brain Model.

you on, and some that turned you off. That exercise should have affirmed for you the role that alignment of your preferences with your work plays in determining your personal motivation to do the work you do.

Consider now the array of creative processes displayed in the four-quadrant model. Wouldn't there be an advantage for individuals engaged in creative problem solving to choose processes that best match their mental preferences? In contrast, think how hard it is for individuals to apply a process that turns them off instead of turning them on, unless they are consciously seeking to stretch themselves. I am convinced that, given the freedom to select from this universe, individuals would naturally gravitate to the processes they understand and are comfortable with, and that provide effective tools and techniques to aid in their problem-solving processes. These individuals would not only select the ones that are in strong alignment with their own mental preferences, but avoid picking processes they don't understand and are uncomfortable with and that don't produce the desired results.

"The product and the process are both important. Without the process, there would be no product. Without the product or evidence of action or achievement, there might not be more than fantasy. Creativity is to be regarded as both process and product."

—

Eugene Brunelle

Imagine for a minute a major creative problem-solving situation. This could be a business process that needs to be reinvented, a product design that needs to be completely rethought, or a customer situation requiring maximum creative effort to resolve. It is decided that due to the severity of the problem, a team of people needs to be assembled to work on this situation and resolve it in the most creative way possible. A conclusion advanced in this book is that such a team should be heterogeneous—that is, diverse in terms of mental preference. In the typical case, the team leader would approach the problem-solving task by applying a single creative process such as brainstorming and, typically, the brainstorming process would result in several alternative solutions. The team leader would typically report those alternative possibilities to the problem owner, who would attempt to select one for implementation. This is an approach with small issues, let's say $1,000, but is grossly inadequate when dealing with large issues, such as $10 million-dollar problems. Major problems deserve multiple solution approaches that will generate optimal creative alternatives by "chunking up" from brainstorming to "creative process storming." The chances for an optimum solution are enormously increased. Experience has demonstrated that most heterogeneous teams have members who are experienced in one or more of the 77 creative processes. Having these individuals develop expertise and become champions in the processes they are aligned with and apply them in rotation to the common problem, greatly increases likelihood of breakthrough solutions.

Organizations that are serious about applying creativity to their business problems can identify individuals interested in creative problem solving and facilitate their advanced training in specific creative processes. This will allow them to be, in effect, champions in those processes that turn them on and to join ad hoc creative problem-solving teams.

As I write this, I am reminded of Red Adair, who created a firefighting organization comprised of world experts in various aspects of firefighting. Some were champions in the use of explosives, some in the use of high pressure water, some in the replacement of the oil-well cap known as a Christmas Tree, and others in the use of specialized bulldozers. Taken together, these specialized champions could mount the optimal creative attack on the out-of-control fire. The Red Adair group became one of the world's best firefighting teams because (1) they were using multiple processes to solve major problems and (2) the individuals applying those different processes were world-class champions of that particular technique.

While all businesses can't afford to have a Red Adair caliber team on standby, few can afford *not* to have such a team available to deal with their major business problems.

> *"A invasion of armies can be resisted, but not an idea whose time has come."*
>
> —
>
> *Victor Hugo*

So What?

- Managements that want to encourage creativity need to be aware of this and actively campaign to change the culture from "killing" creativity to stimulating it, supporting it, and rewarding it.

- Some company problems are so significant that the application of single processes falls short of providing real answers to complex problems.

- Individuals who are motivated to champion their favorite creative process can join with others to form a whole brain problem solving team that applies discrete processes in an effective sequence.

- Multiple creative process approaches greatly increase the likelihood that breakthrough solutions will occur on major problems.

> *"The world of reality has its limits, the world of imagination is boundless."*
>
> —
>
> *Jean Jacques Rousseau*

Going Creative

"The difficulty lies not so much in developing new ideas as in escaping from old ones."

—

John Maynard Keynes

Chapter Headlines

♦ Strongly motivated individuals can become creative process champions and serve as members of whole brain creative process teams.

♦ The more creative the organization, the greater the need for idea management.

♦ An idea management system can be tailored to an organization's culture to capture, process, apply, and reward idea generation.

♦ All good ideas should be either applied or saved and all should be rewarded—none should be wasted.

♦ All organizations, particularly large ones, can benefit from idea management. Such a system can make a business more competitive, more profitable, and more successful.

Whole Brain Creativity Champions

In the context of this book, my definition of *champion* is some-body who is so strongly motivated that he or she is self-actu-alized (i.e., the doing of the work is a reward in and of itself) when carrying out applications of Whole Brain Technology, such as creativity, teaching and learning, communication, and team activity. Champions are those with an almost effortless dedication to being involved. We have experienced many champions along the way. Two good examples are Dave Tan-ner, formerly of DuPont, and Ray Alvord, formerly of Shell;

another is Byron Collins of GE. All three are individuals strongly motivated to be involved, and it is apparent, from my work with them, that they derive a great deal of personal satisfaction simply from involvement with the subject matter. It is for them a turn-on. It almost seems as if they are captured by the whole brain idea and find fulfillment in pursuing it.

We are now embarking on a separate challenge in the domain of champions and that is developing champions of specific creative processes. (See the list of 77 creative processes in figure 23-1 on page 227.) The new concept involves finding people who are highly interested in a particular creative process, like electronic brainstorming, the Six Thinking Hats, Kepner Tregoe, or Synectics, and having these individuals become so expert in implementing that process that they achieve mastery in it. The challenge then is to apply that mastery, so that each champion joins with other aligned masters to work together in solving a major problem. Together, these creative process masters represent a composite whole brain team, and therefore they are able to develop a quantum improvement in the quality of the creative solutions that are obtained. The potential synergy that results from masters working together from different domains on a common problem can be enormous.

I do not believe that creative championship can be forced. I think it springs from being naturally turned on to a particular set of mental preferences that are aligned with a particular creative process. This establishes a very natural linkage between things that you prefer to do and processes and techniques that facilitate your doing them. Work becomes effortless, joyous, and fulfilling under these conditions.

It is possible to establish a school for creative champions that allows candidates to sort through the various creative processes available to them and choose those processes that make use of their preferences in very natural ways, and then to provide them with an opportunity to achieve personal mastery in those processes.

One could dream about an organization that provided an opportunity for creative process champions to make application of their mastery on business problems as they develop.

On the following page is a list of the necessary steps to establish a pool of creative process champions and whole brain problem-solving teams.

"Some things arrive in their own mysterious hour, on their own terms, and not yours, to be seized or relinquished forever."

—

Gail Godwin

1. Arrange for top management sponsorship.

2. Identify interested candidates.

3. Invite them to learn their mental preference by administering the *HBDI*.

4. Identify their existing creative process expertise.

5. Diagnose the degree of alignment between their mental preferences and the mentality of the creative process in which they have expertise.

6. If the level of existing expertise is inadequate, arrange for the needed training to help them achieve mastery of a given creative process.

7. Arrange with direct reporting management for the creative process champions to be given temporary assignment to a creative process problem-solving team.

8. When a major problem occurs, select from the pool of creative process champions a group of five or six who represent a corporate whole brain group with the mix of expertise that would optimize the solution to that major problem.

9. If there is a problem owner, let that person be the team leader; if there is no problem owner, let the role of leader be determined by the team.

10. Provide the team with a dedicated room to apply their creative mastery—a room that has a full spectrum of creative materials to support model making and experimentation with alternative solutions.

11. Make it easy for the team to communicate its problem-solution recommendations to the senior management problem owners.

Supervising and Managing Creative People

Even though applied creativity is by its nature whole brained, some of the visible behavior characteristics of creative people are consistent with right mode, particularly D-quadrant qualities. Creative people have a low tolerance for rules and regulations and resist being closely supervised on the basis of detailed step-by-step processes. They are more inclined to break rules than to make rules. They are more likely to take risks and experiment. Therefore, the job of supervising creatives is always a challenging one. It requires a mixture of trust in the process, patience, encouragement, and realistic goals. The job of many administrators and operational managers, however, is to run a tight ship by monitoring quality, maintaining consistency, and providing structure and control. The differences are so sharply defined that we are dealing with oil and water. When creativity is part of the job description, managers and supervisors need to be sensitive to the conditions under which the creative process can be most productive. The best way to supervise creatives is to be clear about the objectives and deadlines from the start and then manage with some distance. Too many rules and conditions placed on the individuals will inhibit the natural flow necessary to creativity. Although it may seem inefficient to incubate ideas or potential solutions, it actually takes less work and time.

The styles typical to a shop foreman or technical supervisor/manager may be perilous to the creative solution. When managing a creative person or team, steer away from:

1. close supervision

2. adherence to procedures

3. application of quantitative performance measures

Even though applied whole brain creativity requires some of these disciplines in order to follow through and implement creative ideas, these steps are often performed automatically by the individuals because of their self-motivation. If you state the desired outcomes up front, there should be no need for close supervisory techniques. By striking a balance between firm project control and a totally open-ended and undefined process, the manager in charge of the creative individual or team can promote productivity instead of hampering it.

It is important to emphasize this point, because our database indicates that the thinking-style norm for lower- and middle-level managers is strongly left mode-oriented. Therefore, the management styles of this population tend to go against the grain of creativity until we get to the senior levels of both managers and professional employees. Typically, it is only at the higher levels that creativity and innovation become legitimized. It is at these higher levels that creative champions begin to encourage and even sponsor creative behavior. Because the processes inherent to creativity and innovation are typically in conflict with the mental preferences of foremen, supervisors, and the culture at large, leaders who attempt to change an embedded culture like this feel as if they are running into a brick wall. In this case, some sort of creativity campaign may be required.

Changes that would allow the creative and innovative potential of the organization to be unleashed would first require a top-down companywide educational program that provides needed understanding to everyone in the organization, including managers, supervisors, and foremen as well as knowledge workers and production workers. Several of our clients have created videotapes to prove the worthiness of pursuing creativity and innovation. And, in parallel with that, I would suggest an education program that reveals the nature and source of creativity and innovation. Until individuals understand who they are and why they do the things they do and the way they do them, creativity will remain a mystery.

Creating the Right Climate

A major consideration in building a creative organization is establishing a climate that will support the creative process, particularly when heterogeneous teams are involved. Here are some considerations:

1. Creativity needs to be free of precise scheduling.

2. Creativity is an inefficient process from a productivity standpoint. The more you structure it, the faster you shut it down.

3. Creative results cannot be guaranteed.

4. Mistakes will be made.

5. Personal relationships may be stressed.

It is essential that the manager in charge of a creative team first establish a climate that encourages diversity of thinking, tolerates ambiguity, and is flexible in terms of schedule, outcomes, and personal behaviors. This climate must allow for a fundamentally messy process to take place in an otherwise orderly organization. When traditional business approaches to encouraging innovation don't work, management has been known to take a chance on nontraditional ones. Generally speaking, these approaches are outside the regular corporate system. A good example is the skunk works approach. A *skunkworks* is a small subset of a high-powered organization working on a special project in a secluded facility that has everything necessary to achieve success. The approach is based on the idea that certain work requires unique people working in authentic ways that are different from ways of the ongoing culture of the business. So a special place must be found for them within the organization, within a facility that allows them to be authentic in their work habits, (such as flexible work hours, relaxed dress codes, and specialized physical environment) that visibly differs from the daily work habits and facilities of the parent organization.

History of a Skunk Works

The first most successful corporate skunk works was created by Kelly Johnson of Lockheed Aircraft. Kelly Johnson was a legendary figure who has been responsible for some of the most important technological breakthrough designs in American aviation history. Working with his Lockheed skunk works (officially, Advanced Development Projects) team, Johnson designed the world's highest performance aircraft—including the U-2, the SR-71, and the YF-12. Kelly Johnson is an extraordinary engineer and his work was exclusively oriented to the design and development of secret military aircraft.

In his autobiographical book, *Kelly*, written with Maggie Smith, Kelly describes how he had been pestering top management to let him set up an experimental department where the designers and shop artisans could work together closely

"Extraordinary people visualize not what is possible or probable, but rather what is impossible. And by visualizing the impossible, they begin to see it as possible."

—

Cheri Carter-Scott

in the development of airplanes without the delays and complications of intermediate departments to handle administration, purchasing, and all the other support functions. He wanted a direct relationship between design engineer and manufacturing engineer. In essence, he needed all the functions required for the project to operate independently of the main plant. What he created became the first corporate skunk works. Johnson doesn't know exactly where the name came from, but the legend goes that one of Lockheed's engineers asked, "What the heck is Kelly doing in there?" "Oh, he's stirring up some kind of brew" was the answer. This brought to mind Al Capp's popular comic strip, *Li'l Abner* and the hairy Indian who regularly stirred up the brew, throwing in skunks, old shoes, and other likely material to make his "Kickapoo Joy Juice." Thus, the skunk works was born and named.

Johnson enumerates the basic operating rules of the skunk works. Since I believe the application of this approach goes beyond the strictly secret military high-tech project, I have adapted Kelly's rules for a more broadly based and creatively oriented project.

Successful business skunk works require:

1. A highly competent champion, with strong authority, in full charge. As a manager, he or she must be in complete control of the program in all aspects.

2. The champion/manager should report only to a divisional vice president or higher level.

3. The manager must have the ability and freedom to make immediate decisions.

4. The manager must have a hot line to top command to be used at his or her discretion.

5. The skunk works staff should be limited to a small number of especially capable and responsible people, perhaps 25 percent or less of the typical organization.

6. Reports and paperwork should be reduced to an absolute minimum, but all important work must be thoroughly recorded.

7. The entire skunk works staff should be fully involved in the project.

8. All required functions (engineering, advanced design, manufacturing, finance, personnel, strategic planning, etc.) should be represented in the staff and, to the extent possible, it should comprise a composite whole brain work group. Work groups within the skunk works should be small and heterogeneous.

9. All skunk works staff members should have close contact with the actual work. The design of the individual work tasks should take into account the mental aspects of the work to be performed. The assignment of individuals to specific work should be based on the highest correlation of their mental preferences and the mental requirements of the work to be performed.

10. Any and all changes in the work situation should be explained to everyone as they occur.

11. All families should be kept aware of the project status and familiar with the work activities.

12. The motivation of individuals should come from their interest in and challenge of the work rather than a forced draft schedule imposed upon them.

13. Individuals should be allowed to take advantage of their best work times, consistent with the needs of the project.

14. All essential equipment and creative materials should be available to all individuals on a free access basis.

15. The limited staff should be supplemented with needed competence by bringing in experts as situationally required on a timely basis.

16. The facility should provide the team with the necessary privacy for them to carry out their work without being invaded or unduly influenced by the surrounding organization.

17. The leadership of the skunk works should be characterized as exemplifying good human relations.

Important lessons can be learned from Kelly Johnson's success. What he did and how he did it was generally outside and, in many cases, in spite of, the so-called regular system. He created a unique new form of leadership. He felt that he owed the members of his skunk works team challenging work, worthwhile jobs, stable employment, fair pay, a chance to advance, opportunity to contribute, good management, sound projects, good equipment, and good work areas. What makes him different from other leaders? He didn't just talk about it—he did it.

Expanding further on Kelly Johnson's ideas, the theory of a skunk works is to learn how to do things quickly, inexpensively, collaboratively, and creatively, and to tailor the approach to the degree of risk involved in each project. Johnson managed risk taking based on need. When top management and project champions involved in this type of work situation understand what they are doing, a skunk works approach has been known to work well, even spectacularly. This surely was the case with Lockheed, where they had the right people, under the right leader, working under the right top management providing the right support.

So a skunk works is far more than just a place. It is a complete enterprise that arises spontaneously out of an organization, usually powered by the vision and drive of one or two people—*champions* who take advantage of the loopholes in an organization or a culture that allow for such endeavors to grow. Such champions see a situation that requires special handling and subsequently reach for and claim the necessary creative space. The top management wise enough to identify and acknowledge the champion and allow the endeavor to take place can contribute to its success by providing the right environment for the skunk works to flourish.

In the most effective cases, the manager is a true champion of the creative process. Kelly is an example of such a leader. His understanding approached the expert level. He knew how to build a team and create a climate in which it could function, and that included protecting the team from onslaught from above.

Consider this comment from one of our clients at DuPont

who started a creativity and innovation training program: "If you want to make your organization more creative and innovative, it has to start with the leadership of your organization. It has to start with your management."

Creative champions seem to have a knack for establishing an enclave in which creative space can be claimed and creative activity can be pursued even if the surrounding culture is not fully aligned.

Approaching Change Creatively

There are significant consequences to the pursuit of creativity because some rules will have to be broken, some traditions will have to be changed, bureaucracies will have to be overcome, counterproductive management styles will have to be avoided, counterculture behavior will have to be tolerated, and the implementation of creative results will have to be accepted.

Creativity always involves change. However, not all organizational change is approached creatively. There is a significant advantage to doing so because creativity is almost entirely a positive process. It converts the usual negativity of change to the positive action of problem solving. If the reason for change in the first place is a problem issue in the organization, such as a process that doesn't work or a strategy that isn't successful, then these need-for-change issues can be thought of as problems to solve creatively. Creative problem-solving task teams can be organized to develop alternative solutions. In fact, if the problem issue is pervasive, the entire organization can be mobilized as a creative problem-solving organization.

Idea Management

Imagine that all the things necessary to establish the ideal creative climate have taken place, that there are multiple champions in key management positions, and that the CEO is the most effective champion of all. The organization is a beehive of creative activity with ideas being generated like a popcorn machine—so rapidly, in fact, that they cannot be captured, developed, and applied. The vision of the leader had been for the whole organization to go creative and al-

"The best idea is fifteen minutes ahead of its time. Those that are light-years ahead get ignored."

—

Paraphrasing Woody Allen

most all of the ingredients are in place. What is missing is *idea management*.

Maslow's hierarchy of needs starts with the foundation of survival and progresses through successively higher levels of need to self-actualization. This is where the work itself is rewarding, where the performing of a work task is so satisfying that external awards are not needed. Creativity can be the highest form of self-actualization. The exhilaration of an AHA!—the satisfaction of having an idea solve a perplexing problem—is amongst the most fulfilling of all activities. Since synergy is one of the basic ingredients of the creative process, creativity feeds on itself, and therefore organizations that have a climate of creativity can achieve accelerating momentum to the point where that becomes the sustaining culture. Idea generation becomes the thing to do, and everybody begins to do it. The challenge now is to manage this proliferation of ideas.

While there aren't too many organizations that are at this level of idea generation, most organizations either don't know how, or don't want, to take the time to manage the ideas they do have, and probably 80-90 percent of them are wasted. Even the best of suggestion systems are inadequate to process creative ideas. The people in charge of such systems are likely to be administrative people who focus on the procedural aspects of the system rather than on the creativity of the ideas offered, or are idea generators who don't care about organizing the ideas, just creating them. What is needed is a team charged with the creative management of ideas. Its members should be skilled in the creative process, able to recognize the value of an idea, and able to design effective storage and retrieval systems.

What kind of system will work for you or your organization? Can it be done on computer, with categories displayed by icons like the menus of on-line services? Or are there people who don't have a desktop computer and would need a public facility? Let me provide an example. I visualize a central room specifically designed for the capturing and processing of ideas. The core of this facility would be a computer network with specialized software that would capture and save incoming ideas throughout the organization. The names of the individuals contributing the ideas are permanently tagged to that idea as it is moved about in the system.

Creative specialists would conduct daily reviews of submitted ideas and categorize and prioritize them for display on monitors. Creative champions, representing the different functions of the business, would review the accumulated ideas at least once a week—or more often if needed—to determine the idea candidates for review and potential testing and application.

A separate system, linked by network, would capture unsolved problems of the business. These would be sent in from the different components of the business and categorized and prioritized in the same manner as the ideas are processed. Creative specialists would constantly monitor the database of problems and the database of ideas and would make connections wherever there were sufficient alignment between problem and potential solution to be worthy of specific review. When that occurs, the problem owner and the idea generator whose name had similarly been tagged would be brought together for a face-to-face discussion of how that particular idea could be directly applied or modified to meet the problem needs.

This idea management facility would have a creative materials room for modeling of both a problem situation and a potential solution. The problem owner and the idea generator would be able to jointly model the problem and the proposed solution. An adjoining conference space where computerized brainstorming could occur and a room with a wide array of toys, games, and creative objects that would stimulate idea generation would be nice additions.

In the ideal situation, company problem owners and idea generators would take advantage of this specialized facility to focus on a particular problem or idea and move it toward solution or completion. Individuals who contributed ideas would be rewarded appropriately.

Now this system I've described is much too complicated and expensive for a small company of 500 to 1,000 people, but for a company with 10,000, 50,000, or 100,000 employees such a system would not only be cost-effective but could actually save the life of the corporation. If we are wasting 80-90 percent of our ideas by not having an idea management system, then the installation of one would immediately begin to pay for itself. Properly conceived and executed, the creative idea management facility would become the most popular place in town. It could even be featured in the annual report and in the company's commercials. For organi-

"Dixie Cups (and) Life Savers were 'conceived, failed and reborn' thanks to ingenuity, enthusiasm and determination."

—

Michael Gershman

zations who aspire to "go creative," the creative idea management system could be the company's proud logo. Even if your company has fewer than 50 employees, like ours, you can allocate resources on a much smaller scale. We use our learning center, where we conduct seminars and workshops, as model-making space and for other problem-solving activities. E-mail systems with work group definitions can be set up for idea exchange. The main point is, the system must achieve these criteria:

- User-friendly capturing

- Categories that make sense

- User-friendly retrieval

- Identification of the idea generator and the problem finder

- System for ongoing review

- Linking of idea with problem

- Vehicle for problem-solving process face to face

- Acknowledgment and reward for the individuals involved

Achieving Critical Mass

When enough individuals have achieved competency in a common area such as creativity and those individuals can be focused on a common task, it is possible to achieve a critical mass. When that happens, the combined creative potential can become not only extremely powerful but also self-sustaining. With this focused energy emanating from the group, creativity can be more readily applied to organizational tasks. As a result of the predictably greater than normal success that results, the group energy seeks continuing engagement and this results in a continuous loop of creative application.

As the group enjoys repeated success, its skills, techniques, and confidence build in such a way that additional success is achieved. In nuclear physics, when critical mass is achieved, a chain reaction occurs. The metaphor also fits applied creativity. In nuclear physics, the chain reaction produces a quantum leap in energy release. When an organization develops creative critical mass, a quantum leap in both the quality and quantity of creative output occurs.

When you compare a critical mass of individuals in an organization engaged in a common task using multiple creative processes to achieve their results, to a single individual applying a single creative process and working on the same problem independently, the choice becomes clear. For this reason, it is well worth the effort and the investment to produce a critical mass of individuals with a common background in creative process to come together and apply those creative processes in a multiple format to a common problem.

It is quite possible for an organization to have a sufficient number of individuals trained in creativity without having achieved a critical mass. For that to happen, there need to be champions who bring those trained individuals together to apply their combined creative potential to a common organizational issue or problem. Without a champion serving as a catalyst, those trained people will function and perform at best as independent individuals. This will not take advantage of the potential synergy that can result from a group of competent, motivated people working together toward a common end.

There is a phenomenon I would like to tell you about. In it may lie the answer to how organizations can achieve creative critical mass and "go creative." It is the story of "the hundredth monkey" that I am adapting to make this point.

The Japanese monkey, *Macaca fuscata*, has been observed in the wild for a period of over 30 years. In 1952 on the island of Koshima, scientists were providing monkeys with sweet potatoes dropped in the sand. The monkeys liked the taste of the raw sweet potatoes, but they found the dirt unpleasant.

An 18-month-old female named Imo found she could solve the problem by washing the potatoes in a nearby stream. She taught this trick to her mother. Her playmates also learned this new way and they taught their mothers, too. This cultural innovation was gradually picked up by various monkeys before the eyes of the scientists. Between 1952 and 1958 all the young monkeys learned to wash the sandy sweet potatoes to make them more palatable. Only the adults who imitated their children learned this social improvement. Other adults kept eating the dirty sweet potatoes.

Then something startling took place. By the autumn of 1958, a certain number of Koshima monkeys—let us say 99—had learned to wash their sweet potatoes. Let's further suppose that one morning, the hundredth monkey learned to wash potatoes. THEN IT HAPPENED! By that evening, almost everyone in the tribe was washing sweet potatoes before eating them. The added energy of this hundredth monkey somehow created a breakthrough! BUT NOTICE! A most surprising thing observed by the scientists was that the habit of washing sweet potatoes then jumped over the sea. Colonies of monkeys on other islands and the mainland troop of monkeys at Takasakiyama began washing their sweet potatoes!

Thus, when a certain critical number achieves an awareness, this new awareness may be communicated from mind to mind. Although the exact number may vary, the hundreth monkey phenomenon means that when only a limited number of people know of a new way, it may remain the conscious property of these people only. But there is a point at which, if only one more person tunes into a new awareness, a field is strengthened so that this awareness is picked up by almost everyone!

Your awareness is needed in achieving a critical creative mass in your organization. And you may be the "hundredth monkey".... You may furnish the added conscious energy to create the shared awareness of the creative potential of your organization.

Creativity Defined

I have tried to explain creativity from many different perspectives, but I have avoided trying to define it. The reason is that creativity means different things to different people. To attempt to rigorously define it would limit our personal understanding. From a brain dominance perspective, each one of us is unique. We experience the world in ways that are determined by our particular array of mental preferences. Therefore, it is unlikely that there ever will be a single, comprehensive definition of the meaning of creativity.

"What is creativity?

Among other things, it is an ability to

challenge assumptions,

recognize patterns,

see in new ways,

make connections,

take risks,

and seize upon a chance."

I offer this quote, which is my own expression/rewording of Bill Moyers' original one, as a series of action steps that each of us can take as we try to increase our own creative potential.

Challenge Assumptions

When we are dealing with a problem situation, instead of accepting what somebody tells us or how the problem is stated in writing, or even how we define the problem ourselves, it is creatively healthy to challenge the basis of these statements by questioning the facts upon which they are based, or the premise upon which these statements are based. Our assumptions are often the filters through which we perceive the problem situation. Oftentimes when these are challenged, important new understandings are revealed. A problem well stated is a problem half solved.

Recognize Patterns

In seeking to understand complex problems, we are often blind to the presence of patterns which, when recognized, lead us to the solution to those problems. Have you ever wondered why freeway traffic seems to be jammed for no apparent reason? And then, suddenly, traffic opens up and is free-running for a while and then starts jamming up again? Until a short distance later, it again opens up and is free-running? If you changed your vantage point by going up in a helicopter and looking down at the freeway, you would see that there are absolutely no obstructions, but that the cars are bunched up every few miles, with open segments in between. It turns out that a pattern forms, based upon a few cars slowing down, which causes other cars to slow down, forming a jam until the lead cars see that there is no reason for them to be jammed up and they regain speed until the next occurrence. If the helicopter were high enough to see for ten miles, you would see a distinct pattern of alternating traffic jams and open driving every few miles. No doubt each driver assumes that there is a reason ahead of them for traffic to slow down and therefore they do slow down and a jam is created.

I am certain that technology exists to provide radar information that would illuminate signs every mile or so that would say "open driving ahead, maintain legal speed." Such a system would reduce driver frustration and increase the number of cars that a freeway could handle without incurring any of these pattern-type traffic jams. Patterns can be effective diagnostic tools in that they can reveal the true problem.

See in New Whole Brain Ways

Recognizing patterns is for many of us a totally new way of seeing. You will recall the Problem-Solving Walk-Around which deliberately examines a problem from the perspective of the four quadrants. The logical, rational A quadrant; the organized, procedural B quadrant; the interpersonal, emotional C quadrant; and the experimental, holistic D quadrant. Since most of us have our favorite way of looking at things, based on our brain dominance preferences, this walk-around technique provides an easy way for us to be facilitated to seeing in new ways.

Make Connections

A high percentage of creative ideas are the result of synergy occurring between two thoughts or perceptions. Making connections between them can stimulate synergy, which will increase the yield of fresh new ideas. Some of these connections take place naturally, but often seeking out different perceptions and forcing a connection between them can yield creative results. Doing this is, in fact, a distinct creative process.

Take Risks

Those among us who have a D-quadrant preference enjoy risk taking and make use of this creative step naturally. Others of us who have preferences in the other quadrants need to overcome our resistance to risk taking. The way to do that is to practice taking small risks on purpose until a comfort level is achieved. In this way, risk taking can become a tool in the creativity tool kit.

Seize Upon a Chance

Many already creative people are opportunistic as they engage in a problem-solving situation. Their past experience has demonstrated that taking a chance pays off. Others of us who would like to be more creative need to add this, as well as risk taking, to our tool kit. With a little practice we can improve our responsiveness to creative opportunities. In most cases we are dealing with a dynamic, rather than a static, issue. We are dealing with changing situations somewhat similar to a highway round-about where cars are entering and exiting from a circular roadway. All of us have been frustrated by somebody in front of us who doesn't respond to an opening in the traffic pattern. They are too safekeeping, or security-minded, or fearful that they can't maneuver their car quickly enough to fill in an open space in the traffic. Seizing upon a chance in a potentially creative situation is analogous. We have to take a calculated risk in order to take advantage of an opening that will allow us to move forward toward a creative solution. The consequences of not seizing a chance are that we are stuck in our own mental traffic jam and there is no creative outcome.

By digging into this quote and unbundling its main points, I believe we add to our understanding of creativity. By considering these descriptive terms as action steps, we can make this quotation a path forward to an increased level of personal creativity.

In PART IV I have tried to touch on some of the key elements involved in applying creativity and innovation in organizations. It's not enough just to *want* to unleash it, the nature and source of creativity must be understood in order to apply it with positive results. Key considerations are the **organizational climate** required and the **consequences** that result from the unleashing process. I have introduced the idea that not only are creativity and innovation **whole brained,** but there are at least **77 discrete processes** available to apply it. A **quantum leap** in results can be obtained by "chunking up" from brainstorming to "**process storming.**" And finally, I have advanced the idea of whole organizations achieving a **critical mass** and **going creative.** To do that requires the unleashing of individual **creativity.**

So What?

- High interest in Whole Brain Technology leads to individuals becoming whole brain creativity champions in their organization and companies.

- Champions are experts in Whole Brain Technology who can bring about important applications of the technology within the company that would be otherwise unavailable.

- A new application of the champion concept is now available in the form of creative process champions.

- Whole brain teams made up of creative process champions who are experts in a particular creative process can be assigned to solve major problems by applying multiple processes to the solution.

PART V

Whole Brain Personal Development

Creativity for the Businessperson

Chapter Headlines

◆ Jobs are often incorrectly classified as "creative" or "noncreative."

◆ Creative potential is lost by assigning people to noncreative jobs.

> "The most sad way to kill creativity is to place creative individuals in an organization that demands uncreative ways of thinking and has no reward structure for initiative."
>
> —
>
> *James J. Tritton*

Now that we've discussed the overall advantages of going creative organizationally, it's time to focus on a key step in this process. I have stated the importance of cultivating creativity in the individual. Business leaders can talk creativity all they want, but until there is some permission granting and empowering going on, the individual will be leery of taking a risk. This is especially true for those who are concerned about job security and performing well at creativity. In essence, most jobs, even those requiring repetition, will benefit from creativity training. Creativity is what differentiates us from other mammals. It's what makes us human. It allows us to think on the fly and pinch-hit when needed, even in the most structured and defined positions. You may not consider your job creative and neither may your boss; but the following is an example of how jobs can be typecast unnecessarily.

During the course of my 35 years with General Electric, I held a number of jobs that were officially "creative" and a number that were not. The tunnel vision of the late 1940s lent credence to the idea that only certain jobs in certain departments were creative. For example, I worked for a while in General Electric's General Engineering Laboratory as a developmental engineer. Although I was a physicist and thought like a physicist, I was called an engineer and needed to think like an engineer. Because it was a developmental engineering laboratory, I needed to *think* like a developmental engineer, and that meant that I had to *invent* things. I needed to be "creative," although the word creativity was never mentioned. It was not part of the official language of GE back in those days. Meanwhile, other people in the laboratory who were not development engineers were *not* "creative."

I recall vividly one of the wonders of the laboratory facility. It was a self-service stockroom, filled with every electronic and mechanical gadget, device, or part that you could imagine. It was like an inventor's flea market. But the only people who had access to this resource were developmental engineers; in other words, only those who were officially "creative" could benefit from this facility, even though there were at least three times as many "noncreative" people in support of the developmental activities.

Well, it seemed odd to me at the time, and when viewed from the perspective of 50 years later, such a policy was not only ridiculous, but obscene. In point of fact, every job in the organization was, to a certain degree, creative. Some jobs had creativity implied in the job title, such as Developmental Engineer, while others in direct support of those positions were called Technicians, who did the bidding of the developmental engineers and were thought of as noncreatives because of their subordinate position. Even the head of the self-service stockroom was considered a noncreative. In retrospect, the hourly-rated toolmakers in the laboratory's machine shop had to be extremely creative in translating the developmental engineering sketches into experimental hardware. The non-exempt secretarial pool, whose members translated the technical dictation of the development engineers and tried to make sense out of the notes on paper napkins drawn in the cafeteria, had to be actively creative in order to survive the nearly impossible role that they played.

Even in my own small organization, it would be quite

"The microwave oven was invented by an 'inquisitive, self-educated . . .engineer who never finished grammar school.' "

—

Ira Flatow

difficult to identify a job that did not have some element of creativity in it. However, in those long-ago times, the culture of GE was like an iceberg: the small part above the water line was visibly creative, while the main body of the iceberg beneath the surface represented the huge, unrecognized, and invisible domain of creativity. It seems odd that so many people could be blind to the obvious in such a smart company. But, as Henry Mintzberg, one of my favorite management professors has said, "People seem to be smart and dull at the same time." GE is a vastly different company today.

If we now pull back from this microscopic view and look at business and industry through a wide-angle lens, we will find hundreds, thousands, and probably millions of employees whose job title and description are officially deemed "noncreative." Yet many of these jobs have opportunities for creative functioning. These creative job elements are not visible to management. Creative performance is neither encouraged nor rewarded when it occurs. Incredibly, creative initiatives are often grounds for punishment.

Some companies ignore the creative capabilities of existing employees and outsource their creative needs to consulting organizations with individuals who are officially "creative." I have some personal expertise here because my creative capability was overlooked for 20 years until I "officialized" myself by becoming a professional artist. In so doing, I took advantage of the fact that management wouldn't understand the difference between artistic creativity and business creativity. .

As I write this, I'm thinking about the hundreds of thousands of individuals with enormous creative potential who are assigned to officially noncreative work. Translated into brain dominance terms, this means that a lot of very imagi-

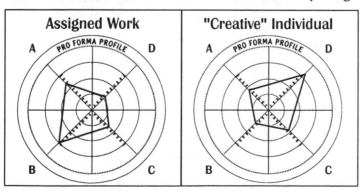

Figure 25-1.
Pro forma comparison profiles of work and creative individuals.

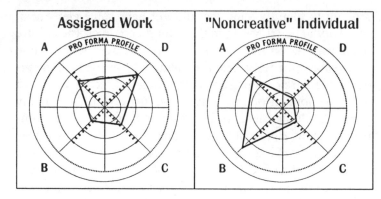

Figure 25-2.
Pro forma profiles of work and non-creative individuals.

<table>
<tr><td>**Assigned Work**</td><td>**"Noncreative" Individual**</td></tr>
<tr><td>A PRO FORMA PROFILE D
B C</td><td>A PRO FORMA PROFILE D
B C</td></tr>
</table>

native D-quadrant-oriented people are assigned to relatively boring A- and B-quadrant work. Most of them have demonstrated that they can do the work, but as in the iceberg example, most of their capability and motivation lie below the water line. In many cases, it's painful for these people to go to work in the morning because only a small portion of their job assignment represents personal turn-on activities. *Most of their job is made up of work that turns them off*, but, largely for economic reasons, they are sufficiently motivated to perform that work at an acceptable level. But there is no joy in Mudville.

Turn now to people who are not so creative, who have been assigned to work that has a high creative content. This is another form of misery, but not as long-lasting, since the obvious lack of performance reveals the mismatch early in the job cycle. That is, of course, if supervisors and managers are able to see what is happening. I can't visualize too many things more painful than to be expected to produce creative results on schedule if creativity is not your idea of fun. However, I am reminded that for some, to have to squelch your creativity is equally painful. In both cases this is a lose, lose, lose situation. It's lose for the employee; it's lose for the manager; and it's lose for the company.

Ted Coulson and Alison Strickland, leading creativity experts, tell this story about Karen Gammon, a secretary in DuPont's Spruance plant. Karen was a participant in the Applied Creative Thinking Workshop, which I had originally designed for GE, but which is now led by Ted and Alison. Karen revealed that she was not fulfilled as a secretary. She had more to offer than she felt the position allowed. During the creativity workshop she decided to do something about her office in the Richmond, Virginia plant. She wanted to clean it up, repaint it in colors she liked, and turn it into a showplace. That night she called her husband, who was head of the maintenance union at the plant, and asked him to get the paint she wanted and remove the furniture from the office so she could paint it when she got back the next weekend.

She did exactly what she planned to do and the place looked great. As she started to move her stuff back into the office, it dawned on her that she didn't need this piece of furniture, and she didn't need that piece, and as a matter of fact she didn't need most of the "stuff" that had crowded her office. She told the story to her fellow workers, who decided they also didn't need a lot of their office stuff. Karen's creative solution was to have an office "yard sale." People came from all corners of the plant and acquired what they needed and contributed what they didn't need. The result was impressive: $100,000 saved for the company, a major charitable gift by DuPont to the city of Richmond, Virginia, a whole lot of great-looking offices, and a group of very pleased and fulfilled secretaries. Some time later, motivated by her creative affirmations, Karen decided to change careers. She entered art school and has progressed rapidly to become an independent, skilled, self-employed professional artist. It is really never too late to try your creative wings. We are all proud of her.

So What?

■ Due to a general lack of understanding of creative work and creative people, many management decisions regarding jobs and people are counterproductive. Everybody loses—the employee, the manager, and the company.

■ Professor Henry Mintzberg observes that people can be smart and dull at the same time—this goes for managers at all levels in both large and small companies. Investment in the managers needs to become "smart" about creative people and creative work in their area of responsibility. Understanding people and work is a necessary beginning.

■ It is never too late to start.

"I never think of the future. It comes soon enough."

—

Albert Einstein

"Take your brain out and jump on it—it gets all caked up."

—

Mark Twain

"Outside the Box" Thinking

Chapter Headlines

♦ "The box" for most of us represents the self-built walls that constrain our everyday thinking.

♦ There are open gates in these walls that allow our thinking to go outside the box.

♦ This type of thinking needs to be practiced in order to make it part of our repertoire of thinking.

For most of us "the box" represents the walls that define our normal everyday thinking. In a sense, it's like a mining claim that is carefully surveyed and registered in the government land office. We get a map with lines drawn on it showing where we can dig; where we can't dig lies outside the prescribed boundaries. This becomes our "box," and because it is so well-defined, it becomes comfortable. It is the "known." On the other side of the line is the unknown, the uncomfortable territory outside the box. For many, "outside the box" thinking means coming up with imaginative ideas, risking criticism, etc. Most of us have lived within prescribed boundaries for so long that going outside of them is like breaking the law. Because "over there" is foreign territory, with its own language, you will need a passport *and* a dictionary so that you can ask for directions and deal with emergencies.

Every once in a while when you look over the wall that you have erected on your property line, you see other people, apparently immune from the constraints you feel, moving about with complete freedom. They look different and they talk oddly and you think they must be weird. You tell yourself that you could risk your life wandering around in that foreign wilderness.

People who have just been assigned to a creative problem solving team but do not feel adequate to the task often feel like aliens in a foreign land. The boss has asked for an "out of the box" solution which they have never attempted and about which they feel very uncomfortable. Walk for a moment in those people's moccasins as they deal with the wall between them and the territory outside the box. Find the opening in your own wall and walk through it in your moccasins.

How to Get Comfortable with "Outside the Box" Territory

Now imagine you are walking along your property line and you come to an open gate in the wall and a person on the other side says, "Would you like to come through and see what's over here?" And you answer, "Yes, I'd like to. I'm curious, but I don't think I'm ready." And the other person says, "Don't be afraid. It's completely safe and I know the language. I can translate for you and I can show you around. You'll love it." And so you think for a minute and suddenly you hear yourself saying, "O.K. I'd like to, but promise me I won't get hurt and that you can bring me back to this gate leading to my own area of comfort."

So you allow your guide to escort you through the gate and across the meadow and up the nearby hill, where you can see into the distance. When you get to the top, the sun is out and the air is pure and people seem to be moving about much more freely than back home behind the wall in your box. It's as if there's less gravity and more oxygen. As a matter of fact, while just standing there, you're beginning to

"Take a chance! All life is a chance. The person who goes farthest is generally the one who is willing to do and dares. 'The sure-thing boat' never gets far from shore."

—

Dale Carnegie

get odd and exciting ideas about how high you can jump and how fast you can run. From the top of this hill it seems as if you can see forever. There's nothing to block your view compared to back home where there are trees and hedges and walls. It's so unusual that you're not ready to believe it, but it seems that distance is like time in that what's a hundred feet away is actually into the future. It's tomorrow over there and those things really in the distance are into next *year*. "I don't know what's happening, but this is too weird for me. I'm going to go back and sit in my favorite chair and think about this some more. So, Mr. Guide, would you please take me back to the gate in my private wall so I can figure out what's happened? Thank you for the guided tour; it was really interesting and I'm glad it was safe, and I didn't get lost and I didn't get hurt. And *maybe* if you're here next week, I might let you take me up the same hill again but then down into that distant valley. But before I commit to doing that, let me have a quiet reflecting time in the comfort of my personal space, my private box."

This fantasy excursion outside the box is a mental exercise in testing your willingness to let yourself go in stages of experimental thinking. Try it yourself. It's a way of getting comfortable with "out of the box" thinking. First, let your imagination take you outside your wall to a place such as I have described. Let your mind explore this open space. Let your fantasy run free for a few minutes. Stay there until you feel comfortable. Now, recall a past event requiring you to think "outside the box," which you were unable to do. Relive that experience, only this time let yourself out of the box—explore a new ending to the story.

The reason for getting personally comfortable with this form of thinking is that it can contribute to your creativity. To qualify, you don't have to be outrageous. At this writing, probably the most extreme example of sustained, public, "out of the box" thinking is David Letterman's *Late Show*. Letterman is outside the box 60 minutes a night, five nights a week. For businesspeople, I see this form of thinking as a tool to be applied situationally and occasionally rather than continuously. It provides openness and flexibility when needed. To be available as a tool, it must be understood and practiced.

> "If there is something that you think you can do, even dream that you can— begin it! Boldness has mystery and power and magic in it."
>
> —
>
> *Johann Wolfgang von Goethe*

Mavericks

My interest in unusual people includes independent, "out of the box" thinkers often referred to as mavericks.

I have decided to avoid going to the dictionary for a definition of *maverick* until I have reached into my personal experience for three real-life examples. The first one that comes to mind is Bill Cronkite. Bill was a GE apparatus products salesman during the 1940s and 1950s. His exploits were legendary. He would routinely sell big-ticket, heavy apparatus, such as steam turbine generators, large transformers, and large switchgear. These products were often priced in the millions, and a total order from a single utility client might be as large as $5 million or $10 million. Bill loved to cater to his customers. He would sometimes invite them on bear hunts and deep-sea fishing expeditions as part of his relationship-building strategy. Hunting lodges and chartered boats were included. He almost always came back with the order, but along with the order came a hefty expense account. An expense charge of $1,500 in 1950 dollar values really got the attention, not only of the finance department but also of the vice president in charge of the sales division. During Bill's tenure two vice presidents failed to control his excesses and it wasn't because they didn't try. Bill always had a way to "explain" the large amounts that he charged to a particular sale. He made it seem totally logical to behave as he did. Even though the vice presidents had set personal goals to correct Bill's behavior, neither of them succeeded.

As a salesman Bill was three layers below the division vice president. Therefore he had a sales manager that he actually reported to who had tried to bring Bill into compliance with the expense account ground rules. The sales manager reported to a district manager, who also failed, after repeated attempts, to bring Bill into line. Therefore it was up to the vice president. At the time of the story as I'm telling it, there was a new vice president who was determined to bring Bill Cronkite down on his knees in abject contrition about the numerous sins he had committed in achieving his sales record. The division VP held a meeting with the district manager and the sales manager to research the sins that Bill had committed. There were dozens of specific incidents that, when fully detailed, occupied eight pages of documented occurrences. Even though Bill's sales had exceeded $40 million during the

Figure 26-1.
Pro forma profile of Bill Cronkite.

same period, these expense account aberrations just could not be tolerated. Brimming with confidence, the vice president wrote what he felt was the definitive letter to accompany the lengthy litany of expense account infractions.

Bill Cronkite was no more than five feet four and about as feisty as you could get. The previous vice president was five feet six, and no match for Bill's aggressive behavior. The new vice president was six feet two, and felt that no little shrimp was going to get away with these shenanigans under *his* management, so he wrote the cover letter to the memo with as much authority as his rank would allow. He was certain that, when confronted with this documented evidence of transgression, Bill would be humbled into submission. The letter was as strong as he could write and still be typed on company stationery. After several drafts that strengthened the initial attempt, the letter was duly signed and mailed.

A week later the vice president received his original letter back with the following message, handwritten across the top of the letter. "Dear George: Look what some son of a bitch sent me and had nerve enough to sign your name to. Your friend, Bill Cronkite." Bill's behavior exemplified a form of outrageous humor characteristic of technical guys with a strong D quadrant.

The second maverick who comes to mind is Gerhardt Neuman. Like Bill, Gerhardt was an engineer with a strong A quadrant and a very strong D quadrant. I first met him when he was Vice President and General Manager of the Aircraft Engine Division of General Electric. He was a hero, both inside and outside GE. He received his U.S. citizenship by an Act of Congress for having assembled the first Japanese Zero from pieces and parts of downed aircraft. He was a brilliant engineer who ran a 20,000-person division as a wartime pilot would handle his flight crew—hands-on leadership, personal knowledge of every member, love and affection for both the machine and the people, and high expectations of everyone, including himself.

He interviewed me in a swimming pool. On my first day of work, he called me at twenty minutes to eight and asked me how all the thousands of engineers in the Evendale, Ohio, plant were doing that day. I told him that I had just arrived and that I would find out. He said, "You better find out and I'll call you tomorrow." The next day he called me at quarter to eight and said, "Herrmann, tell me about those engineers."

And I said, "Gerhardt, I'm still finding out." He said, "You better find out quicker." The next morning, which was my third day on the job, he called me at ten minutes to eight and said, "Herrmann, how are all those manufacturing people doing down there at Evendale?" And I said, "Gerhardt, I'm still trying to find out about the engineers." And he said, "Herrmann, you better find out about the engineers in manufacturing, too." By the end of the week, I knew a lot, not only about the engineers but about the whole operation and was able to answer specific questions with factual answers. That was Gerhardt's way of getting me onboard.

Several months later, he asked me "How's the morale of those engineers?" and I said, "I think it's pretty good, Gerhardt." He said, "Herrmann, you come with me and I'll show you how to find out about morale." Together, we walked out into the large open engineering space and immediately ran into one of the engineers. Gerhardt poked his finger into the man's chest and said, "How's your morale?" The man answered, "Well, gosh, Mr. Neuman, I don't know. I think my morale is o.k." Whereupon Gerhardt turned to me and said, "You see, Herrmann, this is the way you find out about morale in this place." We walked a few feet further and came upon a mature engineer with a distinctly foreign accent. Gerhardt repeated his finger-in-the-chest question about morale and the man stood an inch taller and said, "What my morale is, is none of your goddamn business. What my morale is, is the business of my supervisor and you ain't my supervisor." Gerhardt turned to me and said, "Herrmann, let's find out about morale in the next building."

In my position, I was one of 13 key employee relations managers in General Electric and therefore had a dotted-line responsibility to corporate headquarters. I was expected to attend monthly meetings in New York City. Gerhardt knew about this, but he did not like it at all. *He* was in charge of his division and he had full authority to run it as he saw fit. He didn't want me going to New York and reporting on events in his division and receiving instructions from corporate headquarters. After a year of this infighting, I was in the GE Headquarters Building at 570 Lexington Avenue and was heading down the elevator following the completion of the Key ERM meeting. The lobby of the GE building was rather long and narrow, so that the two banks of elevators were only about 20 feet across from each other. As my elevator door opened and

I stepped into the lobby, the doors of the elevator directly opposite opened and there was Gerhardt Neuman, flanked by an executive vice president on one side and a vice chairman on the other side. He spotted me across the lobby and shouted, "Herrmann, what the hell are you doing in New York? Goddamn it, your job is in Evendale." I stopped dead in my tracks and said, "Gerhardt, I am on my way back to Evendale now." Meanwhile the senior officers on either side of Gerhardt were laughing uproariously, knowing by past experience that this was Gerhardt doing his thing.

The aircraft engine business thrived under Gerhardt Neuman. He knew everything that was going on both day and night. He would often prowl the plant at three in the morning and use pass keys to open doors and closets, including offices of general managers. He would leave notes in places; for example, in a maintenance closet there would be a note saying "This closet is a mess. Clean it up because I'm coming back tomorrow night." On another occasion, he discovered that work was still taking place on an engine project that had been cancelled five years earlier. The next morning there was a note on the general manager's desk, demanding to know why this work was still going on.

Gerhardt's style was hands-on management, 24 hours a day, seven days a week. It was a challenge to work for him, but he was universally loved and respected even though his leadership style was distinctly "out of the norm," even "out of the box." I would describe him as one of the most unusual people I have ever met. I also think of him as a visionary with a sure grasp of the future. And for me, he is the epitome of a maverick. Thirty years after the incidents I have just described, I noted him on Tom Peters' list of outstanding leaders to emulate.

Not only by association, but by his own brand of outrageous behavior, I would also nominate Tom Peters as a maverick. He is brilliant, charismatic, opinionated, and is clearly an "out of the box" thinker. He is also frequently right. Mark Twain once said, "You've got to take your brain out of your head every once in a while and *jump* on it." This is not a bad description of Tom Peters' impact on business leadership around the world. He delights in finding examples of leadership that breaks the rules and then he breaks the rules of reporting those examples of business success. The man is nothing short of terrific in his writing and speaking, but what

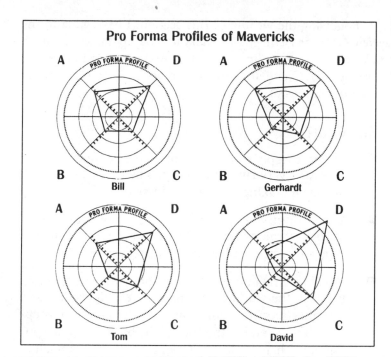

Figure 26-2.
Pro forma profiles of
four mavericks.

he does and says is entirely individualistic, unique, and outrageous. I can't imagine many businesspeople who have not read Tom's books, heard him speak, or listened to his tapes.

He is not above promoting his books with a life-size cardboard cutout photo of himself dressed in a business suit above the waist and swimming trunks below the waist. His idiosyncracies have gained momentum since his blockbuster landmark book in the early 1980s titled *The Search for Excellence* and his most recent book *The Pursuit of WOW*. Tom Peters is brilliant, charismatic, *and* a maverick. Just as a multitude of businesspeople read and listen to Peters to profit from his business advice, millions tune into David Letterman to enjoy his adventures "outside of the box." They both offer fresh, stimulating, and often outrageous, views that cut through the stale, tried-and-true approaches of others in their field. Businesspeople can learn much from both their content and style. They are professionals at the cutting edge. There is plenty of room for the rest of us to try our wings without getting hurt.

I don't have personal profile data on Bill, Gerhardt, Tom, or David, but based on their track records, I offer the *pro forma* profiles displayed in figure 26-2.

Following the writing of this section, I have gone to the *New American Heritage Dictionary* to look up the word *maverick*. It offers two definitions: "(1) An unbranded range calf or colt; (2) One that resists adherence to a group." I think both definitions fit.

"Only the mediocre are always at their best."

—

Jean Giraudoux

So What?

■ Businesspeople can break out of the confines of their ordinary, everyday thinking styles by using their imagination and taking some mental risks.

■ You can test your willingness to explore your "out of the box" thinking potential by letting your imagination take you to new and exciting mental places.

■ David Letterman in the field of entertainment and Tom Peters in the world of business are examples of world class practitioners of this thinking technique. They represent the far end of the "out of the box" thinking continuum. There is plenty of room for others to stretch in that direction.

Reclaiming Your Lost Creativity

Chapter Headlines

♦ Children are naturally creative, but only half the adult population considers itself creative.

♦ The creativity of youth can be reclaimed by businesspeople.

♦ Claiming creative space requires expanding the mental profile of preferences to include what is needed for the creative task.

> *"Everyone is born a genius, but the process of living de-geniuses them."*
>
> —
>
> *R. Buckminster Fuller*

Children are naturally creative. They begin to lose that spark as they gain self-discipline, learn language, accept their parents' discipline, and obey society's rules. Data on over 110,000 adults in our files indicates that 49 percent of them think of themselves as creative. There were an equal number of men and women in this total, and all of them felt they could be *more* creative. This leaves 51 percent who apparently do not think of themselves as creative.

This data is largely confirmed by a separate study of 2,000 men and women workshop participants, 51 percent of whom felt they were creative. This group also felt there was enormous room for creative growth. If we extrapolate these studies to include the general population, my guess is that we would get about the same answer. I believe the same would also be true of the business population. What happens to half our business employees? What happens to the other half who think they are creative, but not nearly at the level they could be? What happens to those who think they are creative, but not at work? If they were creative as children, the chances are good that they can reclaim much of what was lost in the maturing process. It's a little bit like riding a bike. Once you experience success, you can reclaim that success even after 20 or 30 years. All you need is permission, encouragement, and the right circumstances.

A prime reason that many people have temporarily lost their creativity is they didn't feel they had *permission*. Well-intentioned parents, teachers, and bosses behaved in ways that partially or even totally shut down their natural creativity as children, adolescents, and employees. Can this lost creativity be reclaimed? I think the answer is yes, particularly for business employees who function in an organization that has a leadership motivated to take action.

I am confident that most adults can reclaim their creativity because I did so myself, and I have witnessed thousands of others in the process of doing so. In order to understand how this may be accomplished on a large scale, it is necessary to examine some of the major components of the solution.

1. **Attitude**. A significant aspect of adult creativity is that at least half the people don't think they have it, so somehow we must convince them that they were naturally creative as children and can regain enough of that early creativity to be usefully creative as adults. I use the strategy of *personal affirmation* as the primary method of accomplishing this. Since people tend to equate drawing with their early creativity, and since most of them lost what they thought were their natural drawing skills at about age 10 when they acquired a significant language capability, I affirm them by demonstrating that they can draw again. We teach people the basics of how to draw and a very high percentage (80-90 percent) actually can. They are then confronted with indisputable evidence of a regained capability. Included in this group are some adults who claimed that they never could draw even as children. Nevertheless, relatively simple techniques can be used to provide a stunning affirmation. Karen Gammon, whom I referred to in an earlier chapter, is

one of the many who launched a creative career as a result of such affirmation.

A second potential area of affirmation is in the ability to visualize in your mind. Again, this is a natural mode of childhood. Just recall how you once played with toy soldiers, or baby dolls, or forts, or dollhouses, or kitchen sets, or construction models, or empty cardboard boxes as children. We got lost in these fantasies and were able, through our natural ability to visualize, to make real castles out of simple blocks, or real operating rooms out of plastic toys. This is another domain where affirmation is readily available. Individuals who claim that they can no longer do this discover that they can, and the success level is again over 80 percent, and as high as 90 percent with typical business groups. When confronted with indisputable evidence of success, participants are hard-pressed to deny this capability.

2. **Technique**. Specific techniques exist to achieve these affirmations. Betty Edwards, the author of *Drawing on the Right Side of the Brain* and *The Artist Within*, describes in detail the precise steps in the "learning how to draw" process. There are hundreds of experts throughout the world who can facilitate Betty's techniques.

Many adults claim that they used to be able to write rather creatively, but can no longer do so. Gabriele L. Rico, the author of *Writing the Natural Way*, provides specific techniques for opening up people to their natural latent creative writing ability. She provides a specific path toward affirmation. There is nothing quite as persuasive as being impressed by your own creative "stuff," whether it be prose or poetry.

Another technique to provide affirmation of creative expression is that of modeling a problem situation. Workshop participants can build creative models out of such materials as paper towel rolls, wood blocks, styrofoam packing, old washing machine parts, dowels, used tennis balls, shoe boxes, feathers, and string. This involves the use of creative materials to assemble a three-dimensional metaphoric model of a problem or a situation. Through this hands-on experience of creating something visual, natural imaginative ideas surface and are applied to the evolving model. The resulting models represent such strong physical evidence of people's ability to think creatively (when they didn't think they could), that the models are described with great pride in calls to home and often actually taken home to show the family and coworkers.

Participants in a high-level series of workshops on strategic thinking felt that their models of their company and its relationship with key customers were so significant that photographs of them were incorporated into official strategic planning reports.

3. **Tools**. First on the list of tools is the creative process itself. By providing individuals with a take-away process that they can independently apply, we can give self-described "noncreatives" a golden key that unlocks their own closed door of creativity. In Chapter 23 I identified 77 discrete creative processes (p. 227) that can be selected and applied by people with any mental preference in the four-quadrant model. Through specific training and practice, affirmations lead to individuals becoming creative champions of a particular process that suits their thinking style.

4. **Teams**. Many individuals who have lost their creativity have also lost their confidence in trying to regain it by themselves. While creativity is a very personal process, it also can be very lonely. Pairing up two or more lonely people can be positively reinforcing. Building a team of individuals in various stages of creative reclamation can be very mutually supporting and also very exciting. Through team activity, individuals can model stages of the creative process to each other in ways that greatly facilitate creative growth. It's very hard to resist the momentum of successful creative group involvement. People are caught up in the process and, before they realize it, they have demonstrated their own creativity. It is thrilling when they do, and it's hard for them to deny that they did it.

5. **Climate**. In order for any of this to happen, there must be a climate that provides permission and support and reward for creative behavior. For many people who lost their early creativity, this is a crucially needed reversal of what turned them off in the first place. Many didn't feel

they had permission. They didn't feel they had any support and sometimes they were even punished for their creative attempts. This is where business managers must demonstrate their own understanding of creativity by metamorphosing into creative managers. Their goal should be to become creative champions.

If creativity is a specific business goal, then to achieve that goal the people in charge must understand the opportunity they have to assist their employees in the process of reclaiming the natural creativity of their youth. Managers who do so are also unleashing the creative potential of the organization, and this means that everything will now be different. The more managers become champions, the more likely it is that the corporate goal of "going creative" can be achieved.

The track record of success is our own 15 years of business application of this Whole Brain Approach to reclaim creativity in the work space.

Creative Courage

Many people do creative things without giving a second thought to the courage it takes to deal with the consequences. I think it is primarily in the area of consequences that creative courage becomes a significant issue. In most instances the creative act is pleasurable, and quite frequently it is downright *fun*. It's a release from the pressures of everyday work. As the renowned psychologist Abraham Maslow might describe it, "it is a reward in itself to have the opportunity to engage in the creative process." It is an example of what I believe he meant by "self-actualization."

Courage can come into play when your behavior is observed while doing your creative thing. Some coworkers may be seeing you so animated, so energetic, and so happy and your work space so cluttered and messy that they wonder about you. Creative behavior can be so different from the everyday norm that others who have not let themselves experience it may consider it disruptive and even strange. Under these conditions it takes some courage to continue to behave in this seemingly abnormal manner. The risk is that the critical opinion of others might force a level of self-control that shuts down your applied creativity. You just can't do it dressed in a three-piece suit with a worried look on your face. For you, it's a no-coat-and-tie, sleeves-rolled up, happy-times kind of behavior. Censoring that behavior can stop your creativity dead in its tracks.

Assume for a moment that your creative process has not been adversely affected and you have developed a highly creative solution to a long-standing problem. However, some influential people feel that your solution is laughable, impractical, and, in fact, weird. It's totally off-the-wall, "out of the box" thinking and you are ridiculed for even suggesting such an outlandish approach to a serious problem. This is where courage is required. It takes a lot of guts to stand up for your creative idea in the face of severe criticism from the security-minded, status quo, traditionalists. There are always enough of these people standing in the wings to throw cold water on any ideas that deviate from the norm. A whole language has been developed to kill creative ideas. It is likely that all of us have heard these kinds of idea-killers, and maybe inadvertently used them ourselves.

Attitudes that Kill Creative Ideas

The high ranking VP-level idea-killers that I have personally experienced seemed to wear the scalps of dead creative proposals with great pride. On one occasion, I was presenting a creative proposal to a senior vice president heading up a roomful of managers whose approval was required, when he asked the following question at the end of my presentation: "Ned, is what you are recommending something that our leading competitors are doing?" Even though that was totally beside the point, I had to answer, "No." He responded, "Well, that does it for me," and he stood up and left the room. Without a word, everybody else stood up and also left the room.

I was blindsided. I was caught by surprise and was unable to spontaneously counter his idea-killing comment. That incident could have terminated the work of my task force that had devoted several weeks of creative effort, but I was so convinced of the soundness of the proposed solution that I made a conscious decision not to cave in, even though this guy was a powerful vice president. With the help of the task force members, I prepared and sent to him a written *restatement* of the proposed creative solution and ended it by saying, "As you well know, this is an industrywide problem, and

Attitudes that Kill Creative Ideas

1. Don't be ridiculous.
2. We tried that before.
3. We've never done it before.
4. It costs too much.
5. That's beyond our responsibility.
6. It's too radical a change.
7. We don't have time.
8. We're too small for it.
9. That will make other equipment obsolete.
10. Not practical for operating people.
11. The union will scream.
12. Let's get back to reality.
13. That's not our problem.
14. Why change it? It's still working okay.
15. You're two years ahead of your time.
16. We're not ready for that.
17. It isn't in the budget.
18. Can't teach an old dog new tricks.
19. Top management will never go for it.
20. We'll be the laughing stock.
21. We did all right without it.
22. Let's form a committee.
23. Has anyone else ever tried it?
24. Are our competitors doing it?

if our competitors got wind of what we propose to do, they would immediately steal our solution and get ahead of us with our key customers." To my surprise, I got a note back from the senior vice president that said, "I have reconsidered your recommendation and I think you are right. Thanks for not giving up. I have told the Review Board that I am approving your recommendation." Now, you can argue that he didn't have the unilateral right to take that action, but I elected not to use a "killer" phrase to stop him.

"Go and wake up your luck."

—

Persian Proverb

There will be times like this when killer phrases can be challenged by having the courage of your own convictions. People who use these idea-killing phrases enjoy a great deal of success. They provide power to people who seek power. I have discovered that in most instances there is no substance in these killer phrases. People who use them expect to be challenged, and when they are not, their suspicions appear to be correct and they quickly claim victory. As a result of my own successful experience, I prepared myself not to be blindsided again, particularly by high-level officers whose primary weapon was their rank. I now come ready to deal with any idea-killing phrases that might be made.

The net result was a sharp increase in my creative-proposal batting average. If courage is involved, it comes from the worthiness of the creative recommendation. If courage is involved, it is supported by the success of applying this strategy of positive confrontation.

Claiming Creative Space Exercise

> ⚑ Applied Creativity is whole brained.
>
> ⚑ All quadrants are situationally involved in the Creative Process.

Instructions:

Indicate your "Creative Space" in the diagram below by shading in the appropriate portions of each of the four quadrants, "enclosing" the space that you need to claim to become more fully effective.

Then, on the lines provided within the quadrants, write in some key descriptive words of the work that "turns you on" to help you establish your personal ownership of that space. This can provide you with the basis for a personal action plan.

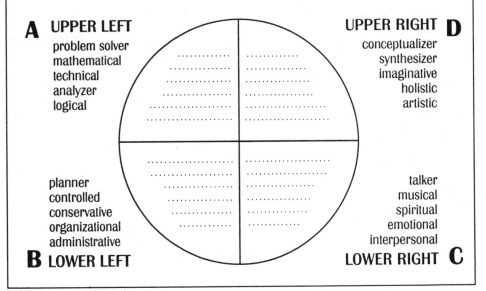

A UPPER LEFT
problem solver
mathematical
technical
analyzer
logical

UPPER RIGHT D
conceptualizer
synthesizer
imaginative
holistic
artistic

planner
controlled
conservative
organizational
administrative

talker
musical
spiritual
emotional
interpersonal

B LOWER LEFT

LOWER RIGHT C

Figure 27-1.
The Claiming
Creative Space
Exercise.

Claiming Your Creative Space

One of the best ways for people to help themselves become more creative is for them to claim their own creative space. By *creative space* I mean the mental, the psychological, and the physical space that allows for, gives permission for, and encourages personal creativity to take place. Some forms of creativity demand enough private *physical space* to engage in the creative act. What we are creating is too big, it's too messy, it's too long-lasting to be done on the kitchen table, in front of the TV, or on your desk at work. So you need your own private skunk works where you can do what you need to do without cluttering up other people's work space, without getting in the way of your everyday tasks, and where you have the freedom to do "weird stuff."

"Never kill an idea, just deflect it."

—

3M Slogan

After physical space the next space to consider is the psychological space that we all need when privacy is essential to our process, and where personal risks can be explored before they are committed publicly. *And* where we are simply comfortable enough to eliminate the self-generated "ogres" that tend to get in the way of the creative process.

Finally, there is the mental space that needs to be claimed. By this, I mean those portions of the whole brain mental spectrum that need to be accessed in order to function at a fully applied creative level. Tap into your own instincts to identify mental areas that you are currently not using and perhaps actively resisting, but need to access in order to be fully creative. A proven tool to aid in this process is the Claiming Creative Space Exercise.

In completing the exercise, you have used your increased understanding of your mental self developed by reading this book to sketch in an approximation of your own profile. You have also used this understanding of the whole brain premise to sketch in a pro forma profile that approximates the mental options you need to access in order to be fully creative in the situation you have in mind. There is typically a gap between the two profiles, indicating those portions of the mental spectrum that have to be added in order to accomplish the creative task, but which are not now an active preference for you personally. What to do about that?

Shown on the next page is my personal profile, along with a pro forma profile of the creative space that I need to write this book.

As you can see from the profiles in figure 27-2, the writing of a book requires more creative space than is typically available to me under ordinary day-to-day circumstances. The implications are clear. If I am to write this book in accordance with the book proposal accepted by the publisher, and to deliver a manuscript complete with illustrations and graphics and do so within the allowable budget and on time, then I am going to have to substantially supplement my normal

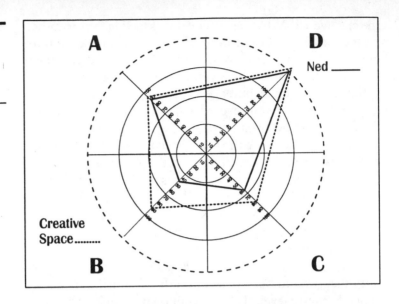

Figure 27-2.
The creative space the author claimed when writing this book.

profile of A- and D-quadrant preferred mental activity with a substantial amount of additional B- and C-quadrant creative space in order to perform the creative tasks that I have committed myself to do. *Further*, to accomplish my creative goals, I will have to consciously, deliberately claim, not only my everyday creative space, but this new, enlarged creative space required by the task at hand.

You will notice that I have not only increased my normal creative profile in the D quadrant, but I have added a significant amount of creative space in the B quadrant. This is where the budgetary, procedural, and production aspects of the creative process are located. This is where the signed contract takes precedence and where due dates need to be met as committed. This is where writing discipline is located and where much of the editorial work needs to take place.

I believe a good personal example of how I have applied this exercise to the writing of this book is the discipline to which I have committed myself of writing each morning, seven days a week until the creative phase is completed. The habit that has been formed over the months of applying this discipline now allows for the editing, rewriting, illustrating, and quote selection processes to take place each morning, seven days a week. This illustrates the point that once creative space has been fully claimed, it provides the basis of a significant increase in my creative capability. As a result of claim-

"Alas, for those who never sing, but die with all their music in them."

—

Oliver Wendell Holmes, Jr.

ing this space, I have acquired a habit that greatly increases my productivity, not only on this book project, but in the everyday accomplishment of my business tasks.

As I think is already clear, the kind of creative space I am talking about is not something that can be given to you by your boss or your spouse or your parents. For this new space to work for you it must be *owned* by you, and there is only one good way that I know to own it, and that is to personally claim it.

So What?

■　Creativity is sensitive to evaluation and criticism and it takes personal courage to withstand the many ways of killing ideas and stopping the creative process.

■　A high percentage of ideas developed in an organizational setting are wasted.

■　Managements that want to encourage creativity need to be aware of this and actively campaign to change the culture from "killing" creativity to stimulating it, supporting it, and rewarding it.

■　Key components to successful application of corporate creativity programs are: top management's understanding of the creative process and its consequences, and the presence of a knowledgeable creativity champion to provide inspirational leadership and protective air cover.

> *"Creative activity could be described as a type of learning process where teacher and pupil are located in the same individual."*
>
> —
>
> *Arthur Koestler*

28

Creative...Who ME?
Tools and Techniques
for Personal Creativity

"The best part of one's life is the working part, the creative part. Believe me, I love to succeed; but the real spiritual and emotional excitement is in the doing."

—

Garson Kanin

Chapter Headlines

♦   Trying to be creative is rewarded more often than poor execution is punished.

♦   Three key steps in getting started are affirmation, facilitation through coaching, and granting of permission.

♦   In a business setting, the negative space between individuals can help define their relationships with one another.

♦   Personal creative habits can provide the discipline needed to help insure professional success.

I resisted my own natural creativity for half my life—at least any public demonstration of it. The parental values handed down to me were along the lines of "do it right the first time." At least that is how I interpreted what my family was saying to me, so it was easy for me to have a fear of failure. If there was any risk of failure, I tried things out in private. It was only when a midlife medical crisis occurred that I was able to see how silly and self-defeating this behavior was. I had provided myself with an excuse to fail in public, but that never really happened. In the domain of art I discovered that the public rewarded *trying* to be an artist to a far greater degree than it punished poor execution of the finished art. I found that the rewards outweighed the risks to such an extent that my activity level soon gave me the practice that I needed to overcome the skill deficits of a beginner.

Moving away from art per se and thinking more of creativity in general, I have pondered the question of "how to begin" for many years. It doesn't need to be so difficult that you waste half your life wondering if you are good enough to even start. Since this is such a personal issue, I will avoid rank-ordering my considered answers, but high on the list has got to be *affirmation*. Attempting something that you always wanted to do and doing it successfully is an affirmation that can convince even the most practiced skeptic that he or she has what it takes to succeed. I have written about this in a number of places in this book because it is such a successful technique. Teaching people how to draw, teaching people how to sculpt, teaching people how to visualize, teaching people how to use creative materials are all examples of techniques that allow people to achieve in areas of low self-esteem. They didn't think they could do these things and so they avoided trying. When they were guided into attempting them and discovered that they could succeed, they were confronted with their own accomplishment.

A key to affirmation is *facilitation* of the activity that leads to affirmation. For the person whose creativity is blocked as if by an insurmountable brick wall, facilitation is a ramp up to a door in that wall. I am thinking of being blocked as a temporary disability that can be overcome through understanding. Through skilled facilitation, a person with natural capability can have that ability released in very effective ways. Think for a minute about a coach who can facilitate a youngster who is riding a bicycle or batting a ball or ice skating or drawing a likeness. Amateur athletes use coaches throughout their careers; professional teams use coaches on a full-time basis; professional golfers and opera singers rely on coaches. However, it would never dawn on a *businessperson* to employ a coach to facilitate them into the release of their natural creativity. Such *creative coaching* or facilitation is available from many sources.

Along with affirmation and facilitation comes *permission*. Many of us hang back until we think we have permission. By that I mean permission to try, permission to experiment, permission to fail. I have discovered that this is very hard to come by. We are reluctant to give ourselves permission and

Figure 28-1.
A sample "Creative
Space Certificate"
awarded to
individuals who
complete certain
NHG workshops.

THE NED HERRMANN GROUP CERTIFIES THAT YOU,

John Doe,

ARE HEREBY GRANTED ENTHUSIASTIC PERMISSION
TO CLAIM YOUR OWN CREATIVE SPACE. THIS SPACE
WILL TAKE EFFECT AS SOON AS YOU ACCEPT THE
RESPONSIBILITY FOR IT AND WILL REMAIN SO AS
LONG AS YOU USE IT AND PROTECT IT.

we are prone to decline the permission granted to us by others. There is a certain inherent shyness that comes to the surface when a chance to be creative is offered. It is all too easy to turn down the invitation. For this reason, permission must be overt. It must be obvious. It must be without strings or consequences, and in this regard the hardest permission to come by is that which we give ourselves. To help get past this self-denial, I present workshop participants with a formal certificate that gives them permission to claim their own creative space.

I encourage them to actually hang this certificate in their work space so that whenever they become unsure of their own permission or of the organization's permission, they can refer to their "official certification of permission" as documentation that they have what it takes to behave in a creative way. Claiming your creative space implies that creativity is a priority. It is more than just a personal urge. It is actually legitimate work. Unfortunately, there are many business cultures that consider creative activity to be something other than work. Instead of being on task, it is thought of as a loss of focus and a deviation from assigned work. For these reasons, the priority that I am alluding to needs to be held not only by the person attempting to establish his or her creativity but also by those people who manage that individual. To be most effective, this sense of priority has to be established simultaneously by the individual and his or her manager. A very effective way to establish and communicate the manager's priority for creative behavior is to have that person sign the certificate of permission for the individual to claim creative space. There should be room on that certificate for the next higher level of manager also to officialize this priority with his or her signature.

Along with affirmation, facilitation, priority, and permission, I recommend creating *a portfolio of creative accomplishments*. Successful artists have a portfolio of their prize-winning work. Authors have a shelf of books. Photographers have a portfolio of pictures. Businesspeople have a résumé or curriculum vitae that lists their accomplishments. Businesspeople can assemble a portfolio of their creative accomplishments. This can include such things as ideas submitted to the suggestion system, creative accomplishments as a member of a task force, or documented ideas submitted to management. It won't take long to accumulate an impressive body of creative work. In surveys that I have conducted over the past few years, I have discovered that more than a third of the thousands of people responding have a body of creative work suitable for documentation. I think it is revealing to note that most of them never thought in terms of a "body of work" until I asked the question. I believe that recognizing that a personal body of work exists is a major affirmation of one's creative ability. I could tell from the brightness of the respondent's eyes and the broad smiles on their faces that these individuals felt very good about their accomplishments over the years. I can tell you that I have kept a portfolio of my creative accomplishments and find it personally inspiring to review this growing body of work. It is, in fact, a very real affirmation that reminds me to give myself permission to "go for it" again.

> *"I need problems. A good problem makes me come alive."*
>
> —
>
> *"Tiny" Roland*

Acquiring Personal Creative Habits

During the 15 years that art was my second professional occupation, I developed a habit that contributed in a major way to my artistic success and productivity. I typically painted a picture a week and completed a sculpture every two months. I discovered that at any given time I had four or five compelling scenes or subjects in my mind for the next painting or sculpture. The problem was making a choice among a number of very desirable subjects. I would usually start a painting on Saturday morning and finish it for framing a week later, typically on Sunday afternoon. On one occasion at the beginning of this highly productive period, I decided to make the decision for the next painting *before I left* the studio after finishing the current painting. After signing the painting that I was working on and removing the watercolor paper from the art table, I would think for a few minutes about the subject that intrigued me at that moment. In a few minutes of contemplation I was able to sort out the one that was of primary interest, and then, working rapidly with my pencil, I would commit myself to that subject as my next painting. I would often commit myself more completely to that chosen subject by brushing in a color wash in the places appropriate to the final scene. I would then set that new watercolor paper aside and complete the matting and framing of the work I had just finished.

What happened next strongly confirms the stage of the creative process that is called incubation. Between the time that I committed myself on paper and the next time that I could work in my studio, I discovered myself painting that picture in my mind. By the time I returned to the painting several days had passed, or even most of the week, but I was able to quickly complete the preliminary sketch that was the initial phase of the painting and then block in the main elements of the scene with almost complete confidence that what I was doing would be part of the finished painting. This technique worked so well for me that it became an absolute unwritten rule that I would always start the next painting before I left the studio. Tangible evidence of the success of this strategy was that I won prizes (60) and sold paintings (400) at an increasing rate.

I applied the same discipline to my sculpture, but since the processes are so different, I couldn't commit myself with a few lines on paper but had to make a miniature in clay of what I intended to sculpt on a larger scale. Again, the same thing happened. I was able to make progress subconsciously by working through the design of the finished piece in my mind as I went about my other business. I believe this to be a key characteristic of the brain. If you present your mental self with a situation, your mind can work on that situation unconsciously and effortlessly during other activity *or* sleep, so that as you reengage on the task at hand, you have made progress toward its solution. I have used this habit now for about 30 years with great success.

> **"Man's mind, once stretched by a new idea, never regains its original dimensions."**
>
> —
>
> *Oliver Wendell Holmes, Jr.*

A new habit that I have acquired in writing this book is dictating every morning, seven days a week, on topics of interest that come to mind each morning. As I contemplate the next morning's writing before I go to sleep I present myself with subject alternatives. When I wake up I spend 15 minutes in a theta state that is conducive to my creative process, which positions me to engage the subject that I'm interested in. When I go to my private place to dictate, the subject presents itself to me in a manner that I can respond to with great ease and comfort. At this point in my writing, I have dictated each morning for 90 days, and I have 90 topics (100,000 words) that will become chapters or sections of this book.

Another measure of the success of these creative strategies is that I never lost "a painting," "a sculpture," and I have never lost "a topic." In other words, in each case what I started out with I completed in a form that I could frame, display, or publish.

So What?

- Many people who have creative potential are unaware of it because they are afraid to try to apply something still hidden in which they have no confidence.

- A good way to start the release of hidden creativity is to experience the *affirmation* of success.

- Affirmation can be greatly *facilitated* through *creativity coaching*.

- For many the key to locked-up creativity is the granting of permission not only by others such as the boss, but also, hardest of all to come by, *permission from themselves*.

- Once creativity is released, keeping a personal creative accomplishment portfolio is strongly recommended.

- The difference between success and failure, particularly in work requiring creativity, is often the personal discipline and commitment that we provide. By identifying a needed discipline(s) and making a habit of it we help guarantee a successful professional outcome.

"Many people know how to work hard; many others know how to play well; but the rarest talent in the world is the ability to introduce elements of playfulness into work, and to put some constructive labor into our leisure."

—

Sydney J. Harris

29

*"Whenever
you see a
successful
business,
someone
once made
a
courageous
decision."*

—

*Peter
Drucker*

How Decisions and Values Are Influenced by Your Thinking Styles

Chapter Headlines

♦ Mental preferences determine personal decision styles.

♦ Each quadrant has its own decision style.

♦ The Whole Brain Decision-Making Walk-Around is a useful tool to improve decision making.

♦ A value clarification process/exercise helps you clarify your personal values.

Over the years, our decision-making processes develop a consistent pattern, which can be described as a decision-making style. Our style is grounded in our preferences, which arise from our brain dominance characteristics as profiled by the *HBDI*. Strongly A-quadrant people who deal with facts become very rational when there are facts upon which to base a decision. Without any facts, their decision process is less effective. B-quadrant people are looking for details. The *i*'s must be dotted, and the *t*'s crossed, and the fine print scrutinized. They don't want to make a mistake, so they will delay a decision until they feel secure that they know everything that there is to know and, there will be no surprises down the road. The B-quadrant decision process is careful, prudent, and conservative.

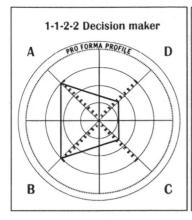

1-1-2-2 Decision maker

A — PRO FORMA PROFILE — D

B — C

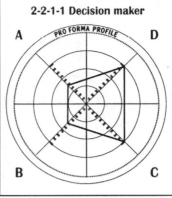

2-2-1-1 Decision maker

A — PRO FORMA PROFILE — D

B — C

The C-quadrant decision process is based not only on a strong preference for preserving relationships but also on a general avoidance of the analysis of facts and figures. Therefore, the C-quadrant decision process is largely intuitive with regard to people issues. The D-quadrant decision process is different from the other three quadrants in that it is inclined to be variable, sometimes bold, assertive, and daring and at other times impulsive and spontaneous.

Because so many businesspeople have double and triple dominances, there are decision styles that are combinations of these single-quadrant styles. The double-dominant A/B left mode style is the most typical. Here there is a need for both facts and details, for both logical analysis and step-by-step processing.

Somewhat less frequent but still often encountered is the double-dominant right mode style, combining the relationship-oriented, intuitive processes of the C quadrant with the more variable, bold and daring, and sometimes vacillating style, of the D quadrant.

The most perplexing style is the one involving double dominance in the B and D quadrants. The operative metaphor here is "having one foot on the accelerator and one foot on the brake." This is an interactive process in which the decision maker alternates between risk taking and safekeeping; between big, bold, daring alternatives and conservative, high-security options.

This decision-making dilemma becomes painfully clear when individuals whose profiles are known are invited to create three-dimensional models of their personal logos or trademark. They use a wide array of creative material to as-

"To vacillate or not to vacillate, that is the question— isn't it?"

———

Bruce Wallace

Figure 29-3.
An *HBDI* profile of a
2-1-2-1 decision
maker. This
person's decision-
making process will
be torn between B-
and D-quadrant
aspects.

Figure 29-4.
The 1-2-1-2 *HBDI*
profile offers an
equally challenging
combination of
quadrant criteria for
decision making.

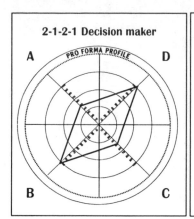

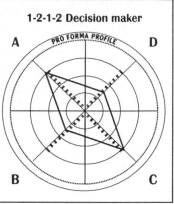

semble these models. If their creative material resources include directional arrows, individuals with B/D duality will
very frequently include contrasting metaphors of, for example,
making money and leading a life of leisure connected by arrows aimed in the opposite direction. This style represents a
decision-making dilemma. Talk to a person who thinks like
this and he or she will express frustration and pain, even in
rendering their everyday decisions—to say nothing about the
major decisions in their life.

The double-dominant A/C-quadrant profile is less frequently encountered in the business world, but also exhibits
internal confrontation between two very different preferences;
on one hand, the strong A-quadrant preference for rational
decision making, and on the other hand, an equally strong
preference oriented to feelings and relationships and people
issues. Businesspeople for whom this is the everyday decision-making style shuttle back and forth between a consideration of facts on one hand and human relationships on the
other hand, and typically agonize over their decisions when
they are hurtful to people.

The two other decision-making styles are double-dominant cerebral and double-dominant limbic. The double-dominant cerebral style (A and D) can be thought of as the scientific approach to decision making. It's a potentially synergistic combination of logical, analytic, rational processing and
bold, daring, and frequently imaginative ideas. A symbol for
this style might be Captain Kirk of *Star Trek* fame. The double-
dominant B/C-quadrant limbic style is more typified by a
social worker's decision-making style—structured, procedural, conservative, yet highly people-oriented. Sensitive but

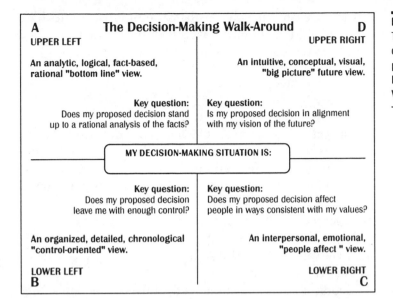

Figure 29-5.
To balance out the decision-making process, try this Decision-Making Walk-Around Model.

careful, spiritual but traditional, lots of detail but a deep concern for human values.

Our personal values as businesspeople greatly influence our decision-making process. Since, as I believe, our values are held in memory, we often rely on our values as we decide what direction to go. Are we willing to risk hurting people? Are we more interested in preserving our career potential or in making a decision in favor of others?

Because all of us are really a coalition of mental preferences involving all four quadrants, we typically shuttle back and forth between different perspectives of a decision situation based on the differing views of our coalition. The Whole Brain Decision-Making Model is a tool to help us in this process. The purpose of the tool is to encourage us to "walk around" the four-quadrant model, asking appropriate questions regarding each aspect of the mental processes involved. For example, have we done a rigorous consideration of the facts? Have we examined the details in the chronology of events? Have we factored in all the people issues, dealt with relationships? Did we take a big-picture view of the entire situation, and have we factored in the future appropriate to our conclusion? The decision-making model provides a discipline to the process that requires a step-by-step consideration of each quadrant-specific aspect of our decision process. And, in so doing, this walk-around helps to bring to the surface the values we hold in memory. Several roundtrips

"To grow as human beings, to guide our conduct, we also look for universal principles: absolute values."

—

Keshavan Mair

provide an even better chance that all appropriate values have surfaced and that all major aspects of the decision situation have been dealt with. A better decision should result.

Values

A manager's values represent an important dimension of that manager's style. Thinking primarily about values in the context of business brings to mind the strong hierarchial nature of an individual's value system. Let's take the function of finance as an example and assume that George, the senior manager we are diagnosing, is a CPA. He is also an M.B.A. and he works with a big triple-A company. He got his B.A. from Harvard and his M.B.A. from Wharton. He is married and has two children.

George is a senior member of the finance function and he reports directly to the chief financial officer (CFO). He is called into the boss's office and learns that he is being considered for an important overseas post, manager of the Singapore office, a major foreign assignment. This is a general management position, out of the finance function. He would have marketing, sales, legal, finance, and public relations managers reporting to him. His two children are in high school. One is a senior and the other is a sophomore and they are both looking forward to college. One has already chosen his university and the other one is poring over catalogues. George's wife is very active in community affairs and heads the docent program at the Art Museum. She is in the last semester of her Master of Fine Arts degree and has plans to open an art gallery with a friend.

As he hears his boss describe this new job opportunity, George's mind begins to diagnose and categorize the consequences of such a promotion. The career implications are enormous. He would be moving into a highly visible general management position, which could lead to candidacy for the London office or perhaps vice presidency of the international division, and considering the globalization of the company, that could lead to strong candidacy for a future CEO opening. Wow!

His mind flashes to his wife and family. This move would upset Mary. She would have to give up a ten-year involvement with the museum, her gallery dream, and maybe her

"Leaders have the greatest responsibility. Without the compass of absolute values, what instrument do they have to guide others?"

—

Anonymous

M.F.A. degree, lose all her friends, and give up the house they just upgraded. Could she do that? And, oh my God, the kids! John would have to leave home anyway and with a little adjustment he could stay with uncle Bill until college starts. But Peter is only a sophomore. He would have to come to Singapore and go to private school. And what about Peter's ability to survive the culture change?

In the midst of these thoughts, it suddenly dawns on George that he would be leaving his lifetime career function. He has spent over 20 years climbing the career ladder in the finance function and has established credentials, not only within the company, but also within the CPA fraternity. All his key relationships have been developed in the field of finance. To make such a move would require him to sever the career ties that he has built up throughout his career. Could he do that?

His twenty-fifth reunion at Harvard is six months away and he is on the reunion committee. As a matter of fact, he has just completed his personal write-up for the reunion book, in which he extols the virtues of sticking to one's career path.

As these personal issues flash across his mind, he is hearing his boss say that there will be an immediate 10 percent salary increase plus an overseas supplement of 7 percent, a housing allowance of 25 percent, and the use of a company Mercedes. What to do? George is so excited he has trouble adding up the benefits. This is too good to be true. He never even imagined that such a job would open up for him.

His mind flips back and forth between the issues. Peter, Mary, Harvard, the value of his house, the security of his function, his lifetime career path, the culture change. What would happen if he didn't succeed? Would he be stranded in Singapore? Suppose John flunked out of college or got into trouble? What about Peter? Was the money worth the risks?

He hears the boss saying, "I hate to lose you in the finance function, but this is a job that needs your experience, and the CEO is high on you as the prime candidate. We know you have a lot of issues to resolve to undertake such an assignment, but time is of the essence and we'd like you to make a decision in two weeks. While we want you to accept this job, George, we are aware that there may be good reasons why you choose not to. Your present job is secure. You're going to have to figure out what's important to you. Now, why don't you just take the afternoon off and talk this over

"New occasions teach new duties."

—

James Russell Lowell

with your family? And call me if you have any questions. I know you well enough to know that you will make the right decision."

A lot of George's values are located in his memory, some of them deep. He was already beginning to realize that he hadn't really known what they were until now, when they were tested. For example, his church just came from no-where to third or fourth in his hierarchy of values. That pushed Mary's gallery career down to fifth place and her museum job to eighth. A bunch of things like his commit-ment to recruit for Wharton dropped way down the list. What was number one? Was it the exciting job? The money? The new career path? Was it Mary? Was it Peter? He kept revis-ing the list, and the more he thought, the more new items of importance injected themselves into his already crowded hi-erarchy of values. Subconsciously George was asking him-self what was really important. How do I make a decision? Who am I and what do I stand for? What are my values? What is really important to me?

Here is a value clarification exercise that George would find helpful in thinking through his career decision:

> *"The worst sin towards our fellow creatures is not to hate them, but to be indifferent to them; that's the essence of inhumanity."*
>
> —
>
> *Heintz Holzer*

---

1. George, consider first what is most important in life for you. Stop here and note down five or six items on a pad.

    wife, home, church, children, neighbors, wife's gallery, finance function, community, children's schooling, country, personal career

2a. Now, George, arrange your items of importance in a ranked list.

    1. *Wife*
    2. *Children*
    3. *Home*
    4. *Children's schooling*
    5. *Wife's gallery*
    6. *Finance function*
    7. *Church*
    8. *Country*
    9. *Personal career*
    10. *Neighbors*
    11. *Community*

b. Stop for a minute and review your list. Does it check out?

    No! Here is my revised list:
    1. *Wife*

    2. *Children*
    3. *Children's schooling*
    4. *Home*
    5. *Wife's gallery*
    6. *Finance function*
    7. *Church*
    8. *Country*
    9. *Personal career*
   10. *Neighbors*
   11. *Community*

3. Now, select the most important item on your list and explore in some depth why this item is number 1 by writing down five or six reasons why you have put this item in first place. Again, stop and give this request a few minutes' thought.

Why my wife is number 1 on my list. Mary is number 1 because:

> *She is my life partner.*
> *She helped put me through graduate school.*
> *She is the mother of my children.*
> *She is really the CEO of the family.*
> *She is my connection to my church and community.*

4. Now select the top supporting reason you have written down in step 3 and explore why this is the most important supporting reason for your choice by noting down a few additional reasons why you selected this item as the most important reason. (Take your time. If this is the first time you have explored your values, what you discover could be an important learning experience for you.)

> *Mary is the love of my life and an equal partner in my nonwork life. I would be lost without her.*

5. Consider repeating steps 2-4 on the basis of the second-most important item on your values list.

> *My children, John and Peter, could share first place with my wife. My children are my future. Their school situations are of special concern.*
>
> *I am investing much of my working life and most of my nonworking life in the development and support of my children. Their schooling, religion, education, sports, and family activities are second only to my wife's well-being.*

6. Go back and take a look at what you have done. Review your set of number-1 and number-2 items and the supporting reasons for their selection. Does a common theme emerge? When you feel ready, write a short statement using these references in describing your most important values. Take a few minutes to think this through and write it down. If the first try doesn't satisfy you, try again.

> *The common theme is clearly my wife and children—my family—and*

> *having said that, I must include the number-1 issues involving wife and children. These are:*
>> *Schooling for the children*
>> *Mary's gallery hopes*
>> *Our home*
>> *Our church and our neighborhood community*
>
> *Other values are much less important than these, and therefore my decision must be based on these written values being satisfied first, even before my personal career opportunities. On this basis I must decline this excellent job opportunity.*

7. Find a favorite place and read your statement out loud to yourself several times. How does it sound? How do you feel about what you have written and said? Think about it. Do these final words come close to expressing what is most important in your life? If they do, you are fortunate. You have come to an important understanding of yourself.

> *My words say it all. My decision is made and I am comfortable with my choice. I believe my family will support my decision.*

"Truth in data and opinions promotes better decision making. When we see the situation for what it really is, the decision is forged on the anvil of truthful debate."

—

John G. Pollard

I developed this clarification exercise as a result of a consultation with Mansfield Elkind, an associate in Whole Brain Technology and a good friend and valued colleague. I offer it to you as a take-away tool that you can reproduce and use to clarify your own values or give it to family or friends. It works well with couples, families, or teams.

So What?

■ Each quadrant and combination of quadrant preferences results in specific, identifiable decision-making styles.

■ Decision-making styles can be improved through quadrant interactivity.

■ Use of the Decision-Making Walk-Around Model will stimulate synergy and improve decision-making results.

■ Each person has a hierarchy of values developed during their life experience located primarily in long-term memory.

■ It is easier to make critical decisions wisely after you have assessed your personal values, tested them against a specific situation, and then rank-ordered them on the basis of real-time priority.

Entrepreneurship

Chapter Headlines

- ◆ You think you have what it takes to make it on your own, but you need some reassurance that you're on the right track.

- ◆ The typical entrepreneur's profile is 2-2-2-1. What if your preferences are different?

- ◆ Intrapreneurs are entrepreneurs functioning inside an organization.

- ◆ There are a few schools for entrepreneurs, but none for intrapreneurs.

"The entrepreneur is essentially a visualizer and an actualizer. He can visualize something, and when he visualizes it he sees exactly how to make it happen."

—

Robert L. Schwartz

How Do Your Thinking Preferences Compare to the Average Entrepreneur's?

You've got this terrific idea. You think it will work, but you need some reassurance that you are on the right track and an affirmation that you've got what it takes. There are numerous experts who can help you get your act together—financial experts, business process experts, motivational psychologists, and friends, neighbors, and family. Many of them have written books or offer seminars or motivational phrases such as "go for it." What I have to offer is not in competition with any of these sources. What I have to offer is a tool and an idea.

The tool is the *Herrmann Brain Dominance Instrument*. I believe it is essential for someone contemplating starting a

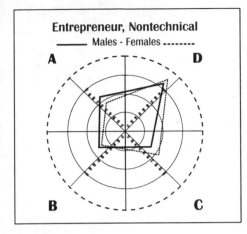

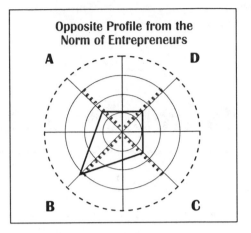

Entrepreneur, Nontechnical
——— Males - Females ....

Opposite Profile from the Norm of Entrepreneurs

business to know what their thinking preferences are and the influence of those preferences on their business behavior.

A 2-2-2-1 profile is the norm for nontechnical male entrepreneurs. The female norm is 2-2-1-1. Such a profile implies that you have ideas, concepts, and a vision of the future. You are also able to deal with risk and ambiguity, and probably are pretty optimistic about your chances for success. From a business perspective, the dark side of the entrepreneur's profile implies that they have: (1) only moderate levels of interest and capability in the rational, analytic, financial domain; (2) perhaps some knowledge but not much skill in business planning; and (3) limited skill in recognizing that certain other people may have to be involved in the venture. The typical entrepreneurial mentality is: Legal advice costs money, and since this is a low-risk venture, I don't believe I'll need a lawyer *or* a financial expert *or* a business planner *or* a human resource mentor. The implication here, however, is that you *do* need to supplement your strong preferred modes with additional interests and competencies, never forgetting the critical importance of legal advice.

Suppose your *HBDI* profile is 2-1-2-2, the opposite of an entrepreneur. Perhaps you have been persuaded by others that the idea is too good to pass up. But such a profile strongly implies that you are far too interested in safety and security, far too traditional and conservative in your approach to life, and far too detail-oriented to allow a big-picture approach to serve as your guiding star. You need to know with clear objectivity that should you start a business, you will likely be "riding the brake" throughout its birth and infancy stages.

"And the trouble is, if you don't risk anything, you risk even more."

—

Erica Jong

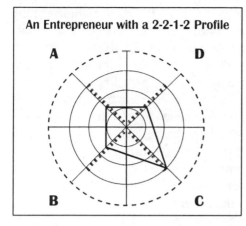

An Entrepreneur with a 2-2-1-2 Profile

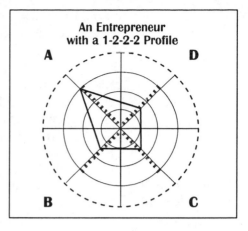

An Entrepreneur with a 1-2-2-2 Profile

You would need to partner with an entrepreneur whose vision, enthusiasm, and risk orientation could carry you through the first few years of your business journey.

So you want to start a business and your *HBDI* profile is 2-2-1-2. You *love* people. Your profile confirms what you already knew, which is that you don't know much about business. You've never been good at organizing and planning, and your new business idea is much more of an urge than a concept. You kind of "feel" that this could be a success. You have strong intuition that you could make a go of it, but when you compare your profile to that of the occupational norm for an entrepreneur you quickly grasp the significant differences and the risky consequences of attempting to mount your business with a nonbusiness mentality.

With a profile of 1-2-2-2 you have a tiger by the tail. You are a technical whiz and you have a business idea that won't quit. The logic of it is overwhelming. You have analyzed the need and diagnosed the market potential. And you have a good handle on the needed finances. What you don't have yet is a business plan and a time-line run-out of your new product development. You don't have a big-picture concept of where your proposed business could go, because your focus has been extremely narrow, if not tunnel-vision. The weakest link in your business experience has to do with people. You are simply not interested in this aspect.

There is a strong likelihood that all four of these aspiring businesspeople would go for it in spite of the predictable consequences of their particular coalition of mental preferences. The quest to have their own business is so strong that

Figure 30-3.
An entrepreneur with a strong C-quadrant orientation.

Figure 30-4.
An A-quadrant entrepreneur with a 1-2-2-2 profile.

it would likely override any inadequacies they might feel along the way. Since the statistics on business failures are so frightening, I believe that people who want to start their own business need to be absolutely objective about their own mental capability to undertake such a risk. So the first order of business is to understand themselves. The second order of business is to supplement their low areas of preference—and therefore low levels of established competence—by bringing in people to provide those competencies. Business development, I believe, is a whole brain activity. All four of these profiled individuals need to supplement their single quadrant dominances with the other three.

Imagine for a moment, a four-person volley ball team where only one of the players is really skilled in the game and the other three are generally familiar with volley ball but have only played it once or twice. This is an analogy or metaphor of the four selves that make up each of our mental capabilities. What I am saying here is that the business world requires four skilled players on each team. Without all four, not only are the chances of winning greatly decreased, but even staying in the game becomes a critical question.

Supplementing the three less-skilled players can be accomplished in many ways. If your financial assets allow, you can hire them. One or two could be family members, or you can get the needed input from established contacts, such as bankers and lawyers. But there is another possible source.

A colleague here in the Lake Lure community, Russell Meade, started a very successful legal practice by involving retired lawyers in the Florida city where he set up his first practice. As a young person who had never set up a business, he found an enormous pool of successful people who were energetic, smart, and available. Russ was able to take advantage of several hundred years of accumulated experience in launching his legal practice. The level of competence these highly experienced people provided was beyond his ability to pay, but because of their circumstances and his need, he got a dollar's worth of ability for ten cents. No matter how you do it, if you want to start a business, you need to know your own strengths and limitations and find ways to fill in the business gaps so that you don't become another statistic in the annual report of business failures. At a bare minimum, line up a CPA and a lawyer you trust and pledge to listen to them. Trust your instincts, but take their advice.

"The freedom to fail is vital if you're going to succeed. Most successful people fail time and time again, and it is a measure of their strength that failure merely propels them into some new attempt at success."

—

Michael Korda

Thinking Like an Entrepreneur

Our data and experience reveal the special nature of entrepreneurial thinking. The data I collected at the reunion of entrepreneurs who had attended the School for Entrepreneurs at the Tarrytown House led by Bob Schwartz showed a high degree of homogeneity among the 70 people surveyed. It is seldom indeed that an occupational group has such a clearly defined norm. The composite average of males and females in that group was 2-2-2-1+. What was striking was that all the profiles were within five or ten points of each of the quadrant scores making up the average. In other words, the norm really was the typical profile of this entrepreneurial group. In interviews with them, I discovered that almost all of them were currently successful but had failed at least once during their entrepreneurial career.

Does this mean that aspiring entrepreneurs who have profiles such as 1-2-2-2 strong A-quadrant preferences or 2-1-2-2 strong B-quadrant preferences could succeed in an entrepreneurial venture? Based on this initial study of 70, plus the experience of profiling hundreds of entrepreneurs in the intervening 12 years, I would have to say that these people would be poor candidates to undertake an entrepreneurial venture. This is not to say that someone with these profiles, with a low D-quadrant score, could not survive, but it is clear to me that to succeed in a true entrepreneurial situation dealing with high-risk new products and unknown markets, it takes a very strong D-quadrant thinking preference to achieve the level of success that I believe is fundamental to entrepreneurial behavior.

"Entrepreneurship is business behavior resulting from a specialized form of thinking greatly influenced by an individual's D-quadrant mental preferences."

—

Ned Herrmann

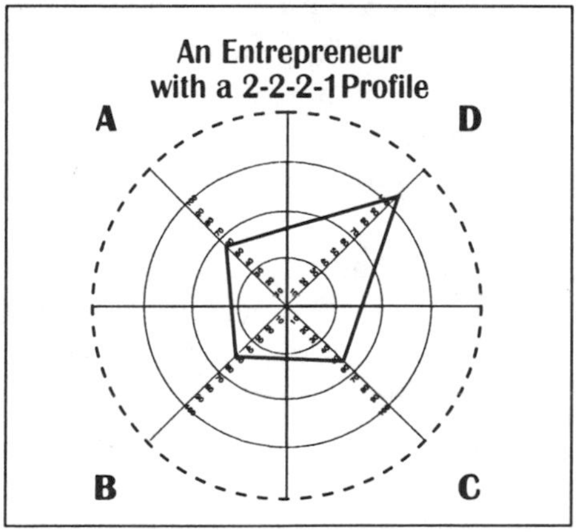

An Entrepreneur
with a 2-2-2-1 Profile

Figure 30-5.
2-2-2-1 Profile — the classic profile of a nontechnical entrepreneur.

I believe that true entrepreneurs have the "entrepreneurial bug." I believe that they are interested in the adventure, in the pursuit, in the chase of a business venture that has never actually been launched in this unique way. It is not just the thrill of the investment risk; it is the need for the spirited chase of the personal dream. For these reasons, the strong, overriding D-quadrant mentality is almost essential to playing the role to the hilt. No other strong quadrant preference provides the needed ingredients for entrepreneurial behavior.

Of course, there are significant consequences to unleashing that behavior based upon a strong, single primary in the D quadrant. It would be typical of this mentality to want to continue to "entrepreneur" even though it was time to change gears and focus on building and delivering the product. This is frequently a fatal consequence of D-quadrant thinking, not appropriately moderated by contributions from A, B, and C quadrants. Entrepreneurs need to be smart enough to be aware of their own obsession and also to seek out objective advice and counsel regarding their stewardship of the entrepreneurial enterprise.

International Management Consultant Ichak Adizes describes the life cycles of a business from its "infancy" to its achieving of "prime." During these growth stages, through infancy and adolescence, entrepreneurial thinking is almost always the key mentality required for success, but as the business matures and begins to enter a state of optimization and stability, the leadership style must change and the "obsessive" entrepreneurial behavior must stop, or the business will suffer and ultimately fail.

The *HBDI* profile is based on a coalition of differing mental preferences. The secondary preferences and resulting competencies need to be situationally engaged as the primary entrepreneurial focus declines. I believe most entrepreneurs are capable of shifting their mental processes if they become alert to the need. It requires a wake-up call of reality from staff advisors or consultants to affect the mid-course correction that many entrepreneurs need to make in order to survive "infancy" and "adolescence" and achieve mature success.

How do you get the attention of an entrepreneur who is so obsessed with a dream that he or she can't see that it won't happen? The most effective way is first to arrange a financial audit by a CPA whom the entrepreneur trusts and have the

"If you see a bandwagon, it's too late."

—

Sir James Goldsmith

results shared with all the key players in the enterprise. Then, following the audit results, an entrepreneurial statement of business objectives should be developed and passed to all key personnel for their annotated comments. Encourage the entrepreneur with the help of the CPA to walk the audit results and the statement of business objectives around the four-quadrant model, testing for viability in each quadrant. With the help of the CPA, come to terms with each nonviable aspect of the business, in the presence of all key personnel. Prepare a revised statement of business objectives that all concerned consider viable.

My continuing research on entrepreneurship led me to Cornell University's Entrepreneurship and Personal Enterprise Celebration 1995 honoring N. Arthur Goentsler as Cornell's Entrepreneur of the Year. The one-day conference following the celebration was hosted by Cornell's President Frank Rhodes and attracted well over 100 participants from around the United States.

What surprised and pleased me was to discover that Cornell University has a formal academic program on Leadership for the 21st Century. In 1992, with strong support from a group of inspired entrepreneurially-oriented alumni, Cornell launched a universitywide Entrepreneurship and Personal Enterprise (EPE) program. Through prestigious endowed professorships and lectureships, the EPE program has attracted outstanding educators to teach its courses.

While a small number of academics were involved in the conference, a much larger group of successful entrepreneurs played a key role in the presentations and discussions. It became clear to me that the heart and soul of the Entrepreneurship and Personal Enterprise program lies with its advisory council. This consists of 36 Cornell graduates, all of whom have a successful track record as entrepreneurs. As visiting faculty members and contributors to such events as this one, they have a direct interface with the students, who are drawn from many colleges and schools throughout the university. I was surprised, but shouldn't have been, by the relatively large number of students from the College of Agriculture and Life Sciences, the Cornell Hotel School, and the Johnson Graduate School of Management. I found the students, the faculty members, and the advisory council members all extremely sharp, highly animated, high-energy people. I felt some passion among the students on campus. These positive impressions were in contrast with most of my previous experience with academia, alumni groups, and students.

While I did not have an opportunity to profile all of these groups involved with the conference, their behavior strongly suggested the characteristics of D-quadrant thinking. What I like about what Cornell is doing is their integration of the active input from successful entrepreneurs with the academic aspects of entrepreneurial management and the essential business skills for successful personal enterprise into one multidisciplined program. Many schools have M.B.A. programs and business courses, but the only other school I know of that has both undergraduate and graduate entrepreneurship programs like Cornell's EPE is the Center for Entrepreneurship at the University of St. Thomas, in Minneapolis. The outstanding curriculum offered by the Center for Entrepreneurship has been recognized nationally, with awards from numerous independent and governmental business organizations. What a break for the aspiring entrepreneur! I would love to go back to school and acquire the skills that I missed completely as I learned the hard way. These programs make a real contribution to business education.

"Every successful person has had failures, but repeated failure is no guarantee of eventual success."

—

Anonymous

One More Time, Do You Really Want to Own a Business, or Are You Looking for Intrapreneurship?

The descriptive term *entrepreneur* is a very familiar business word and most people seem to have a good understanding of what it means. In the business world the word conjures up the image of an independent person with a unique product or service idea that is brought to market by the wits, skill, energy, and risk taking of that highly motivated person. Many fail, and some, like Lazarus, rise from the ashes of defeat and ultimately succeed. In the previous section, I reported on a study of 70 entrepreneurs that I conducted in 1980 at the Tarrytown School for Entrepreneurs, headed by Robert Schwartz. In that study I learned that most of that group, even though they were now successful, had experienced failure one or more times. This implies a level of motivation to succeed that overrides trouble along the way and is often so strong that it could be described as an obsession. They have caught the "entrepreneurial bug" and usually will not be satisfied until the business idea has been fully explored. The typical entrepreneur is almost always working outside the formal company organization, unless it's a company that he or she personally owns. If that's the case, the entrepreneur has freedom of action that doesn't exist inside an organization—freedom to take risks without justifying them and to fail without the usual organizational consequences.

The word *intrapreneur* was coined by Gifford Pinchot, who was associated at the time with Robert Schwartz at the Tarrytown School for Entrepreneurs. By *intrapreneur* Pinchot meant an individual's functioning in an entrepreneurial way *within* an organization. The concept is great, but the intrapreneur's circumstances are very different because, unlike the entrepreneur, the intrapreneur is tied to an organization that has a climate, culture, leadership, policies, budgets, audit procedures, *and* supervising management. In every sense, it has a bureaucracy. Catching the entrepreneurial bug and going it alone is not often possible under these conditions. In most cases the reality is that others who have managerial decision-making authority are also involved in the intrapreneurial project. The true entrepreneur would never buy into this situation. The conditions are too limiting for freedom of action, and freedom of action is an entrepreneurial requirement.

On the other hand, if the organizational climate can be developed to support risk taking and freedom of action, then it might work. But my experience tells me that in order for the intrapreneur to be able to function in an entrepreneurial manner, the mentality of the intrapreneur and of the sponsor need to be in very good alignment. My personal belief is that it takes a high-level "champion" who thinks like an entrepreneur to create intrapreneurial air cover. I don't have a thinking-preferences norm for intrapreneurs because this is not an occupational title. If it were, I have reason to believe that the norm for intrapreneurs would be generally similar to the profile for entrepreneurs. However, I *do* see a Catch-22. Entrepreneurs don't want to have anything to do with bureaucracies. They don't want to have anything to do with people looking over their shoulder. They don't want to have anything to do with externally imposed financial constraints. In general, they don't want to have anything to do with rules, procedures, policies, audits, and strict reporting relationships.

Years ago I talked to Gifford Pinchot at length about his

concept of intrapreneurship and argued the points that I've just made. His idea is, of course, very appealing, and under the right circumstances it can be applied successfully. And when it succeeds, it is wonderful.

I was an intrapreneur in GE for five years before I left the company and became an entrepreneur. Much of what I have described in this book, including the Whole Brain Concept, the *Herrmann Brain Dominance Instrument*, and its application to teaching, learning, and creativity and innovation were all developed while I was an employee of General Electric. During the high-risk developmental phase of this technology, I was given air cover by my direct boss, Lindon Saline, and his financial manager, Dave Dickson, and also by the senior vice president and the CEO. However, there were several high-level managers, including another senior vice president, who felt that what I was doing was not in any way aligned with General Electric's business operations and therefore inappropriate. Because of the air cover my champions provided me and my own wits and ingenuity and the quality of my ideas, I not only survived but succeeded. GE helped me through the infancy stage of my entrepreneurial endeavors in starting my own company by sending participants to my creativity workshops and using me as a consultant in the area of mental diversity.

While I love the idea of intrapreneurship, there are potentially severe personal consequences to playing that role or serving as a champion for others. It takes good ideas, high motivation, guts, a thick skin—a true entrepreneurial spirit. A golden parachute also helps!

> *"Money never starts an idea; it is the idea that starts the money."*
>
> —
>
> *W. J. Cameron*

So What?

■ People who start businesses need to know their own strengths and weaknesses.

■ Many entrepreneurs share a common 2-2-2-1 profile.

■ The dark side of that profile is that three quadrants of needed business competencies may be inadequate or missing.

■ Business is a whole brain activity. Therefore, the chance of startup success increases when interest and competency in all four quadrants is available in the leadership role.

M.B.A.s versus the Creatives

Chapter Headlines

♦ The business community and the creative community think differently and are turned on by different kinds of work.

♦ The Diversity Game reveals mental differences in an informal, fun way.

♦ Some professional creatives want to retain the mystery of their craft.

♦ An M.B.A. program featuring an artist-in-residence as a member of the faculty shifts the entire student body away from the B quadrant toward the C and D quadrants.

> *"Art does not reproduce what we see. It makes us see."*
>
> —
>
> *Paul Klee*

Given the generally left mode preference of the business community, it's not surprising that there is some skepticism about creativity and the creative process from the perspective of traditional, rational thinking. For some business people the creative approach takes on the image of long hair, flamboyant fashions, impractical ideas, and generally weird behavior. But there are rational explanations of this seemingly odd behavior.

1. The creative community thinks differently from the business community. Different preferences engage parts of the mental process that are more expansive, free-flowing, aesthetic, experimental, and risk-oriented.

2. Members of the creative community are turned on by different kinds of work. They have different values and different priorities. They are easily bored by the administrative work activities that turn on many businesspeople.

3. The business community is smart in one way, and the creative community is smart in other ways. And while these different smartnesses should be complementary, they are often misunderstood and end up being mutually antagonistic.

This combination of thinking preferences, types of smartness, differing values, and priorities contribute to what is, in many businesses, an arm's-length relationship between the business types and the creatives. It is often "*we*" and "*they*," and the sad part is that it doesn't have to be. The loss of potential synergy is enormous and costly.

A lot of this animosity simply vanishes when the individuals who think differently discover that the root of their problem is their mental diversity rather than anything personal. One of the quickest and most effective ways of bringing about that understanding is playing the Diversity Game. This is a unique card game developed by Ted Coulson and Alison Strickland of Applied Creativity, Inc., in Seminole, Florida. The game is based on the four-quadrant Whole Brain Model described in this book. Individuals are dealt a random hand of five cards from a deck representing a complete set of four-quadrant descriptors. They are then given the chance to improve their hand in terms of its being representative of their mental self by bartering cards with fellow participants. This interchange is very revealing because it quickly indicates the direction of the preferences of the players. After several opportunities to improve their hands, the players are asked to narrow their choices to the three cards that best represent their preferences and one card that represents their area of least preference or even avoidance. The individual cards are slipped into a plastic sleeve with a velcro backing and are then placed on a flannel display in a sequence, starting with everyone's most preferred, followed by their next-most preferred and finally, on a separate board, the cards that represent their least preferred. Even though this game represents only a rough approximation of an individual's distribu-

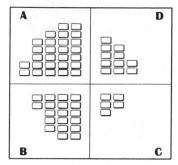

Cards selected by the M.B.A.s

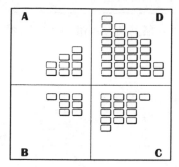

Cards selected by the "Creatives"

Figure 31-1.
Typical display of
Diversity Game
Cards indicating a)
the distribution of
preferences of a
group, and b) the
distribution of each
of the preferences.

tion of preferences, it is still accurate enough to reveal the gross differences between individuals and groups, including, for example, the M.B.A. community and the creative community.

To further reinforce the clear distinctions between the mentality of the two groups, it is almost certain that the least-preferred choices for each group fall into the most-preferred category of the other group. In other words, they are not only opposite in their preferences but also in their lack of preferences. We have found that this kind of understanding almost instantly defuses the personal aspects of thinking-style differences. The creatives are not irritating the business community on purpose with their "out of the box" thinking. And the business people are not boring the creatives to death on purpose with their rational, administrative approach. It is just the natural preference of both communities affecting their work behavior. When the two different thinking groups discover that their differences can stimulate creative synergy, they are more open to work together to develop creative solutions to mutual business problems. Of course, this doesn't happen overnight, but the fact that it happens routinely in many organizations substantiates this application of Whole Brain Technology.

In most cases, the next step is to administer the *Herrmann Brain Dominance Instrument,* which provides an accurate profile of an individual's mental preference. While these *HBDI* profiles will vary for each individual, the group norms will be strongly aligned with the database findings for M.B.A.s and creative individuals.

Supposing, for example, that the occasion is the annual meeting of a large advertising and public relations firm and

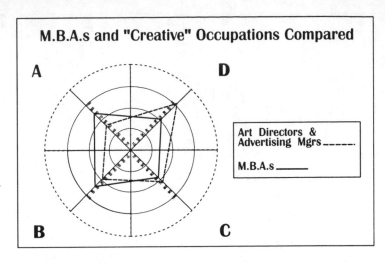

M.B.A.s and "Creative" Occupations Compared

A   D

Art Directors &
Advertising Mgrs ------

M.B.A.s ------

B   C

among the 300 attendees there are 30 art directors and 30 account managers. Ninety percent of the art directors are art school graduates and 90 percent of the account executives are M.B.A.s. They are seated in the auditorium based upon their mental preferences. The 30 M.B.A.s will be seated in a cluster on one side of the room and the 30 art directors will be seated in another cluster on the other side of the room. When it is pointed out to them, by a show of hands, where the two groups are located, they are at first amazed, but then very quickly give evidence of instant acceptance of the group-ings and the locations by the expressions of understanding on their faces. This understanding is reinforced by exercises that reveal the consensus of thinking that exists in each group, and that each consensus is different between the two groups. For example, the creatives often rely on hunches in making their decisions and would enjoy a day alone chewing their mental cud, while the M.B.A. group tends to rely on a step-by-step process to solve difficult problems. During the breaks, members of the two groups mingle together as if they are discovering each other for the first time. When higher man-agement is aware of the consequences of previous hostility between the two occupational communities, and now wit-nesses the beginning of understanding occurring, it can take advantage of this opportunity to orchestrate cross-functional team development assignments.

One such company established teams of account execu-tives and art directors and initiated client visitations as a good-will gesture. This strategy not only helped to integrate the two separate functions but also allowed the client to give face-to-face feedback on both the business and creative aspects of the account. It took a while for the apples and oranges of this joint approach to reconcile their differences, but the net effect was a win for everybody.

In another case, a major corporation that organizes its businesses around brand teams decided to invite members of the ad agency hired by a particular brand team to participate together in a creative problem-solving workshop. The idea was to have the members of the brand team, representing three or four functions of the business, to join with the ad agency representing several different functions of that business, in a learning experience around common problems between the brand team and the ad agency. This was a real stretch because this real-time integration of different functions between two companies had not previously been attempted. In those cases where this process worked, it was like the magic effect of dull silver objects being dipped into tarnish remover. Walls came tumbling down and free-flow mutual problem solving brightened the existing tarnished relationships. It was wonderful. The members of the now better-integrated group couldn't be stopped. The workshop refused to end. They kept working on their mutual problems without regard for time. I almost had to turn the lights out as a signal to them to go home.

In those cases where it didn't work, the reason was not the challenge of integrating different functions, it was the resistance to exposing the mythology of advertising creativity to the client. The strategy of using whole brain creative problem solving as the vehicle for integration was simply wrong. The ad agency creatives were so unsure of their powers that explaining their creative process to the brand team was perceived by them as destroying the mystery of their power. It turned out that the ad agency creatives were not students of the creative process; they were practical applicators of something they really didn't understand. Being highly paid and having the word *creative* on your business card does not mean that you understand the creative process. By explaining the nature and source of creativity to the client, we were in fact exposing the ad agency creatives to the inadequacy of their own understanding. This was a costly strategic error. But like most mistakes, it was rich in its learning potential. Some occupations are so self-contained that they have their own

"An M.B.A.'s first shock could be the realization that companies require experience before they hire a chief executive officer."

—

Henry Ford

educational preparation, professional development process, and occupational culture. To invade that culture as we did broke unwritten rules and became counterproductive. As it turns out, it was not standard practice for professionals in the "creative" roles in advertising to attend training programs—no matter how good they might be, and no matter how badly the client wanted them involved. These cultural walls could not be broken down at that time.

The walls surrounding the M.B.A. culture are being broken down by changes in the ways M.B.A.s are being educated and employed. Creative Problem Solving has been added to the curriculum of a number of M.B.A. schools over the past decade, but none have taken such a dramatic step as Franklin University of Columbus, Ohio. The academic and administrative leaders of that school have added an artist-in-residence to the M.B.A. faculty. The artist Georgia Tangi has developed a curriculum that exposes M.B.A. students to fine art in order to broaden their business perspectives by having them see through perceptual "lenses" that supplement their everyday preferred modes of seeing the world around them. While this program is still in its beginning stages, the very existence of an artist on the M.B.A. faculty changes everything. Changes will take place and all will benefit.

"I didn't see until I believed."

—

Anonymous

Franklin University uses the *Herrmann Brain Dominance Instrument*, the Myers-Briggs Type Indicator, and the Kolb Learning Style Inventory as a battery of assessment tools in providing feedback to the M.B.A. students and input into the academic processes used in the M.B.A. program. Students with differing brain dominance preferences are invited to select and describe examples of the kind of art that appeals to them as seen through the lens of their personal preferences. Through discussion and interaction with examples of different art and artists, students are guided through a development process that broadens their business perspective. The objective is to have the students review business practices and processes through a broader variety of perceptual lenses than those limited to their own initial preferences.

The artist's direct involvement with the students and with the faculty provides dual paths of development. There is as much learning needed at the faculty level as there is at the student level, and the benefits have a multiplying effect. I see this artist-in-residence development as an extraordinarily creative and courageous leap on the part of Franklin

M.B.A. Curriculum 1993-1995

A	B	C	D
Pre-enhancement			
83	85	55	70
Post-enhancement			
83	76	60	76
CHANGE			
0	-9	+5	+6
	p<.00	p<.02	p<.001
N= 45			

University's leaders, giving it almost guaranteed success. The walls of M.B.A. education and practice will surely begin to come tumbling down. As a matter of fact, the composite average of the M.B.A. charter class shows a distinct shift away from the B quadrant toward the right mode, including both the C and D quadrants. As a result of this artistic and aesthetic inclusion in the curriculum, I am certain that the people involved will learn how to do their jobs better and better each month and year and the net effect will be a significant win for the students, the faculty, and businesses everywhere.

Figure 31-3.
Franklin University's MBA Artist-in-Residence program in Columbus, Ohio resulting in a right mode shift of the composite MBA average profile.

The initial results of this unique program are very encouraging. As the pre- and post- data illustrates, the student body of 45 M.B.A.s has shifted away from the structured B quadrant toward the aesthetic C and artistic D quadrant.

So What?

- M.B.A.s and creatives are working the opposite sides of the business street.

- Narrowly defined jobs and status quo education contribute to this sub-optimization.

- Breakthrough educational programs such as the artist-in-residence M.B.A. curriculum, augur well for the future. A shift in mental preference toward the right mode will broaden the M.B.A. graduates' mental perspective and enrich their job performance.

"You have brains in your head, and feet in your shoes. You can steer yourself in any direction you choose."

—

Dr. Seuss

Breaking Down the Barriers to Whole Brain Growth

Chapter Headlines

♦ People change when there is a reason, and most of us have about a 70 percent chance of changing if the conditions are right.

♦ Whole Brain Technology can help change to be positive for all concerned.

♦ While other people are involved in the change process, self-motivation is often the key to successful change.

I am in the process of increasing my computer literacy, and in so doing, I am becoming more aware of the walls that I have built up over the years. These walls have gotten in the way of my making more effective use of the computer earlier in life. Over the years I have become so sensitive to step-by-step, sequential, rule-oriented activities that I find myself becoming exasperated by the unforgiving DOS (Disc Operating System). It requires exact, precise, detailed following of the rules or nothing happens. The computer just sits there looking at you. It's maddening. It has taken me as long as 55 to 60 years to develop the walls that have prevented me from using computers in my own work. I become irritated, and even exasperated, by the incredibly large number of what I consider to be silly operations that are required to perform a simple task.

The other night, I observed my grandchildren, Chris 13, Karim 12, and Selim 8, doing their homework on computers, and they weren't bothered at all by the zillion steps required to open files and locate directories and format an answer to their homework questions. There didn't seem to be any walls. A major reason, I suppose, is they had neither the time nor the inclination to build walls before they started learning how to use the computer. The results of the computer were so intriguing and miraculous that they did not consider the number of steps required to achieve results as irritants that got in the way of accomplishing their task.

One conclusion is that walls are a great deal easier to build than they are to tear down. Another conclusion is that walls are not likely to be built at all if the pathway to successful outcomes is magical, intriguing, and fun. It is clear that these technical pathways are much more readily available to children than to adults. That's why children can set the VCR while adults give up. My experience tells me that at least half, and maybe as many as three-quarters, of the world's adult population is resistant to detailed step-by-step, rule-oriented procedures that are built into the products they try to use. Children, on the other hand, have not developed barriers to making these complex but useful devices work. Apparently, to children, the means justify the ends. For many adults, the means prevent the ends from ever happening.

"Creativity is as common among young children as runny noses. . .and yet, it is quite rare in adults."

—

Joe Renzulli

Can People Change?

Can people change? **Yes.** Most of us are largely a result of what's happened to us. Converting that to percentages, it is my belief, from years of pondering this issue, that on the average about 70 percent of who we are is the result of nurture rather than nature. Of course, in the final analysis it must be both nature and nurture. But if my theory is right, most of us have about a 70 percent chance of changing if the conditions are right. And there are many circumstances under which the conditions for change can be right. Here is a list of what I think are the most important reasons for change.

1. The individual wants to change.
2. The individual's job changes radically.
3. The individual becomes a mother.
4. The individual becomes a father.
5. The individual undergoes a significant values shift.
6. The individual experiences significant learning.
7. The individual loses a job and must find a new one.
8. The individual is mentored by a master.

This list is just a sampling of the reasons why people change. In this section I'm going to narrow the population who might change to businesspeople, and I'm going to focus on the role that Whole Brain Technology can play in bringing about needed change.

There are dozens of developmental opportunities through-out the United States and, for that matter, throughout the world. There are places that provide creativity training, lead-ership training, sensitivity training, organization development, and business training in all functions. Essentially, whatever the need is, there are courses or activities available. Indi-viduals need to be motivated to seek them out and find the time and energy to experience them.

In my own case, I revealed a deficit in the feeling area, so I took five weekend seminars offered by the Esalen Institute located in Big Sur, California. These experiences helped me to become comfortable with my body and my feelings and more effective in my interpersonal relationships. They al-lowed me to become less inhibited and more open and imagi-native. Not only was I a better person for it, but I was more effective in my work. I think most people instinctively know when they have a deficit in their array of thinking options, and I also believe that many people want to fill that deficit with useful forms of mental processing. For many, it's un-comfortable to be incomplete. Often this feeling of incom-pleteness can be satisfied through marriage or partnership. But for those who truly want to develop themselves, the feel-ing of completeness is internal. For example, they realize that they are avoiding dealing with emotional issues; they are avoiding letting their feelings come to the surface in a rela-tionship or in a conversation or in a business situation. In my own case, I became so intrigued with the techniques and processes the Esalen Institute used that I talked about those experiences with my family and my business associates and

"Nothing in progression can rest on its original plan. We might as well think of rocking a grown man in the cradle of an infant."

—

Edmond Burke

subordinates. They were all fascinated. In retrospect I discovered that my talking about emotions, feelings, and interpersonal relationships helped break down the walls that had been built up during my adolescence and went a long way to free me from those self-imposed constraints.

Being laid off is another experience that all too many businesspeople are having during these times of downturning, reengineering, and organizational flattening. Suddenly you are in the job market, and the particular job for which you have the most skills is not one that other companies are seeking to fill. This is when an objective self-understanding of your mental preferences, competencies, and mental options becomes not only a key to self-understanding but also a key to finding the next job. The self-understanding that can come from knowing your thinking preferences allows you to map your current qualifications and also to locate your areas of needed competencies. When these needed competencies are in mental alignment with your existing competencies and preferences, you have a clear path to achievable self-development. When the opportunities you are trying to pursue are not in alignment with your existing preferences and competencies, the likelihood of success is substantially reduced.

We have all heard about individuals who have been laid off from jobs that were out of alignment with their preferences to such an extent that their performance was marginal and their job fulfillment was unacceptable. For these people the trauma of layoff turns out to be an opportunity to find work that turns them on and leads them to greater success and substantially more job fulfillment and personal satisfaction. Experience demonstrates that the likelihood of this happening is greatly improved if the person knows his or her strengths and weaknesses as they translate into job capabilities and can pursue the strengths with renewed confidence. This is the time in your life to become aligned with the work that turns you on and to seek development opportunities that are in alignment with those preferences. This strategy breaks the nonaligned cycle of the past, in which individuals have ended up in work that they don't really like to do and from which they derive little satisfaction. Life is too short to perpetuate this mismatch.

Another key basis for change is experiencing a significant new learning. Take the case of a person who has never managed before and has been promoted into a management posi-

> *"The final forming of a person's character lies in their own hands."*
>
> —
>
> *Anne Frank*

Figure 32-1.
Profiles: Two types
of change.

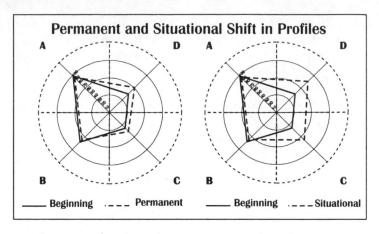

Permanent and Situational Shift in Profiles

Beginning ‒ ‒ ‒ Permanent   Beginning ‒ ‒ ‒ Situational

tion because of technical competence rather than management qualifications. Let's now assume that through a combination of excellent management education and mentoring by a master, this person becomes a knowledgeable, skilled, management practitioner. He or she knows that a significant change is taking place, but the most important feedback comes from the person's employees, peers, and the manager to whom he or she reports. The combined learning from academic courses, mentoring, and coaching has transformed them from someone who managed by instinct to someone who now understands the work of managing and has developed the skills to perform the role effectively. This individual's profile will clearly show the effect of these learnings on mental preferences. In addition to a measurable shift, there will also be a new capability of being situational in response to daily managerial requirements.

I am describing two different kinds of change. One is a relatively permanent shift in preference toward the quadrant direction of the learning enlightenment. The second aspect of change is the increased flexibility of responding for brief periods of time into mental domains that are not primary preferences but are now more available situationally as the work requires.

Consider next an individual who has undergone a significant shift in values. The cause might have been recovering from a major illness, escaping a serious accident, or losing a dear friend or spouse. Whatever the reason, the person has been affected so significantly that his or her values are now different. Value shifts at this level can change how people think and therefore change what they want to do and how they want to do it. Most of us can cite personal examples of people we know or have read about. My point is that these changes do happen and they usually show up as a dramatic change in the person's profile. How to put these shifts in values, interests, and priorities to work is a question worth considering. When a values shift causes a job mismatch, corrective action is called for. I am convinced that most of us know more about our jobs than anybody else, including our managers, and most of us have a great deal more freedom of action than we have thus far claimed. Therefore:

1. Where we have freedom of action, we should make changes in our job to bring it into better alignment with our current mental preferences and those activities which turn us on, and also fulfill the job requirements.

2. Where we don't have freedom of action, we should bring the proposed changes to the attention of our manager and persuade him or her that it's in the best interests of all concerned to make them.

3. If we are the manager, we should make use of our own freedom of action to supplement those changes by encouraging our employees to better align themselves with their work by granting them the freedom to act more independently in making those adjustments.

I see this as a win/win/win scenario. It's a win for the person; it's a win for the manager; and it's a win for the company because a better-aligned employee is going to be more productive and more fulfilled on the job. This is what managers are supposed to do anyway. But by taking advantage of change, we are finding ways for the employees to help managers achieve their bottom-line goals.

So What?

- Resources are available around the world to facilitate change. These include schools, developmental institutes, courses, books, and mentors and coaches.

- Changes that bring individuals into better alignment with their work are often win/win/win. Win for the individuals; win for the manager; win for the company.

"There was an old man who began an orchard upon his retirement. Everybody laughed at him. Why plant trees? They told him he would never live to see a mature crop. He planted anyway and he has seen them blossom and has eaten their fruit. We all need that type of optimism."

—

Deng Ming-Dao

Afterword

In the close to 20 years of application of the *Herrmann Brain Dominance Instrument* and the more than 30 discreet applications of Whole Brain Technology, there is a phrase that characterizes the unsolicited flow of comments from practitioners and participants. That phrase is: "This stuff works."

I seek no higher compliment for myself or my work because the entire objective behind the development of these brain-related tools is that they can be applied to the benefit of all concerned. Since all of this development took place in a business setting to solve business problems and improve business results, it is particularly gratifying to experience such positive feedback from the business community on a continuous worldwide basis.

Some steps provided by this book for becoming a Whole-Brained Businessperson:

1. Acquire a clear understanding of your personal mental preferences.

2. Become aware of your management/leadership style.

3. Understand the consequences of your personal preferences and management/leadership style on your business behavior.

4. Bring about maximum alignment between those aspects of work that turn you on and your actual work assignment.

5. Become skilled in performing those necessary work elements that turn you off.

6. Sketch a time line of your personal career path; become acutely aware of your position on it and what you are doing about it.

7. Recognize that being situationally capable in response to business challenges is the ultimate answer to being a whole-brained businessperson.

8. Make it a part of your personal development plan to engage in those activities that optimize your ability to be mentally situational.

"There is only one thing that will really train the human mind, and that is the voluntary use of the mind by the man himself. You may aid him, you may guide him, you may suggest to him, and, above all else, you may inspire him. But the only thing worth having is that which he gets by his own exertions, and what he gets in direct proportion to what he puts into it."

—

Albert L. Lowell

9.   If you are a manager or leader, provide turn-on work opportunities for members of your organization.

10. Again, if you are a manager or leader, provide opportunities for individuals in your organization to be as fully aligned as possible with their work preferences and/or to pursue training in those areas they wish to develop.

11. Recognize the mental diversity of your organization and pursue ways of taking advantage of personal differences.

12. Encourage the formation of gender-balanced whole brain teams.

13. Understand the business consequences of unleashing creativity and innovation, and become a personal champion within your organization.

14. Discover that much of what succeeds for you is because your actions are whole brained.

15. Many of the whole brain concepts, tools, and techniques described in this book are simple and straightforward. Take advantage of the daily opportunities you will have to begin to apply these tools and techniques in your organization.

16. Applications of Whole Brain Technology are without limit in a business organization. Go beyond what is described in this book and experiment with ways that this new knowledge can help you and your business become more successful.

Appendix A

Answers to Common Questions About Whole Brain Technology

1. *I've heard about the* HBDI. *What are the other applications of the Whole Brain Concept?*

PERSONAL GROWTH
- Education/Training Direction
- Career Direction
- Job Choice
- Personal Creativity
- Job Satisfaction/Fulfillment
- Group Profiling
- Creative Problem Solving
- Team Building

UNDERSTANDING OF SELF
- Relationship with Others
- Thinking Styles
- Learning Styles

COUNSELING
- Educational
- Career
- Job
- Marriage/Family
- Clarifying Relationships

SELECTION
- Job
- Task Force Formation
- Project Team Formation
- Learning Group Formation
- Creative Team Formation
- Staff
- Succession Planning

DESIGN
- Educational Courses
- Meetings
- Presentations
- Learning Materials
- Publications
- Advertisements
- Job Design & Structuring

DIAGNOSIS
- Occupational Profiling
- Thinking Styles
- Learning Styles
- Organization Structure
- Organization Culture
- Mgmt/Leadership Style
- Key Leadership Issues

MODELING
- Creativity
- Teaching/Learning
- Communication
- Organization Development

MANAGEMENT
- Understanding of Management Roles/Styles
- Staff Development
- Communication
- Planning
- Strategic/Operational Planning
- Managing Differences
- Dealing with Diversity
- Dealing with Change
- Alignment of Corporate Issues
- Creative Climate Building
- Improving Productivity

SELLING
- Needs Assessment
- Strategy Development
- Communication
- Sales Training

TEACHING AND LEARNING
- Design and Delivery
- Evaluation
- Presentation Materials
- Training Trainers
- Participant Selections/Groupings

COMMUNICATION
- Writing
- Formatting
- Designing
- Facilitating
- Training
- Clarifying
- Presentation of Materials

CREATIVITY
- Understanding Creative Process
- Whole Brain Creativity Approach
- Claiming Creative Space
- Establishing Creative Climate
- Unleashing Creative Potential

2. *Is this brain dominance stuff like astrology or psychology or phrenology?*

No. There is essentially no relationship between Whole Brain Technology and these three approaches.

I think of astrology as a very complicated construct based on ancient myth and anecdotal data. Even after its existence for well over 3,000 years it remains highly speculative and scientifically invalidated. One of the reasons that the birth date question is included in the research questions portion of the survey form is to attempt to discover the degree to which there are brain dominance correlations with astrological signs.

Psychology is a highly developed science founded on a conceptual base entirely different from the physiological base upon which Whole Brain Technology is based.

Contemporary understanding of the brain renders phrenology as totally without meaning. Even though phrenology flourished for over 50 years in the 1880s there is absolutely no scientific validation of this pseudoscience. A positive contribution to present day understanding that comes out of this now-discarded approach is the notion of brain specialization in many different categories. Even though these proved to be erroneous they did represent an early understanding of the specialization concept. Whole Brain Technology is of course entirely based on the specialized brain, with the specialized modes being allocated to the four quadrants of the Whole Brain Model.

3. *Is the brain dominance theory and the Whole Brain Concept valid? What proof exists?*

The brain dominance concept has been strongly validated in a number of different ways; *First*, through the research and experimentation of leaders in the field including Roger Sperry, Robert Ornstein, Henry Mintzberg, and Michael Gazzanniga. *Second*, it has been validated by the hundreds of EEG experiments carried out personally by Ned Herrmann. *Third*, it has been validated by the public demonstrations conducted by Ned Herrmann over the past 12 years. *Fourth*, it has been validated by specific validation studies carried out by C. Victor Bunderson and James Olsen of WICAT and later by C. Victor Bunderson and Kevin Ho, and in parallel with those studies by validation experiments carried out by Schkade and Potvin at the University of Texas. Additional validation comes from the more than 60 doctoral dissertations based on both the *HBDI* and the Whole Brain Concept.

In addition to these more formal studies and activities, there have been thousands of anecdotal validations coming from people who have acknowledged verbally or in writing their strong personal acceptance of the *HBDI* profile as descriptive of themselves and others in their personal and work lives. When asked the question, "Does this concept help me understand myself, people I know, and experiences I have had and am having?" their answers have been enthusiastically positive.

4. *Why did Ned Herrmann develop the Whole Brain Technology?*

As a professional artist for many years, Ned Herrmann became curious about the nature and source of creativity. Upon exploration, it became suddenly clear to him that the source of creativity was the brain. Pursuing that AHA! led to the Whole Brain Concept and the development of the *HBDI*. At the time this occurred in 1976, Ned was head of Management Education at General Electric's Management Development Institute. His understanding of the brain as a source of creativity was quickly followed by his second insight that the brain was also the central organ in learning. His dual profession as an artist and educator gave him the opportunity to apply his new understanding to whole brain creative learning. GE supported Ned's experiments and applications during the late 1970s, and it was these activities that led to the development of the Whole Brain Concept and the *HBDI*.

5. *Who are the key contributors to Whole Brain Technology?*

Roger Sperry, Robert Ornstein, Henry Mintzberg, Paul MacLean, Joseph Bogen, and Victor Bunderson.

6. *Isn't all this brain stuff just a flash in the pan? Won't it just pass?*

In early Egypt, valued organs of the deceased were preserved in canopic jars; the brain was discarded. In 1989 the U.S. Congress and President Bush declared the 1990s as the Decade of the Brain. It's taken 6,000 years to get to this point in our understanding of and respect for the brain as the central organ of the body. This idea like many other things of great value take a long time to achieve general acceptance. Considering the rapid increase in worldwide attention being given to the Whole Brain Concept, we expect this technology to be a major plateau for understanding the nature of humans.

7. *To what extent is the work (Whole Brain Technology and the* HBDI) *documented?*

Over 50 doctoral dissertations and masters' theses based on Whole Brain Technology and the *HBDI* document this work in a variety of theoretical and practical applications. Over 100 articles published in the *International Brain Dominance Review* further document Whole Brain Technology and the *HBDI* in a wide variety of applications. Many hundreds of letters, study reports, and memos are on file. Over a hundred thousand individual profiles and many hundreds of group analysis and interpretations are on file. We have reason to believe that these materials represent only a fraction of the number that exists in private archives or in the files of our 7 international institutes. In addition to this material, there is on display in the Ned Herrmann Group Learning Center in Lake Lure, 50 books and magazines referring to Ned Herrmann's work, and to the Whole Brain Technology in a wide variety of application areas.

Appendix B

Common Questions and Answers About the HBDI

1. *Is the* HBDI *validated?*

Yes. Psychometric experts in the field feel that the *HBDI* is strongly validated. Validation studies have been under way for over 15 years. The early studies were conducted in Berkeley, California, using a dual left brain/right brain EEG apparatus, plus the first Mind Mirror used in this country. Following these were three separate validation studies supervised by C. Victor Bunderson formerly Chief Scientist of WICAT and later Vice President for Management Research at Education Testing Service. These comprehensive studies are summarized in the validation appendix of *The Creative Brain*. An additional study was conducted in the early 1980s by Schkade and Potvin of the University of Texas. The "Husky" validation of the *HBDI* is continuously affirmed by documented workshop experiences, plus more than 50 doctoral dissertations and studies by students and researchers who have based their work on the *HBDI*. One of these dissertations, conducted by Kevin Ho, Ph.D., strongly supports the validity conclusions. The validation study conducted by C. Victor Bunderson, Ph.D., is described in *The Creative Brain*. Continuing validation studies are conducted as part of the research and development effort of The Ned Herrmann Group. It is significant to note that the result of all of the validation studies carried out over the 14-year history of the *HBDI* are positive. There has been no negative input. Experts in the field consider this to be rare.

2. *Is the profile "me," or how I would "like" to see myself?*

In the vast majority of cases, how a person sees him- or herself is the most accurate and most informative view of themselves that can be held. Even though this self-view might be imperfect, in most cases, it considers more aspects and information than is available to any other person. While it is possible that individuals can tilt their answers toward an idealized view of themselves, the survey questions are framed in ways that minimize this, and in addition, the vast majority of respondents would consider it self-defeating to provide inaccurate information about themselves. Follow-up questions to many hundreds of *HBDI* participants indicate an extraordinarily high (over 90 percent) agreement with their profile.

3. *What do the color designations for each quadrant mean?*

The upper left A quadrant typifies *cerebral* processing and therefore the color chosen to represent this quadrant is *cerulean* blue. The lower left B quadrant

The *HBDI* Profile and training in applications of Whole Brain Technology are available to readers by contacting The Ned Herrmann Group. Workshops in strategic thinking, creative thinking, creative problem-solving, use of the *HBDI* and whole brain training are a few of those regularly offered. Customized

---

▰▰▰ HOBBIES ▰▰▰

Indicate a **maximum of six** hobbies you are actively engaged in. Enter a **3** next to your major hobby, a **2** next to each primary hobby, and a **1** next to each secondary hobby. Enter only **one 3**.

51. **2** arts/crafts	59. _____ gardening/plants	67. _____ sewing
52. **2** boating	60. _____ golf	68. _____ spectator sports
53. _____ camping/hiking	61. _____ home improvements	69. _____ swimming/diving
54. _____ cards	62. **2** music listening	70. _____ tennis
55. **2** collecting	63. _____ music playing	71. _____ travel
56. _____ cooking	64. **3** photography	72. _____ woodworking
57. **2** creative writing	65. _____ reading	_____ other _____
58. _____ fishing	66. _____ sailing	_____

Please review: Only one 3 and **no more than six hobbies.** Correct if necessary.

▰▰▰ ENERGY LEVEL ▰▰▰

73. Thinking about your energy level or "drive," select the one that best represents you. Check box **A**, **B**, or **C**.

    A [☒] day person   B [ ] day/night person equally   C [ ] night person

▰▰▰ MOTION SICKNESS ▰▰▰

74. Have you ever experienced motion sickness (nausea, vomiting) in response to vehicular motion (while in a car, boat, plane, bus, train, amusement ride)? Check box **A**, **B**, **C**, or **D** to indicate the number of times.

    A [ ] none   B [ ] 1–2   C [☒] 3–10   D [ ] more than 10

75. Check box **A** or **B** to indicate whether you can read while traveling in a car without stomach awareness, nausea, or vomiting.

    A [☒] yes   B [ ] no

▰▰▰ ADJECTIVE PAIRS ▰▰▰

For **each paired item** below, check the word or phrase which is more descriptive of yourself. Check box **A** or **B** for **each** pair even if the choice is a difficult one. **Do not omit any pairs.**

A / B		A / B	
76. .... conservative [ ] / [☒] empathetic		88. .... imaginative [ ] / [☒] sequential	
77. .... analyst [ ] / [☒] synthesizer		89. .... original [☒] / [ ] reliable	
78. .... quantitative [ ] / [☒] musical		90. .... creative [ ] / [☒] logical	
79. ... problem-solver [☒] / [ ] planner		91. .... controlled [ ] / [☒] emotional	
80. .... controlled [ ] / [☒] creative		92. .... musical [☒] / [ ] detailed	
81. .... original [☒] / [ ] emotional		93. .... simultaneous [☒] / [ ] empathetic	
82. .... feeling [ ] / [☒] thinking		94. .... communicator [ ] / [☒] conceptualizer	
83. ...... interpersonal [ ] / [☒] organizer		95. ...... technical things [☒] / [ ] people-oriented	
84. .... spiritual [ ] / [☒] creative		96. .... well-organized [ ] / [☒] logical	
85. .... detailed [ ] / [☒] holistic		97. .... rigorous thinking [ ] / [☒] metaphorical thinking	
86. .... originate ideas [☒] / [ ] test and prove ideas		98. like things planned [☒] / [ ] like things mathematical	
87. .... warm, friendly [ ] / [☒] analytical		99. .... technical [☒] / [ ] dominant	

Please review: Did you mark **one** and **only one** of each pair? Correct if necessary.

Page 5   **FOR CONFIDENTIAL RESEARCH PURPOSES**

The questions on this page are not used in scoring the HBDI. However, the answers to these questions are valuable in our continuing brain dominance research. Skip any question you wish, but please answer as many as you feel you can.

Indicate the birth order of your brothers, sisters and self by darkening the appropriate symbols. Then **circle** the symbol representing yourself.

MALE → ♂	(♂)	♂	♂	♂	♂	♂	♂	♂	♂	♂	♂ ←MALE
Oldest	2nd	3rd	4th	5th	6th	7th	8th	9th	10th	11th	12th
FEMALE → ♀	♀	♀	♀	♀	♀	♀	♀	♀	♀	♀	♀ ← FEMALE

Date of Birth _**2/10/22**_ Years in Current Occupation _**15 YEARS**_ Job Satisfaction: [ ][ ][ ][ ][☒] LOW HIGH
Citizenship: _**U.S.**_ Native Language: _**ENGLISH**_ Are You Bilingual? [ ] Yes [☒] No
Ethnicity: [ ] American Indian [ ] Black [☒] Caucasian [ ] Hispanic [ ] Asian [ ] Other _____
Do you consider yourself religious? [ ] Yes [☒] No Religious Affiliation: [ ] Catholic [ ] Protestant [ ] Jewish [ ] Other: _**CHRISTIAN**_
Level of participation: [ ] Minimal [ ] Trained-but-not-practicing [☒] Casual [ ] Devout [ ] Other: _____
If you are a parent, please indicate: Number of Children _**3**_ Age of Oldest _**46**_ Age of Youngest _**38**_
Couple Status: [☒] Married [ ] Separated [ ] Divorced [ ] Living Together [ ] Widow/Widower [ ] Single   Have your parents divorced? [ ] Yes [ ] No

being structured and organized was designated as *green* because green suggested *groundedness*. The lower right C quadrant because of its *emotional*, feeling, and interpersonal orientation was assigned *red* because of the *emotional passion* implied by that color. The upper right D quadrant because of its *imaginative* qualities was assigned *yellow* because of that color's *vibrancy*.

4. *What types of questions are asked on the* HBDI *survey that result in the* HBDI *Personal Profile?*

The best way to answer that question is for you to see it for yourself. The following is a sample *HBDI Survey Form* which I completed.

BIOGRAPHICAL INFORMATION

Please complete **every** question according to the directions given. Each response, including your answers to question 1, 2, 3 and 4 provide important data. When directions are not followed or data is incomplete we are unable to process your survey, and must return it to you.

1. Name *NED HERRMANN*   2. Sex: M ☒ F ☐

3. Educational Focus or Major *BA IN PHYSICS AND MUSIC*

4. Occupation or Job Title *BUSINESS OWNER, EXECUTIVE, AUTHOR, LECTURER, BRAIN RESEARCHER*

Describe your work (please be as specific as possible) *RESEARCH DIRECTOR, BOARD CHAIRMAN, CONSULTANT, SPEAKER, WORKSHOP DESIGNER AND LEADER*

HANDEDNESS

5. Which picture most closely resembles the way you hold a pencil? Mark box **A, B, C,** or **D.**

A ☐   B ☐   C ☐   D ☐

6. What is the strength and direction of your handedness? Mark box **A, B, C, D,** or **E.**

A ☐ primary left   B ☐ primary left, some right   C ☐ both hands equal   D ☒ primary right, some left   E ☐ primary right

SCHOOL SUBJECTS

Think back to your performance in the elementary and/or secondary school subjects identified below. **Rank order all three subjects differently,** even if the choice is difficult, by entering a 1, 2, and 3 on the basis of how well you did: **1** = best; **2** = second best; **3** = third best.

7. *1* math   8. *3* foreign language   9. *2* native language or mother tongue

Please check that no number is duplicated: The numbers 1, 2, and 3 **must be used once** and **only once.** Correct if necessary.

WORK ELEMENTS

Rate each of the work elements below according to your strength in that activity, using the following scale: **5** = work I do best; **4** = work I do well; **3** = neutral; **2** = work I do less well; **1** = work I do least well. Enter the appropriate number next to each element. **Do not use any number more than four times.**

10. *5* analytical	16. *3* technical aspects	21. *4* innovating
11. *2* administrative	17. *2* implementation	22. *5* teaching/training
12. *5* conceptualizing	18. *3* planning	23. *2* organization
13. *4* expressing ideas	19. *3* interpersonal aspects	24. *5* creative aspects
14. *2* integration	20. *4* problem solving	25. *3* financial aspects
15. *4* writing		

Please tally: Number of 5's *4* **, 4's** *4* **, 3's** *4* **, 2's** *4* **, 1's**_____. If there are more than **four** for any category, please redistribute.

KEY DESCRIPTORS

Select **eight adjectives** which best describe the way you see yourself. Enter a **2** next to each of your **eight** selections. Then change one **2** to a **3** for the adjective which best describes you.

26. *2* logical	35. _____ emotional	43. _____ symbolic
27. *2 3* creative	36. _____ spatial	44. _____ dominant
28. _____ musical	37. _____ critical	45. *2* holistic
29. _____ sequential	38. *2* artistic	46. *2* intuitive
30. *2* synthesizer	39. _____ spiritual	47. _____ quantitative
31. _____ verbal	40. _____ rational	48. _____ reader
32. _____ conservative	41. _____ controlled	49. *2* simultaneous
33. *2* analytical	42. _____ mathematical	50. _____ factual
34. _____ detailed		

---

training and consulting are also available. For more information, contact The Ned Herrmann Group at 2075 Buffalo Creek Road, Lake Lure, North Carolina 28746, or call voice lines 1-800-432-HBDI, 704-625-9153, fax line 704-625-1402 or leave an e-mail message at Braintools @aol.com.

■■■ INTROVERSION/EXTROVERSION ■■■

100. Check one box only to place yourself on this introvert–extrovert scale.

introvert ☐ ---- ☐ ---- ☐ ---- ☐ ---- ☐ ---- ☒ ---- ☐ ---- ☐ extrovert

■■■ TWENTY QUESTIONS ■■■

Respond to each statement by checking the box in the appropriate column.

	strongly agree ▼	agree ▼	in between ▼	disagree ▼	strongly disagree ▼
101. I feel that a step by step method is best for solving problems.	☐	☐	☐	☒	☐
102. Daydreaming has provided the impetus for the solution of many of my more important problems.	☒	☐	☐	☐	☐
103. I like people who are most sure of their conclusions.	☐	☐	☐	☒	☐
104. I would rather be known as a reliable than an imaginative person.	☐	☐	☐	☐	☒
105. I often get my best ideas when doing nothing in particular.	☒	☐	☐	☐	☐
106. I rely on hunches and the feeling of "rightness" or "wrongness" when moving toward the solution to a problem.	☒	☐	☐	☐	☐
107. I sometimes get a kick out of breaking the rules and doing things I'm not supposed to do.	☒	☐	☐	☐	☐
108. Much of what is most important in life cannot be expressed in words.	☒	☐	☐	☐	☐
109. I'm basically more competitive with others than self-competitive.	☐	☐	☐	☒	☐
110. I would enjoy spending an entire day "alone with my thoughts."	☒	☐	☐	☐	☐
111. I dislike things being uncertain and unpredictable.	☐	☐	☒	☐	☐
112. I prefer to work with others in a team effort rather than solo.	☐	☐	☐	☒	☐
113. It is important for me to have a place for everything and everything in its place.	☐	☐	☐	☐	☒
114. Unusual ideas and daring concepts interest and intrigue me.	☒	☐	☐	☐	☐
115. I prefer specific instructions to those which leave many details optional.	☐	☐	☐	☒	☐
116. Know-why is more important than know-how.	☐	☒	☐	☐	☐
117. Thorough planning and organization of time are mandatory for solving difficult problems.	☐	☐	☐	☒	☐
118. I can frequently anticipate the solutions to my problems.	☐	☒	☐	☐	☐
119. I tend to rely more on my first impressions and feelings when making judgements than on a careful analysis of the situation.	☒	☐	☐	☐	☐
120. I feel that laws should be strictly enforced.	☐	☐	☐	☒	☐

Please review to make sure you have answered all 120 questions.

To what extent were you formally educated for the field you are now working in? ☐ Not at all ☐ Somewhat ☒ To A Great Degree ☐ Fully

Please indicate the time(s) of the day/night you feel most mentally capable: | 12mid. | 6am | 12noon | 6pm | 12mid.

Have you ever experienced any learning disabilities? ☐ Dyslexia ☐ Reading ☐ Speech Impediments ☐ Hearing Impediments ☐ A.D.D. ☐ Other

Please describe _____ Age of onset_____ Age when ceased_____

If you have filled out the HBDI previously, or under a different name (e.g. maiden) or address, please specify: _6 TIMES_

How do you see yourself? Please distribute 100 points between these four descriptions:

Rational _30_ Organized _10_ Interpersonal _20_ Imaginative _40_

Please check the best descriptor indicating your mood or the way you felt at the time you were completing the survey.

☐ Happy ☐ Enthusiastic ☐ Interested ☐ O.K. ☐ Relaxed ☐ Indifferent ☐ Distracted ☐ Tired ☐ Unhappy

If you have experienced any significant life-changing events, please indicate the date, event, and impact on you: _1 NEAR DEATH EXPERIENCE_
4 MAJOR ILLNESSES, AWARDS IN 6 DIFFERENT DISCIPLINES

NOTE: There is a fee for processing this survey form.

International readers can obtain information on the *HBDI* in their native languages through the international affiliates of The Ned Herrmann Group listed below or through the main office in Lake Lure, North Carolina.

LATIN AMERICA

For information on all Latin American countries, contact the following office.

The Ned Herrmann Group
Latin American Operations

Juan-Carlos Folino
6 North Autumnwood Way
The Woodlands, TX 77380 USA
Phone: 713-367-6889
Fax: 713-367-4911

Satellite Offices are located in:

Argentina

Brazil

Mexico

EUROPE

France
(also serves Belgium, Holland, Switzerland, Portugal and Spain)

Institut Herrmann France
Lionel Vuillemin
102 Boulevard Franklin Roosevelt
BP 238 92504 Rueil Malmaison
France
Phone: 331 47 513 115
Fax: 331 47 513 328

Germany
(also serves Austria and other German-speaking nations)

Herrmann Institut Deutschland GmbH
Roland Spinola
Kausenerstr.4
D-36037 Fulda
Germany
Phone: 49 661 605 380
Fax: 49 661 602 564

Germany & Austria Satellite Office

Dr. Frank D. Peschanel
gfs Gesellschaft fur
Systementwicklung GmbH
Rathausplatz 2 Postfach 1163
83246 Unterwossen
Germany
Phone/Fax: 43 5375 2109

United Kingdom

Herrmann Brain Dominance Institute-UK Central
Sally Cartwright-Bishop
P. O. Box 1
Battle
North Lodge
North Trade Road
East Sussex TN33 OYB
Great Britain
Phone: 44 1424 775100
Fax: 44 1424 775693

ASIA/PACIFIC

Australia/New Zealand

The Ned Herrmann Group
Australia and New Zealand
Mike Morgan
2 Garden Square
Gordon, NSW 2072
Australia
Phone: 612 880 2333
Fax: 612 880 2343

Turkey

Dr. Savas Tumis
Interconsult Ltd. Sti.
Icadiye Caddesi No. 26
81200 Kuzguncuk
Istanbul, Turkey
Phone : 90 216 391 6585
Fax : 90 216 391 6586

Appendix C

HBDI Average Profiles of Several Occupational Titles

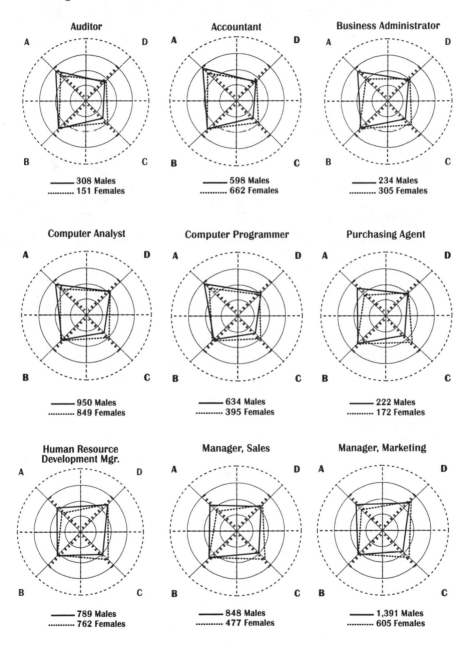

Auditor	Accountant	Business Administrator
A ... D	A ... D	A ... D
B ... C	B ... C	B ... C
——— 308 Males	——— 598 Males	——— 234 Males
.... 151 Females	.... 662 Females	.... 305 Females

Computer Analyst	Computer Programmer	Purchasing Agent
A ... D	A ... D	A ... D
B ... C	B ... C	B ... C
——— 950 Males	——— 634 Males	——— 222 Males
.... 849 Females	.... 395 Females	.... 172 Females

Human Resource Development Mgr.	Manager, Sales	Manager, Marketing
A ... D	A ... D	A ... D
B ... C	B ... C	B ... C
——— 789 Males	——— 848 Males	——— 1,391 Males
.... 762 Females	.... 477 Females	.... 605 Females

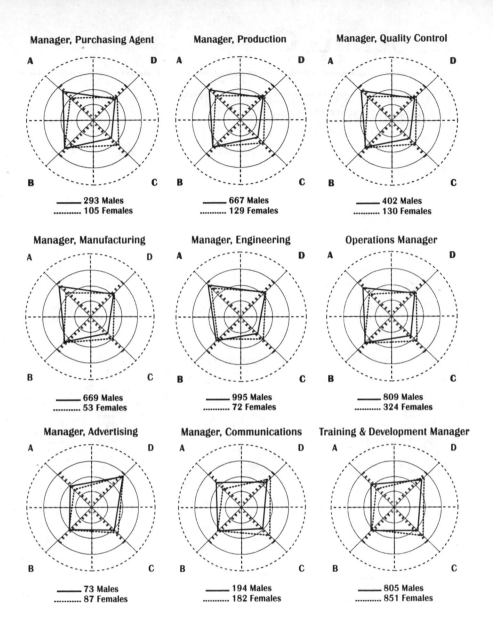

Manager, Purchasing Agent

——— 293 Males
·········· 105 Females

Manager, Production

——— 667 Males
·········· 129 Females

Manager, Quality Control

——— 402 Males
·········· 130 Females

Manager, Manufacturing

——— 669 Males
·········· 53 Females

Manager, Engineering

——— 995 Males
·········· 72 Females

Operations Manager

——— 809 Males
·········· 324 Females

Manager, Advertising

——— 73 Males
·········· 87 Females

Manager, Communications

——— 194 Males
·········· 182 Females

Training & Development Manager

——— 805 Males
·········· 851 Females

Reading List

A Bibliography of Selected Books on the Brain and Brain Dominance

The following is a list of "basic" books, personally selected by Ned Herrmann, that will be useful in your knowledge of the brain, whole brain thinking, and the applications of Whole Brain Technology. All these should be available in bookstores or libraries.

ABC's of the Human Mind, The: A Family Answer Book, Reader's Digest Association, Inc.

*Accelerated Learning: How You Learn Determines What You Learn by Roger G. Swartz, M.A. Ed., M.P.A., Essential Medical Information Systems, Inc.

Adult Learner, The: A Neglected Species by Malcolm Knowles, Gulf Publishing Company

Amazing Brain, The by Robert Ornstein and Richard F. Thompson, Houghton Mifflin Company

Brain Book, The by Peter Russell, Hawthorn Books, Inc.

Brain Has a Mind of Its Own, The by Richard Restak, Harmony Books

Brain, Mind and Behavior by Floyd Bloom and Arlyne Lazerson, W. H. Freeman and Company

Brain, The: How Things Work by Time Life Books, Inc.

Brain, The: The Last Frontier by Richard M. Restak, M.D., Doubleday & Company, Inc.

Conversations with Neil's Brain by William H. Calving & George Ojeruaun, Addison Wesley

*Creative Brain, The by Ned Herrmann, The Ned Herrmann Group

*Creative Problem Solving by Edward and Monika Lumsdaine, McGraw-Hill

Descartes' Error by Antonio R. Damasio, G.P. Putnam's Sons

Drawing on the Right Side of the Brain by Betty Edwards, Jeremy P. Tarcher, Inc.

How the Brain Works by Leslie A. Hart, Basic Books, Inc.

How Your Brain Works by Anne D. Novitt-Moreno, Ziff-Davis Press

* Indicates books containing information on Whole Brain Technology.

"Incredible Machine, The," National Geographic

Left Brain / Right Brain by Judy Springer and George Deutch, W. H. Freeman and Company

Learning Brain, The by Eric Jensen, Turning Point for Teachers, San Diego

Metaphoric Mind, The by Bob Samples, Addison-Wesley

Mind, The by Richard M. Restak, M.D., Bantam Books

Owner's Manual for the Brain, The by Pierce J. Howard, Ph.D., Learncan Press

Psychology of Consciousness, The by Robert Ornstein, Penguin Books

*Sixth Sense by Laurie Nadel, Prentice Hall

*Tao Jones Averages, The by Bennett W. Goodspeed, E. P. Dutton, Inc.

Three Pound Universe, The by Judith Hooper, Dick Teresi, Dell Publishing

Use Both Sides of Your Brain by Tony Buzan, A Dutton Book

* Indicates books containing information on Whole Brain Technology.

Index

A (Rational) quadrant:
competition within, 45
creative process role, 220
fictional characters as exemplars of, 67
male vs. female preference for, 52–57
management style, 103–104
in North American business culture, 181–182
occupational profiles for, 72–73, 76
in Whole Brain structure, 6, 21–25
A/B quadrants (*see* Left mode thinking style)
A/C quadrants, decision-making dilemma, 284
A/D quadrants (*see* Cerebral thinking style)
Academe (*see* Education)
Adizes, Ichak, 296
Advertising:
creative tension vs. business client, 305–306
Whole Brain applications to, 86–89
Affirmation, in creativity building, 266–268, 277
Alignment, thinking style:
in education, 151–154
intrapeneur and sponsor, 299
job to worker:
advantages of, 135
analysis of, 140–143
and creativity, 253–255
importance of, 131–139
as motivational tool, 144
and personal change, 312, 313
leadership statements and actions, 165–170
Alpha brain waves, 215, 221–222
Alvord, Ray, 230
Analytical thinking style [*see* A (Rational) quadrant]
Applied vs. original thinking, 212–213
Artists, as creativity tools for business, 306–307
Asian-Pacific business culture, 181–182
Astrology, brain dominance theory and, 318
Asymmetry of human body, and thinking preferences, 16–17, 35–36
Authoritarian management style [*see* A (Rational) quadrant]
Avoidance of thinking style, importance of, 31, 34–43

B (Organizational) quadrant:
creative process role, 220
as crisis refuge, 171–172
customer service role, 84
fictional characters as exemplars of, 67
management style, 105–106
occupational profiles, 73–74
in Whole Brain structure, 6–7, 21–25
B/C quadrants (*see* Limbic mode thinking style)
B/D quadrants, decision-making dilemma, 283–284
Beer, Janice, 7
Behavior, as mental preferences indicator, 63–72
Beta brain waves, 215–216, 221–222
Bogen, Joseph, 11
Brain dominance:
behavioral clues to, 63–72
definition of, 16–17
development of, 35–36
metaphorical model of, 15–18
physiological basis, 10–15, 18–19
validity of theory, 318–319
Brain wave states, and creative process, 215, 221–222
Brainstorming, vs. process storming, 129

C (Feeling) quadrant:
in Asian-Pacific business culture, 181–182
customer service role, 84
deficit in instruction book writing, 91–92
female vs. male preference for, 52–57
fictional characters as exemplars of, 67
management style, 104, 106–107
misalignment consequences, 165
occupational profiles for, 73–76
in Whole Brain structure, 7, 21–25
C/D quadrants (*see* Right mode thinking style)
Cash management program, 173–174
Center for Entrepreneurship, 298
CEO (Chief Executive Officer):
cross-cultural analysis of, 179–191
and leadership documents, 163–170
multidominance of, 76–77
training in Whole Brain methods, 155–159
Cerebral cortex, hemispheric analysis of, 10–13

Cerebral mode thinking style:
  and decision making, 284
  management characteristics, 109–110
  in reinvention strategy, 176
Certified Public Accountant (CPA), 296–297
Champions, creativity, 230–239, 241, 243, 269, 299
Change:
  creative approach to organizational, 197–200, 204–205, 239
  Whole Brain application to personal, 308–313
Chief Executive Officer (CEO) [see CEO (Chief Executive Officer)]
Claiming Creative Space Exercise, 272
Collins, Byron, 231
Color designations for quadrants, 27, 320–321
Communication, Whole Brain Technology application, 115–122, 146
Compatibility, fallacy that similarity equals, 46
Competence:
  CEO universal, 180
  vs. intelligence, 50–51
  origin of, 38–39, 60
  result of situational thinking approach, 114
  thinking preference vs., 9–10, 30
  (See also Intelligence)
Competition, and similar thinking styles, 44–47
Conflict resolution, Whole Brain Model and, 69
Constructive dissonance, criticism of, 127–130
Consumer-oriented businesses, importance of Whole Brain approach, 48
Cornell University, 297–298
Corporate culture (see Cultural considerations)
Corporate officers, profiles of, 64–66
Corpus callosum, function of, 11
Cost-saving measures, 172, 177
Coulson, Ted, 254
CPA (Certified Public Accountant), 296–297
Creative accomplishments portfolio, 279
Creative Problem Solving, 306–307
Creative Selves Model, 222–223
Creativity:
  brain as source of, 214–217
  as catalyst for Whole Brain theory, 10–11
  champions of, 230–239, 241, 243, 269, 299
  claiming space for, 272–275

crisis as opportunity for, 172–173, 177–178
  establishment of personal, 276–281
  and experimental thinking, 256–264
  heterogeneous teams and, 128
  impact on business success, 102
  in job classification, 251–255
  mental diversity in problem solving, 223–224
  mental processes of, 217–222, 225–229
  methods for stifling, 270–271
  organizational change role, 197–200, 203–213
  reclaiming of, 265–275
  self-sustainment of, 242–244
  steps to enhance, 244–248
  strategic thinking role, 193–196
  traditional business attitude, 186–187, 301–302
Credibility, loss through leadership hypocrisy, 168
Crisis management, improved methods for, 171–178
Critical mass, achievement in creativity, 242–244
Cronkite, Bill, 259–260
Cultural considerations:
  corporate resistance to creativity, 213
  for CEOs, 180–187
  mental preference profiles of ethnic groups, 47, 50–51
Customer service, Whole Brain Technology application, 84–85
Customers, benefits of inclusion in product design, 94–95

D (Experimental) quadrant:
  CEO preference for, 186, 191
  creative process role, 218–219, 233, 256–264
  entrepreneurship role, 292, 295–296
  fictional characters as exemplars of, 67
  management style, 107–108
  occupational profiles for, 75–76
  strategic thinking role, 193
  in Whole Brain structure, 7, 21–25
Dalziel, Murray, 181
Decision making, thinking styles' influence on, 282–286
Delegation, Whole Brain communication and, 145–147
Delta brain waves, 215–216
Dichotomy, human penchant for, 12–13
Dickson, Dave, 300
Diversity, mental:
  and business vs. creative community differences, 302–306

creative problem solving and, 223–224
management of, 98–102
team formation and, 123–127
ubiquity in large population samples, 47–51
Dominance, brain (*see* Brain dominance)
DuPont Corp., creative solutions at, 205–207, 254–255

Education:
creativity programs, 234, 297–298, 306–307
importance of Whole Brain approach, 48–49, 151–154
as method for personal change, 310–312
(*See also* Learning)
Edwards, Betty, 267
EEG (electroencephalography), limitations of, 17
Elkind, Mansfield, 290
Emotions, limbic system's role in, 18
Employees:
analysis of work performance, 140–142
and misaligned leadership statements, 165, 167
motivation of, 143–144
productivity and job assignment, 131–139
responsibilities as followers, 147–148
Entrepreneurship, Whole Brain applications, 95–97, 291–300
Entrepreneurship and Personal Enterprise Program, 297–298
Epilepsy, 11
Esalen Institute, 310–311
Ethnic groups, mental preference profiles, 47, 50–51
European business culture, 182–184
Evolution, human, and brain specialization, 13
Experimental thinking style [*see* D (Experimental) quadrant]

Facilitation of creativity, 277
Family dynamics, Whole Brain Model application, 61–62
Feeling thinking style [*see* C (Feeling) quadrant]
Female thinking style (*see* Gender considerations)
Financial crisis, management of, 171–178
Followership, creation of effective, 147–148
Four-Quadrant Brain Model, development of, 6–19
Four-Quadrant House, 21
Four-Selves Model, 21

Fox, Ayn, 194–195
Franklin University, 306–307

Gammon, Karen, 266–267
Gazzaniga, Michael, 11
Gender considerations:
in CEO thinking style analysis, 188–190
in communication, 117–118
in management style, 108–109
in mental preference, 51–57, 106
General Electric Corp., role in Whole Brain Technology, 1, 17–18, 300
Goldberg, Rube, 96
Greenspan, Alan, 66
Gustavson, Paul, 177–178

Hemisphere specialization in brain, 11–12
Hermann Brain Dominance Instrument (HBDI):
application to CEO study, 184–191
development of, 18
entrepreneurial role, 296
function of, 7
and intelligence testing, 63
international sources for, 324
role in analysis of thinking preferences, 20, 29–33
sample of questions, 321–323
validity of, 320
and work performance problems, 140–142
Heterogeneous teams:
advantages of, 228–229, 231, 237
characteristics of, 125–128
in creative problem solving, 223–224
crisis management role, 173–174
vs. homogeneous, 54–57
High-performance teams, characteristics of, 128–130
Hoestede, Geert, 183
Homogeneous teams, 54–57, 124–128
Human resources, and mental preferences, 48, 100, 106

Ideas:
management of, 239–242
neural generation of, 214–217
stifling of, 270–271
(*See also* Creativity)
Imagination, and high-performance team success, 130
(*See also* Creativity)
Innovation:
CEO preference for term, 186–187.
vs. creativity, 204, 209–212
Creativity and Innovation Model, 218
Whole Brain Technology applied to, 95–97

Intelligence, brain dominance and, 50–51, 59-63
International applications of Whole Brain Technology, 47, 50–51, 180–187, 324
Intrapeneurship, 298–300
IQ tests, criticism of, 62–63

Job classification, creative vs. noncreative, 251–255
Job satisfaction:
  and thinking preferences, 77–78, 311
  work assignment as key to, 131–139, 168
Johnson, Kelly, 235–239
Jones, David, 66

Leadership:
  CEO thinking styles analysis, 179–191
  and competitive thinking styles, 46
  as creative champions, 230–239, 243
  creative element in crisis, 172–173
  cultural patterns, 183–184
  left mode tendencies, 47–48
  statements of, 163–170
  (See also Management)
Learning:
  limbic system's role in, 18
  mental process of, 11
  Whole Brain application to, 150–159
Left mode thinking style:
  CEO compliance with, 158
  and competitiveness, 45–46
  creative process role, 208, 218–220
  decision-making application, 283
  in European business culture, 182–183
  management style, 101, 106, 234
  reengineering role, 177–178
Legal advice, importance for entrepreneurs, 292
Letterman, David, 263
Limbic mode thinking style:
  and competitiveness, 46
  decision-making role, 284–285
  management characteristics, 109, 111
  occupational profile norms, 73–75
Limbic system, functions of, 13–15, 18
Lindh, Hilary, 68–69

M.B.A. (Master of Business Administration), expanding creativity of, 301–307
MacLean, Paul, 13–15
Major, Paul, 69
Male thinking style (see Gender considerations)
Management:
  communication responsibilities, 119

creativity facilitation, 268–271, 278–279
delegation responsibilities, 147–149
gender and team selection, 54–57
job assignment responsibility, 51, 132
left mode tendencies, 47–48, 204, 206
and mental diversity, 98–102
and motivation source, 143–144
and product design, 93
reengineering role, 178
role of thinking styles in, 46
strategic thinking responsibility, 193
styles of, 23–25, 102–114
team supervision role, 130, 230–239
Whole Brain method training for senior, 155–159
(See also Leadership)
Marketing, Whole Brain applications to, 86–89
Married couples, thinking preferences of, 53–54
Mavericks, as experimental thinkers, 259–264
Media, on brain dominance, 13, 18
Memory, limbic system's role in, 18
Men vs. women in mental preferences (see Gender considerations)
Metaphor:
  as basis for Whole Brain Model, 7, 18, 29
  and strategic thinking, 194–195
Mintzberg, Henry, 59–60
Motivation, source of, 132, 143–144, 156
Multidominant thinking style, 76–77, 111–112, 156–159, 179–180

Nature vs. nurture, origin of thinking preferences, 34–35, 309
Neuman, Gerhardt, 260–262
Nicklaus, Jack, 69–70
North American business culture, 181–183
Nurture vs. nature, origin of thinking preferences, 34–35, 309

Occupations:
  consequences of mismatch with thinking style, 136–139
  cultural influence on choices, 51
  gender specific preferences, 53
  HBDI profiles for, 31, 59, 72–78, 325–326
  positions in Whole Brain Model, 28
Opportunity, seizing of, creative process role, 247–248
Organizational thinking style [see B (Organizational) quadrant]
Organizing Principle, Herrmann's, 16
Original vs. applied thinking, 212–213

Ornstein, Robert, 12
"Outside the Box" thinking, creative use of, 256–264

Pattern recognition, creativity role, 245–246
People-oriented thinking style, position in Whole Brain Model, 7, 24
[See also C (Feeling) quadrant]
Perception, subjectivity of, 115–116
Performance, work, Whole Brain applications, 132, 140–143
Permission, importance in creativity building, 277–278
Peters, Tom, 262–263
Phrenology, brain dominance theory and, 318
Pinchot, Gifford, 299–300
Player, Gary, 69–70
Positron emission tomography (PET), 17
Preference Indicator Exercise, 8–9, 25–28
Pro forma profile:
    application to product mentalities, 86–97
    and job alignment with employees, 135
    in strategic thinking, 195–196
    usefulness of, 81–85
Process storming, vs. brainstorming, 129
Product design, thinking style influence on, 86–97
Productivity, and job design, 131–139
Profile Interpretation for HBDI, 31–33
Psychology, brain dominance theory and, 318

Quadrant colors, definition of, 27, 320–321
Quadrant structure of thinking styles, overview, 6–7
(See also individual quadrant designators)

Ragsdale, Floyd, 206–207
Rational thinking style [see A (Rational) quadrant]
Reengineering, creative version of, 175–178
Reinvention vs. reengineering, 176–178
Relations with others, effect of mental preferences on, 44–57, 61–69
Research and development, thinking style of, 45–46, 109–110
Rico, Gabriele L., 267
Right mode thinking style:
    in CEO career progression, 158–159
    and competitiveness, 46
    creative process role, 219–220, 233
    decision-making application, 283

female predominance in, 108–109
of management, 108–109
in North American business culture, 183
Risk taking, 238, 247, 269–270

Safekeeping thinking style [see B (Organizational) quadrant]
St. Thomas, University of, 298
Sales, Whole Brain applications to, 86–89
Saline, Lindon, 300
Scientific research, thinking styles in, 45–46, 109–110
Self-actualization, 132, 168, 240, 269
    (See also Turn-on work)
Sensory experience, subjectivity of, 58–59
Shinn, George, 66
Situational use of thinking styles, 38–39, 102, 112–114, 156–159, 173
Skunk works approach, 235–239
Smartness, brain dominance and, 50–51, 59–63
Sperry, Roger, 11, 14
Sports figures, thinking preferences in, 66–67, 68–70
Stolpen, Spencer, 66
Strategic thinking, 192–196
Street, Picabo, 68–69
Street smarts, difficulty in measuring, 62–63
Strickland, Alison, 205, 254
Suggestion programs, inadequacy of, 240
Supervision:
    of creative problem-solving teams, 230–239
    Whole Brain Technology applications, 140–147, 230–239
    (See also Leadership; Management)
Synaptic activity, associations with creative thought, 216–217
Synergy:
    and business skepticism of creativity, 302
    creative process role, 226, 231, 240, 246
    integration of M.B.A.s and creatives, 304–305
    mental diversity as catalyst for, 223–224

Tangi, Georgia, 306
Tanner, Dave, 230
Task-oriented style [see A (Rational) quadrant; B (Organizational) quadrant]
Teams, problem-solving:
    communication in, 121–122
    creativity and, 268
    gender differences in, 54–57
    heterogeneous:
        advantages of, 228–229, 231, 237
        characteristics of, 125–128

creativity of, 223–224
crisis management role, 173–174
high-performance, 128–130
homogeneous vs. heterogenous, 54–57,
    124–128
maximizing results of, 123–130
Theta brain waves, 215–216, 222
Thinking preferences:
    analysis of, 25–27
    avoidance of certain, 34–43
    basic assessment of, 7–10
    benefits of understanding, 59
    development of, 34–38
    diversity of, 98–102
    entrenchment of, 104–105
    organization of, 21–25
    quadrant overview, 6–7
Training (see Education; Learning)
Trevino, Lee, 69–70
Triune Brain Model, 13
Turn-on work:
    and job satisfaction, 77–78, 131–139,
        168, 311
    as key to good followership, 148
    productivity importance, 131–132
Turn-On Work Exercise, 26–28

Understanding, need to test for, 145–146
Universe-of-Thinking-Styles Model, 23
University of St. Thomas, 298
Unmarried couples, mental preferences of,
    53
User-friendliness, thinking style influence
    on, 90–97

Values, and personal change, 285–290,

312–313
Visualization, creative importance of, 128–
    129, 267
[See also D (Experimental) quadrant]

Wallas, Graham, 217
Weiskopf, Tom, 70
Whole Brain, universality of composite,
    47–51
Whole Brain Exercise, 7–10
Whole Brain Model:
    elements of, 6–7
    organization of, 15–16
    physiological roots, 14–15
    research basis for, 17–18
Whole Brain Teaching and Learning
    program, 154–155
Whole Brain Technology:
    areas of application, 317
    basis of, 6–7
    business problem diagnosis, 81–85
    development of, 319
    elements of, 30
    as key to mental wholeness, 315–316
    and predictability of thinking, 94
    teachability of, 138–139
Wholeness:
    importance of, 35–37, 315–316
    situational nature of, 38–39
women vs. men in mental preferences (see
    Gender considerations)
Work elements, in CEO study, 185–191
Work preferences (see Job satisfaction;
    Occupations)

Zoeller, Fuzzy, 69–70

About the Author

Ned Herrmann is the founder of Whole Brain Technology and a pioneer of creative thinking in the corporation. He began researching the brain during his management career at General Electric and has continued his work as head of The Ned Herrmann Group, which teaches Applied Creative Thinking Workshops on every continent. He has been awarded honorary doctorates of Science and Humane Letters. Upon Herrmann's election to the prestigious *Training* magazine Hall of Fame, his work was cited as "one of the most significant contributions to training and development." He has also been honored by the American Society for Training and Development and profiled in publications worldwide. *Business Week* said of him: "Today, amid a flock of consultants who often sound alike, Ned Herrmann stands out." His previous books include *The Creative Brain* (Brain Books/The Ned Herrmann Group). Herrmann and his company, The Ned Herrmann Group, are based in Lake Lure, North Carolina.